AF702814

The Economics of Pension Insurance

Other publications of the
PENSION RESEARCH COUNCIL

Concepts of Actuarial Soundness in Pension Plans—*Dorrance C. Bronson*

Social Aspects of Retirement—*Otto Pollak*

Positive Experiences in Retirement—*Otto Pollak*

Ensuring Medical Care for the Aged—*Mortimer Spiegelman*

Legal Protection of Private Pension Expectations—*Edwin W. Patterson*

Legal Status of Employee Benefit Rights under Private Pension Plans—*Benjamin Aaron*

Decision and Influence Processes in Private Pension Plans—*James E. McNulty, Jr.*

Fulfilling Pension Expectations—*Dan M. McGill*

Collectively Bargained Multiemployer Pension Plans—*Joseph J. Melone*

Actuarial Aspects of Pension Security—*William F. Marples*

Status of Funding under Private Pension Plans—*Frank L. Griffin, Jr.* and *Charles L. Trowbridge* (out of print)

Guaranty Fund for Private Pension Obligations—*Dan M. McGill*

Preservation of Pension Benefit Rights—*Dan M. McGill*

Retirement Systems for Public Employees—*Thomas P. Bleakney*

Employer Guarantee of Pension Benefits—*Dan M. McGill*

Reciprocity among Private Multiemployer Pension Plans—*Maurice E. McDonald*

A New Look at Accounting for Pension Costs—*William D. Hall* and *David L. Landsittel*

Social Security and Private Pension Plans: Competitive or Complementary? *Dan M. McGill* (ed.)

Pension Mathematics—*Howard E. Winklevoss*

Indexation of Pension and Other Benefits—*Robert J. Myers*

Joint Trust Pension Plans—*Daniel F. McGinn*

Financing the Civil Service Retirement System—*Dan M. McGill* (ed.)

Continuing Care Retirement Communities—*Howard E. Winklevoss* and *Alwyn V. Powell*

Social Investing—*Dan M. McGill* (ed.)

Employer Accounting for Pensions—*E. L. Hicks* and *C. L. Trowbridge*

Pensions, Economics and Public Policy—*Richard A. Ippolito*

Search for a National Retirement Income Policy—*Jack L. VanDerhei* (ed.)

Inflation and Pensions—*Susan M. Wachter*

Pension Asset Management: An International Perspective—*Leslie Hannah* (ed.)

Fundamentals of Private Pensions—*Dan M. McGill* and *Donald S. Grubbs, Jr.*

The Economics of Pension Insurance

Richard A. Ippolito
Chief Economist
Pension Benefit Guaranty Corporation

1989
Published for the
Pension Research Council
Wharton School
University of Pennsylvania
by
IRWIN
Homewood, IL 60430
Boston, MA 02116

© 1989 by Pension Research Council of the Wharton School
University of Pennsylvania

All rights reserved. No part of this publication may be reproduced, stored in a retrieval system, or transmitted, in any form or by any means, electronic, mechanical, photocopying, recording, or otherwise, without the prior written permission of the copyright holder.

Project editor: Paula M. Buschman
Production manager: Bette Ittersagen
Compositor: TCSystems, Inc.
Typeface: 10/12 Melior
Printer: R. R. Donnelley & Sons Company

Library of Congress Cataloging-in-Publication Data

Ippolito, Richard A.
The economics of pension insurance / Richard A. Ippolito.
p. cm.
Bibliography: p.
Includes index.
ISBN 0-256-07474-7
1. Pension Benefit Guaranty Corporation 2. Insurance, Pension trust guaranty—United States. I. Title
HD7105.45.U6I615 1989
368.4—dc19 88–39853
CIP

Printed in the United States of America

1 2 3 4 5 6 7 8 9 0 DO 6 5 4 3 2 1 0 9

To Pauline, Benedic, and Dominic

PENSION RESEARCH COUNCIL

Chairman and Research Director,
Dan M. McGill, *Chairman,* Insurance Department, Wharton School, Philadelphia

Associate Research Director,
Jack L. VanDerhei, *Associate Professor of Risk and Insurance,* Temple University, Philadelphia

J. Vance Anderson, *Counsel for Employee Relations,* Mobil Oil Corporation, New York City

Kenneth Blaylock, *President,* American Federation of Government Employees, Washington, D.C.

Zvi Bodie, *Professor of Finance and Economics,* Boston University, Boston

George W. Cowles, *Senior Vice President,* Bankers Trust Company, New York City

Charles D. Ellis, *Partner,* Greenwich Associates, Greenwich, Connecticut

Michael S. Gordon, Esq., *Attorney,* Washington, D.C.

Donald S. Grubbs, Jr., F.S.A., Grubbs and Co., Inc., Silver Spring, Maryland

Ronald E. Keller, *Senior Vice President,* Principal Financial Group, Des Moines

Raymond C. Lauver, *Member of the Board,* Financial Accounting Standards Board, Stamford, Connecticut

Alicia H. Munnell, *Senior Vice President and Director of Research,* Federal Reserve Bank of Boston

Roger F. Murray, *Emeritus Professor of Banking,* Columbia University, Wolfeboro, New Hampshire

Robert J. Myers, F.S.A., *International Consultant on Social Security,* Silver Spring, Maryland

George J. Pantos, Esq., Vedder, Price, Kaufman, Kammholz & Day, Washington, D.C.

James E. Pesando, *Professor of Economics,* University of Toronto

Samuel H. Preston, *Director,* Population Studies Center, University of Pennsylvania, Philadelphia

Jerry S. Rosenbloom, *Professor of Insurance,* Wharton School, Philadelphia

Sylvester Schieber, *Director of Research and Information Center.* The Wyatt Company, Washington, D.C.

Marc M. Twinney, Jr., *Manager of Pension Department,* Ford Motor Company, Dearborn, Michigan

L. Edwin Wang, *Retired President,* Board of Pensions of Lutheran Church in America, Minneapolis

Howard E. Winklevoss, *Independent Actuarial Consultant,* Greenwich, Connecticut

Howard Young, F.S.A., *Adjunct Professor of Mathematics,* University of Michigan, Ann Arbor

PURPOSE OF THE COUNCIL

The Pension Research Council was formed in 1952 to undertake academic research into those institutional arrangements designed to provide financial resources for a secure and dignified old age. It seeks to broaden public understanding of these complex arrangements through basic research into their social, economic, legal, actuarial, and financial foundations. While generally geared to the long view of the pension institution, projects undertaken by the Council are always relevant to real-life concerns and frequently focus on issues under current debate. The Council does not speak with one voice and espouses no particular point of view. The members do share a general desire to encourage and strengthen private-sector approaches to old-age economic security, while recognizing the essential role of Social Security and other income-maintenance programs in the public sector.

Preface

The Pension Benefit Guaranty Corporation (PBGC) was created by the Employee Retirement Income Security Act of 1974. The PBGC was to insure defined benefit pension benefits in the event of termination of a pension plan with insufficient assets to pay vested liabilities when the plan sponsor was unable to make up the difference. The insurance program was started with almost no information about risk and exposure parameters in the market and little or no information about historical pension terminations. Premiums reflected neither the financial condition of the pension fund nor the plan sponsor; benefits were set at very high levels; and the potential for moral hazard was virtually unconstrained.

Insurance experts at the time predicted the so-called insurance system had the potential to grow into a large federal transfer agency. Many of their predictions came true. By 1986, the cost of the PBGC program was perhaps 50 times original estimates.

Despite this experience, relatively little has been written that evaluates the consequences of creating the new government insurance system. Like most federal programs, it is easier to start than to revamp once it becomes apparent that the cost is higher than anticipated.

This does not mean, however, that the PBGC problem has not been studied or that an understanding of its causes and consequences has not been developed. Various staff in the executive and congressional branches—and the professional staff of the PBGC, in particular—have accumulated a remarkable amount of information and understanding of "the PBGC problem."

After spending approximately one year at the PBGC, I had the urge to try to write down the information I had assimilated from the senior staff in some systematic way. The value of this exercise was not in creating new information available to public policymakers in government. Those involved in assessing the PBGC program have access to the information and expertise necessary to evaluate experience and reform ideas. Instead, my intention was to write a volume for the benefit of those outside the government process.

I hope the book is of some interest to public policy experts and those who operate insurance firms and pension plans. Most important, however, I hope the information in the volume provides a basis for study by students of insurance. The history of the PBGC provides a textbook case study of the consequences of establishing an insurance system that does not adhere to sound insurance principles, and the consequent solvency problems provide a good backdrop for discussion of various reform ideas.

I developed the outline of the book as if a well-meaning Congress created the system with the ultimate idea that, after a suitable understanding of how a pension insurance contract could be written, the insurance program could be transferred to the private sector. Thus, the book is arranged in a way that tries to use historical claims experience and various reform efforts toward developing a pension insurance policy that ultimately would work in the private sector. While I ended up trying to describe a system I thought would work, my main purpose was to provide the information necessary for readers to come to their own conclusions and to formulate their own ideas of how a pension insurance market could actually work.

ACKNOWLEDGMENTS

This book could not have been written without the support of many individuals. I must first thank Dan McGill, whose 1970 Pension Research Council volume on the same subject inspired my attempt. I wrote what might be considered a follow-up volume, which describes "what happened," in answer to McGill's volume, which warned "what will happen if." I am also indebted to my colleague Emerson Beier for patiently teaching me insurance principles, for challenging (and, in many cases, modifying) my ideas, and for his thorough critique of a previous draft. Jack VanDerhei was equally generous with his time in providing information and advice, for making his pension insurance pricing study available for extensive citation, and for a careful review of an earlier draft.

I must also thank my colleagues Vincent Cicconi and John Hirschmann for providing factual and institutional information to me during the process of writing the book and for making extensive corrections to a draft manuscript; and various individuals who were generous enough to provide comments for revision, including William Beyer, Zvi Bodie, Alicia Munnell, and Jim Pesando. This, of course, does not absolve me from any errors that may remain; nor does it implicate any of these individuals with views expressed in the volume.

Many staff members in the PBGC's research and policy office provided various data and information for the book, including Richard Freiman, John Leonard, Linda Mizzi, Gail Sevin, Larry Shirley, and, especially, Fran Morawski. Ronetta Lawson undertook the task of typing all the tables and much of the other appendix materials.

I am especially grateful to Audrey Frazier, who did the bulk of the typing for the book through its various drafts and generated all of the figures for the volume. She did an outstanding job and kept a smile on her face through the entire project. I am also especially grateful to the Executive Director of the PBGC, Kathleen Utgoff, who generously provided me with academic freedom and institutional support for my various research activities at the corporation, particularly for this volume. I would like to emphasize that the views expressed in the book are my own, and therefore are not intended to represent the official position of the PBGC.

Richard A. Ippolito

Contents

List of Tables, xix
List of Figures, xxiii

Part One Description of the Problem **1**

1. **Overview of Pension Insurance** **3**
Background: *Premise of the Volume. The Insured Population. Growth of Defined Benefit Plans.* The Pension Contract, Experience of the PBGC: *Changing Claims Expectations. Reform Efforts.* The Pension Protection Act of 1987. Efficiency Aspects of the New Laws. Characteristics of the Volume.

2. **Insuring a Defined Benefit Contract** **16**
The Defined Benefit Contract: *Pension Formula. Who Pays for the Pension?* Pension Capital Losses: *Losses upon Quitting. Losses upon Plan Termination. Related Issues: Coinsurance and Follow-On Plans. Age Distribution of Coinsurers.* Role of the Interest Rate: *Levels of Claims. Investment Implications: The Principle of Immunization.* Market for Insurance: *Insurance for Termination-Value Pensions. Insurance against Ongoing-Value Pensions. Immunizing a Real Pension Insurance Contract. Why Any Insurance?* Conclusion.

3. **Insurance Principles and the PBGC** **36**
Developing Policy at the PBGC: *Benefit Guarantee. Pricing. Control of Funding. The Insurable Event.* Consequences of Current Policy. Conclusion.

4. Revenue Implications of Claims Experience **50**
Evolution of Claims Expectations: *Evidence from the Early Years, Reappraisal of Claims and Policy: The 1982–1983 Experience, Escalation of Activity: 1985–1986.* Exposure *Measurements.* Calculation of an Economic Premium: *Magnitude of Expected Claims. Translating Claims to Premiums. Sensitivity Tests.* Conclusion.

Part Two Efforts to Reform Program **67**

5. Reform Efforts through 1987 **69**
Regulatory and Litigation Efforts: *Follow-On Plans. Control Groups.* Maximum Guaranteed Benefits: *Actuarial Reduction of Maximum Benefits. Alternate Approach to Maximum Guaranty. Costs of Special Early Benefits.* Legislative Efforts: *SEPPAA. MPPAA. Pension Protection Act.* Conclusion. Appendix: Excerpt from Opinion Letter 81–11—Follow-On Plans.

6. Pricing Solutions **88**
Insurance Pricing Principles. PBGC Proposal for Pricing Reform. Comparison to Market Rates: *Estimation of Market Rate Structure. Comparison to the PBGC Proposal.* Provisions of the 1987 Legislation. Conclusion. Appendix: Other Features of the PBGC Pricing Proposal.

7. Underfunding Exposure: The Evidence **105**
Overall Underfunding since ERISA: *Impact of ERISA. Some Reasons for Persistent Underfunding.* Defunding Prior to Termination. *Methods of Defunding Prior to Termination. Quantitative Effects of Defunding.* Conclusion. Appendix: Impact of ERISA on Funding Levels.

8. Toward Controlling Exposure **132**
PBGC Funding Proposal: *Faster Amortization Rules. Other Rules and Provisions.* Provisions of the Pension Protection Act of 1987: *Faster Amortization Schedules. Transitional Rules.* Shortcomings of New Minimum Funding Rules: *Defunding. Falling Interest Rates. Actuarial Asset Values.* Implications of the New Full Funding Limit: *Impact on Pension Plan Funding. Potential Impact on PBGC.* Other Reform Proposals: *Benefit Reductions. Lien against Underfunding. Bankruptcy Law.* Conclusion.

Part Three Toward Economically Rational Pension Insurance **155**

9. Efficiency Aspects of Pension Insurance Rules **157**
Illustration of Efficiency Concepts. Pension Insurance and Efficiency: *Potential Problems with Market Prices. Problems with Mandatory Coverage with Market Prices. Optimal Insurance under Mandatory Coverage: Market Prices and Benefit Reductions.* Nonprice/Benefit Reforms: *Outlawing Underfunding. Bankruptcy Changes. Arguments for Mandatory Participation.* Distortion for Overfunded Plans: *Trust Fund Balance: Pre-1988 Rules. Trust Balance: Post-1988 Rules. Tax Assessment. Balanced Work Force.* Conclusion.

10. Proposal for an Economic Insurance System **175**
Underlying Characteristics of Proposal: *Congressional Constraints. Role for the Industry Group. Assigned Risk Pool.* Illustrative Policy by a Private Insurer. Default Risk. Exposure at Existing Asset Values: *Liability Calculation. Control of Defunding. Exposure Calculation. Administration of Insurance.* Adjustments for Portfolio Risk: *Factors Affecting Risk. Calculations of Additional Exposure.* The Insurable Event. The Assigned Risk Pool: *Special Benefit Limitations. Special Funding Rules. Portfolio Exposure. Termination While in the Pool. Participation in the Pool.* Conclusion.

Part Four Appendixes **205**

Appendix A: Statistical Tables, 207
Appendix B: Adjusting Liabilities to Common Interest Rates, 224
Appendix C: Factors that Affect PBGC Interest Rates, 227
Appendix D: The Largest PBGC Claims, 234
Appendix E: Summary of Major Pension Protection Act Provisions Affecting Single Employer Plans, 241
Appendix F: References, 255
Dissenting Comments **259**
Statement of Howard Young
Statement of Michael S. Gordon

Index **267**

LIST OF TABLES

1–1 PBGC Facts, 1986, 4
1–2 Single Employer Defined Benefit Plans, 1987, 7
1–3 Growth in Defined Benefit Plans, 1976–1986, 8
1–4 Pension Terminations and Formation Data, 8
2–1 Capital Losses from Quitting, 20
2–2 Pension Losses from Termination, by Age, 23
2–3 Role of Interest Rate in Pension Insurance, 25
2–4 Immunization Strategies, 32
3–1 PBGC Net Claims and Deficit, 41
3–2 The Twelve Largest Claims against the PBGC as of 1986, 42
3–3 PBGC Claims from Steel Industry, 43
3–4 Steel Plan Terminations, 50 Largest Claims, 44
3–5 Claims by Union Status, June 1986, 45
3–6 Sensitivity of Net Claims to Interest Rates, 45
3–7 Exposure Levels Facing the PBGC, 46
3–8 Pension Underfunding on an Ongoing Basis, 47
4–1 Characteristics of Insufficient Plans, 1972, 51
4–2 Losses from Terminated Plans, 1972, 52
4–3 The PBGC Deficit, 1976 and 1981, 52
4–4 Waivers Example—Rath Packing, 55
4–5 The Alan Wood Steel (Hourly) Termination, 55
4–6 Risk Exposure to the PBGC, 59
4–7 Risk Categories of Ten Largest Terminations after 1981, 59
4–8 Claims Experience, Adjusted for Interest Rates, 61

4–9 Economic Premium: Baseline Model, 62
4–10 Economic Premium: Sensitivity Tests, 64
5–1 Important Steps toward Reform, 70
5–2 Maximum Benefits for Single Life Annuity, 1988, 76
5–3 Distribution of Retirement Benefits, 76
5–4 Costs of Supplemental Early Retirement (SER), 80
5–5 Major Provisions of the Pension Protection Act, 84
6–1 Funding Ratios, 1986, 91
6–2 Percent of Participants in Overfunded Plans, 1978–1986, 91
6–3 Pension Liability per Insured: Selected Industries, 92
6–4 Schedule of Premiums: PBGC Proposal, 93
6–5 Schedule of PBGC Premiums with No Maximum, 94
6–6 Risk- and Exposure-Related Market Premiums, 1985, 96
6–7 Market Rates for Selected High-Risk Firms, 100
6–8 Comparison of PBGC Proposal and Legislation, 101
6–9 Schedule of PBGC Premiums: Pension Protection Act, 101
7–1 Termination versus Ongoing Funding Ratios, 1986, 108
7–2 Thirty-Five Poorly Funded Terminations, 115
7–3 Waiver Amounts in Relation to Claims, 116
7–4 Unpaid Contributions, 117
7–5 Relation of Assumed Interest Rates to Type of Plan, 120
7–6 Changing Interest Rate Assumptions, 121
7–7 Illustration of Lump-Sum Effects, 122
7–8 Defunding Prior to Termination, 124
7–9 Results of the GAO Study, 126
7–10 Funding Ratios: PBGC Claimants versus Universe, 127
7–11 Impact of ERISA on Funding Levels, 128
7–12 Impact of ERISA on Contribution Rates, 130
8–1 PBGC Proposed Amortization Periods for Past Service Credit, 134
8–2 Funding Provisions of the Pension Protection Act, 136
8–3 First-Year Contributions for New Past Service Liability after 1988, 137
8–4 Illustration of Faster Amortization Schedule, 138
8–5 Funding Ratios Using Four-Year Treasury Rate, 1986, 146
8–6 Relation of Termination to Ongoing Liabilities, 147
8–7 Potential Reduction in Funding Levels under New Full Funding Limit, 149
8–8 Ideas for Reform Not Legislated, 151

9–1 Tax Cost of New Funding Rules: Illustration, 170
10–1 Assumed Congressional Constraints, 177
10–2 Features of an Illustrative Economic Insurance Policy, 180
10–3 Coinsurance in an Illustrative Indexed Insurance Policy, 183
10–4 Factors Affecting Default Risk, 186
10–5 Distribution of Exposure Levels, 191
10–6 Illustration of Portfolio Risk, 193
10–7 Portfolio Exposure: 1960–1987, 195
10–8 Special Rules for the Assigned Risk Pool, 201
A–1 Trends in Employment and Wages, 208
A–2 Employment in Small and Large Establishments, 208
A–3 Growth of Participants in Insured Defined Benefit Plans, 209
A–4 Pension Plan Terminations and Formations, 210
A–5 Distribution of Plans by Industry, 211
A–6 Distribution of Plans by Size, 212
A–7 Distribution of Termination Funding Ratios, 1978–1986, 212
A–8 Distribution of Ongoing Funding Ratios, 1978–1986, 213
A–9 Reversions in Excess of $1 Million, 1980–1987, 213
A–10 Claims Experience: Single-Employer Program, 214
A–11 Distribution of Net Claims by Size, 1986, 214
A–12 PBGC Financial Summary: Single-Employer Fund, 1975–1987, 215
A–13 Largest 100 Claims Excluding LTV, 1974–1987, 215
A–14 Participants in Pay Status, 219
A–15 Maximum Monthly Benefits, by Year, 220
A–16 Stock Price Indexes, 221
A–17 Long Term Bond Rates, 222
A–18 Treasury Bill Rates, 223
B–1 Illustrative Interest Rate Conversion Factors, 225
B–2 Sensitivity of Liabilities to Interest Rates within Plans, 225
B–3 Sensitivity of Liabilities to Interest Rates across Plans, 226
C–1 Illustration: Deferred Interest Rates, Private versus PBGC, 230
C–2 PBGC Interest Rates, 1974–1988, 231
D–1 Largest PBGC Claims, 235

LIST OF FIGURES

2–1 Insured and Uninsured Losses on Termination, 25
2–2 Coinsurance, 1950–1987, 26
3–1 Termination Underfunding, 1978–1986, 46
3–2 Ongoing Underfunding, 1978–1986, 48
3–3 Variation in Funding, 1978–1986, 49
4–1 Observation on Underfunding, 1977, 58
4–2 PBGC Claims, 1975–1986, 62
4–3 Indexed vs. Flat Premiums, 63
5–1 Maximum Benefits Alternatives, 79
6–1 VanDerhei Study
  Part a: Estimated Market Premiums, 1985, 98
  Part b: Exposure and Default Risk, 99
7–1 Funding Ratios, 1950–1987, 107
7–2 Inadequate Funding Rules
  Part a: Flat Benefit Plan, 110
  Part b: Salary Related Plan, 111
7–3 Adequacy of Minimum Funding Rules, 1975–1985
  Part a: Flat Benefit Plan, 112
  Part b: Salary Related Plan, 113
7–4 Decline in Ratio of Actual to Minimum Contributions, 125
9–1 Trust Funding: Old and New Funding Rules, 169
10–1 Changing Funding Ratios, 1960–1987, 196

PART ONE

Description of the Problem

CHAPTER 1

Overview of Pension Insurance

BACKGROUND

On Labor Day 1974, the *Employee Retirement Income Security Act (ERISA)* was enacted into law. The legislation was designed to improve the security of pension promises made by private firms. Part of this security was attributable to the creation of the *Pension Benefit Guaranty Corporation (PBGC)*. The PBGC ensured that workers would be paid their vested pension benefits on termination of their pension plan. Workers would receive their benefits even if the funding levels in the plan were insufficient to pay benefits and the firm was unable to make up the difference.

The price of the insurance for single-employer plans was set at one dollar per participant per year.[1] This price was set after a 1972 government study showed that insufficient terminations occurred rarely, affecting only 1 in every 10,000 participants per year. Little was known about how to write a controllable pension contract; and there was widespread doubt in the private insurance industry that such a contract could be written. These concerns were articulated in *Guarantee Fund for Private Pension Obligations*, a book published by Dan McGill in 1970.

The McGill book foresaw many of the pitfalls involved in writing pension insurance contracts. He warned of the potential problems if behavioral reaction by insureds (moral hazards) were not taken into account. McGill suggested contract provisions that, if adopted by ERISA, would have gone a long way toward reducing the magnitude of

[1]Multiemployer plans were assessed a premium equal to 50 cents per person per year.

the ensuing problems. These provisions included stricter funding rules, lower benefit guarantees, and tougher standards to qualify for insurance payments.

In fact, ERISA incorporated a pension insurance contract much more liberal than that suggested by McGill, one rife with moral hazard problems. These problems were aggravated by regulations issued by the PBGC early in its history that made insurance protection even more generous. Until 1987, no attempt was made by Congress or the PBGC to alter the pricing scheme from a flat rate to one that reflected benefit levels, risk, and funding ratios.

Largely as a result of enacting such a loose insurance contract, the PBGC has become a large insurance company. As of 1986, it had accepted more than 1,300 claims, was paying $260 million in annual benefits, held almost $2 billion in assets, and maintained almost a $4 billion deficit (see Table 1–1). This deficit accumulated during the first 12 years of its history despite a more than eight-fold increase in the per participant premium charge over the same period, which generated revenues of over a quarter-billion dollars per year.

As of 1986, the PBGC estimated that premiums needed to pay for the insurance contract were in the range of $25 to $50 per participant, indexed to wages. A study by Jack VanDerhei for the PBGC put the premium at $65.

Given the experience of the PBGC, there has been widespread interest in revisiting the issues that should have been considered when ERISA was enacted: How to write a controllable insurance contract,

TABLE 1–1 PBGC Facts, 1986 (dollars in millions except average annual benefit)

Category	*1986*
Insufficient terminations (cumulative)	1,345
Participants in current pay status	90,750
Participants in deferred pay status	100,000
Premium income (during year)	$201.4
Benefits paid (during year)	$260.5
Average annual benefit	$2,870
Assets	$1,740
Liabilities	$5,491
Deficit	$3,826
Claims	
During year*	$2,895
Average cumulative ($ 1986)	$ 329
Per plan (during year)	$ 8
Average funding ratio at termination (all years)	41%

NOTE: Deficit and claims data for 1986 include the then-pending pension terminations affiliated with the LTV Corporation.

* Includes pending claims at end of fiscal year (September 30).

and how it can be priced to reflect rational insurance principles. This book traces the history of the PBGC problem and the efforts by its staff and Congress to control it and works toward a model of insurance that reflects sound insurance principles.

Premise of the Volume

The lack of sound insurance principles embedded in ERISA suggests to some that the PBGC was not set up to be an insurance firm, that a pricing scheme and insurance contract could have been enacted in 1974 but was not because of a deliberate attempt to effect transfers to workers and shareholders in troubled firms. By creating a generous insurance contract that was not priced in relation to risk and exposure, Congress in effect erected an institution to transfer billions of dollars from workers in well-funded, healthy firms to those in underfunded, troubled firms.

An alternative explanation is that Congress misjudged the effect of creating a simple insurance policy—that at a cost of one dollar per participant, it was not worth creating a more complex policy to reflect sound insurance principles.

For the sake of setting a theme for this volume, I will adopt the second explanation. That is, my working hypothesis is that Congress intended to erect a bona fide pension insurance firm and chose a simple policy and an arbitrary price out of sheer unavailability of good information. This was a new line of insurance, one where no basic research had been done, and barely anything was known about expected claims. Neither the insurance event nor the amount of benefits guaranteed were well defined. Further, little was known about how firms would try to "game" the new insurance system.

Thus the PBGC can be viewed as the embodiment of a national research project designed to accumulate information about claims, moral hazard, and sound premium structures and ultimately leading to the transfer of its functions to the private sector, perhaps with the government remaining in a reinsurance or regulatory capacity.

Initial regulations were issued without the benefit of much information, which greatly increased the PBGC's exposure. The most costly regulatory decision was to guarantee full, unreduced benefits at *any* age specified in the plan (subject to the PBGC's maximum benefit schedule). Included was the guarantee of shutdown benefits: payment of full benefits to workers as young as age 45 who were affected by a plant shutdown prior to plan termination. The guarantee of full benefits (instead of actuarial reductions from, say, age 62) led to the imposition of hundreds of millions of dollars in additional claims against the PBGC.

As claims arrived, the staff of a newly created agency began accumulating information about how pension insurance contracts worked. The consequences of various provisions of the insurance contract gradually became apparent (for example, those that permitted the Internal Revenue Service to grant waivers to troubled firms, inadequate funding of plans, and inclusion of shutdown benefits in guaranteed claims). And a series of court cases involved firms dumping losses on the PBGC through either spin-offs of poorly funded plans or attempts to effectively continue terminated plans after receiving a transfer from the PBGC. Reform ideas were developed gradually as more information about pension insurance was accumulated.

The Insured Population

The Pension Benefit Guaranty Corporation insures most participants in *defined benefit plans.*[2] The nature of these plans is discussed in Chapter 2, but essentially they involve a promise to pay a benefit at retirement. The plan sponsor is responsible for implementing a funding policy and for accepting investment risks. The problem for the PBGC arises when these plans are terminated midstream with insufficient assets accumulated to pay these benefits and with insufficient net worth to make up the difference.

Various data describing the single-employer (private-sector) defined benefit universe are shown in Table 1–2. In 1987, 228,000 plans held over $900 billion in assets. Twenty-four million workers were covered in these plans. Seven million retirees collected benefits totaling $47 billion.

In general, plans are well funded. In 1987, corporate defined benefit plans held assets sufficient to pay their collective economic (ongoing) pension obligations. (Economic liabilities account for indexing of pension promises to wages at retirement and partial indexing to prices beyond retirement.) Funding on a termination basis was much higher: plans held $167 in assets for every $100 in legal (termination) pension obligations. (Legal liabilities make no provision for indexing to either wages or prices after the date of termination.)

Growth of Defined Benefit Plans

While participation in defined benefit plans has increased dramatically over the post–World War II period, some evidence suggests this growth has slowed over recent years. That is, though employment and the

---

[2]Section 4021 of ERISA excludes certain defined benefit plans from coverage. Most of these are professional service plans that cover fewer than 26 participants. ERISA does not cover pension plans administered by federal, state, and municipal governments.

TABLE 1–2 Single-Employer Defined Benefit Plans, 1987

Category	*Estimate*
Number of plans	
Over 100 participants	23,000
Under 100 participants	205,000
Total*	228,000
Assets	$909 billion
Active participants	24 million
Retirees	7 million
Pension benefits paid	$ 47 billion
Funding ratio†	
Legal (termination concept)	167.9%
Economic (ongoing concept)	101.8%

* Only 110,000 plans, however, are insured (see footnote 2 in text).

† Derived from the Wyatt Company, *1986 Survey of Actuarial Assumptions and Funding*, 1987. The mean funding ratio for beginning of plan year is 158 percent, based on an average 7.7 percent interest rate. The ratio is converted to a 8.49 percent interest rate for the legal calculation (Moody's Aaa) in January 1987 and to a 2 percent interest rate for the economic calculation. (The interest rate conversion method is discussed in book Appendix B.)

SOURCE: U.S. Department of Labor, unpublished data.

overall number of pension participants in the United States continue to grow, the share covered by defined benefit plans may be falling. Some concern has been expressed since ERISA was enacted that growing regulation has discouraged firms from using defined benefit plans and instead has encouraged a switch toward *defined contribution plans*. In these plans, firms guarantee a rate of contributions, not benefits. They are akin to tax-preferred savings accounts.

Some data are consistent with this point. For example, data from the form 5500 annual pension plan reports submitted to the Internal Revenue Service show virtual stability in participation over the 1976–84 period (column 3, Table 1–3). Other data suggest continued growth. For example, the number of PBGC premium payers has grown steadily over the 1976–86 period (see column 2); and from 1976 to 1986, assets in defined benefit plans increased in real terms by 150 percent (column 1).

Data in Table 1–4 also suggest stability in defined benefit plan coverage. In columns 1 and 2, the ratios of defined benefit to defined contribution formations and terminations are shown over the period 1975 through 1987. These ratios have been relatively stable during that period.

Part of the impression that defined benefit plans are losing popularity is attributable to an unusual amount of reversion activity during the 1980s. A *reversion* occurs when a firm terminates a defined benefit plan that has excess assets beyond those needed to pay legal pension liabilities. Columns 3 and 4 of Table 1–4 show that between 1980 and

TABLE 1–3 Growth in Defined Benefit Plans, 1976–1986 (absolute numbers in millions)

Year	Assets* ($1986) (1)	Premium Payers† (2)	Partici-pants* (3)	Employment in Large Firms: Firm‡ (4)	Employment in Large Firms: Plant§ (5)	DB Participation by Firm Size‖: Small (6)	DB Participation by Firm Size‖: Medium (7)	DB Participation by Firm Size‖: Large (8)
1976	$364,000	25.6	25.9	48.2%	14.7%	5.7%	36.4%	54.1%
1978	402.000	25.2	27.8	47.4	14.2	5.2	34.3	49.6
1980	472,000	28.1	29.6	48.0	14.3	5.6	33.7	50.3
1982	541,000	29.7	30.0	47.5	13.9	5.8	35.4	53.7
1984	640,000	30.2	29.3	46.6	13.3	5.5	33.6	55.1
1986 (est.)	909,000	31.0	—	—	—	—	—	—

NOTE: Single-employer plans only.

* Data from annual 5500 pension plan reports, U.S. Department of Labor.

† Data from PBGC Form 1.

‡ Data from U.S. Small Business Administration, unpublished; large firms ("enterprises") are those with more than 1,000 employees.

§ Data from U.S. Census, *County Business Patterns, Annual Summary,* 1986; large plants ("establishments") are those with more than 1,000 employees.

‖ Estimates are made by comparing premium payers in small, medium, and large plans with employment in small, medium, and large firms. Small is defined as 1–99 workers, medium as 100–999, and large as 1,000 or more.

TABLE 1–4 Pension Termination and Formation Data

Year	Ratio of DB to DC Formations (1)	Ratio of DB to DC Terminations (2)	Reversions*: Plans (3)	Reversions*: Amount (4)
1975	.9	1.3		
1976	.2	1.3		
1977	.2	.5		
1978	.2	.4		
1979	.4	.4		
1980	.4	.5	9	$ 18
1981	.4	.5	35	159
1982	.5	.5	82	404
1983	.5	.6	166	1,608
1984	.5	.8	331	3,564
1985	.6	.9	580	6,666
1986	.5	.7	263	4,287
1987	.4	.7	169	1,426
Total	.4	.7	1,635	$18,134

* Amounts in millions; includes reversions of $1 million or more. Data not available prior to 1980.

SOURCE: See book Appendix A, Tables A–4 and A–9.

1987, over 1,600 plans that had at least $1 million in overfunding terminated and received $18 billion in reversions (these plans had 1.8 million total participants). While these data appear to suggest the abandonment of defined benefit plans, studies have shown that in the majority of these cases, the plan sponsors that obtained reversions reestablished defined benefit plans identical to the ones terminated.[3]

Even if some drift toward defined contribution plans has occurred during the 1980s, this is not necessarily attributable to growing pension regulation. Another explanation may be the slow growth in employment in large firms (see Table 1–3, columns 4 and 5). Large firms offer defined benefit plans more often than small firms (columns 6 through 8 in Table 1–3). The shift in employment toward small firms could imply lower participation in defined benefit plans owing to a firm-size compositional effect.

There is no conclusive evidence that defined benefit plans have lost their popularity since ERISA. Nevertheless, it is important to recognize that defined benefit plans, though potentially valuable to firms and workers, presumably can be replaced with defined contribution plans. The nature of the pension system in the United States could be altered if the government—through premiums, regulations, and changes in tax law—makes the relative cost sufficiently high for defined benefit plans.

Since the cost imposed by pension insurance is placed only on defined benefit plans, the insurance system has a potential role to play in these decisions. This is a fundamental motivation behind policymakers' concerns that the pension insurance system is losing control of its claims and thus imposing an unreasonable and growing burden on well-funded defined benefit plans.

In the remainder of this chapter, I outline the main content and results of the book. The detail supporting the rather sketchy remarks made here is found in the ensuing chapters.

THE PENSION CONTRACT

The volume begins with a development of the pension insurance contract. The fundamentals derived in Chapter 2 are used throughout the book. It is impossible either to evaluate the current insurance system or to formulate systems that might work better without understanding the pension contract implicitly agreed to by workers and firms and how the insurance policy is related to these promises.

Workers pay for and expect pensions indexed to final wages (even if benefits are stated in flat dollar terms). The difference between expected benefits and insured benefits is the amount workers lose if

[3]See Hay-Huggins Company, 1986. All references are found in Appendix F.

their plan is terminated. This tells us about the coinsurance factor implicit in any pension insurance system, including the one administered by the PBGC.

Because the PBGC insures nominal pension benefits and workers pay for and expect real benefits, a significant coinsurance factor is present in the current system. The problem, however, is that this coinsurance can vary from 10 percent to 90 percent of expected pension benefits, depending on the interest rate and the worker's age.

While the great variation and volatility of the coinsurance factor are shortcomings of the PBGC insurance policy, it nevertheless is important that some significant coinsurance factor be incorporated. This explains why the PBGC historically has worked to prevent ongoing firms from offsetting losses incurred by workers following an insufficient termination.

Chapter 2 also discusses the market for voluntary insurance. In an unregulated environment, do firms/workers want to insure against underfunding attributable to asset value volatility and/or against systematic underfunding over the long run? On the supply side, what kinds of policies can be written to protect the insurance company? If pension insurance is offered, can the contract be written to insure that claims will be paid regardless of investment returns earned by the carrier? Does the potential for catastrophic claims make it necessary for the government to play a role in this market?

EXPERIENCE OF THE PBGC

Changing Claims Expectations

The market for insurance discussed in Chapter 2 has little to do with the policy written and enforced by the PBGC. Chapters 3 and 4 discuss the policy that has been in effect and consequent claims experience.

There are many problems with the way PBGC's insurance system is structured. Prices essentially are unrelated to exposure and risk elements. In addition, except for a maximum payable benefit and phase-in rules, benefit guarantees are almost unrestricted. For example, if a pension provides for full benefits at age 50, the PBGC also pays these benefits (subject to the maximum benefits limit). And the system is rife with moral hazard: funding levels were seemingly unaffected by ERISA; defunding prior to termination has been routine; and firms have terminated plans and made claims even though they have continued as ongoing entities.

It is not hard to understand that the availability of insurance in almost any amount that costs potential claimants almost nothing will generate lots of claims. And this describes the short history of the PBGC. Initial studies of terminations suggested that a premium equal to one dollar per participant would pay for expected claims. This, in fact, was consistent with initial claims in the first year or two of the corporation's existence.

With time, however, as firms learned to use the system, claims escalated. Chapter 6 describes a series of PBGC studies to update estimates of its exposure and to recalculate its premium requirements. These calculations persistently were wrong by orders of magnitude, as claims grew much faster than PBGC expectations. By 1986, the PBGC's evaluation of premium needs were 25 to 50 times higher than they were in 1974.

Reform Efforts

Claims experience over time provided information to the agency upon which reform ideas were based. Chapter 5 discusses various insurance principles put in place through either regulation, litigation, or new legislation. An important early decision was to interpret ERISA language conservatively so that the maximum guarantee as of age 65 (established in ERISA) reflected full (not subsidized) actuarial reductions for earlier ages of receipt. This became important in light of the generous early benefits available in the majority of large plans that made claims against the PBGC.

Litigation efforts were made to vigorously enforce the control group concept, which prevented firms from terminating insufficient plans in subsidiaries while, at the same time, trying to avoid the PBGC's claim against 30 percent of the employers' net worth. Strong efforts were made in negotiations and in court to prevent firms from establishing follow-on plans designed to evade the coinsurance for workers. Legislation was enacted to constrain the insurable event to meet various distress criteria.

The discussion in Chapter 7 shows that these efforts were insufficient to stop the growing flow of claims into the PBGC. One reason was the ineffectiveness of minimum funding rules after ERISA. Despite these rules, funding ratios among the most underfunded plans in the pension system became even more underfunded. And it was demonstrated that firms could engage in rapid defunding over time and yet be in compliance with minimum funding requirements. It was not unusual for plans to arrive at the PBGC with funding ratios of less than 20 percent.

Many avenues were used by plan sponsors to accomplish defunding, including increasing benefits prior to termination, paying out lump sums to workers otherwise affected by the PBGC maximum, establishing "springing" shutdown benefits that provided generous pensions to very young workers (with no provision for pre-funding), obtaining contribution waivers from the Internal Revenue Service, changing actuarial assumptions, and simply not making required contributions.

THE PENSION PROTECTION ACT OF 1987

In December 1987, as a part of the Omnibus Budget Reconciliation Act (OBRA), perhaps the most significant single-employer pension insurance legislation since ERISA was enacted into law. The legislation within OBRA that amends Title IV of ERISA (pension insurance rules) is known as the Pension Protection Act and is the subject of Chapter 8 in this volume. This legislation was the culmination of debate centered around the growing deficit of the PBGC, which amounted to $4 billion by 1986. Because the PBGC financial situation is indirectly reflected in the U.S. budget, the need to make larger benefit payments from the insurance program was beginning to cause perceptible increases in the overall U.S. budget deficit. This is why reform was included in the budget law.

The hallmark of the legislation was the introduction of stricter minimum funding standards for all large plans less than 100 percent funded on a termination basis.[4] Except for underfunding existing at the time of the legislation, which was subject to transitional rules, all new underfunding is to be amortized at faster rates. Simulations showed that, had the rules been in effect during the post-ERISA period, underfunded plans would have posed significantly lower exposure to the PBGC.

The new law is far reaching and could have an important impact on PBGC claims. However, owing to transitional rules and exemptions for large integrated firms in the steel industry, the full impact of the new rules will not be felt for perhaps 20 years, though measurable effects ought to be observed sooner.

In addition, the legislation for the first time abandoned a strict flat rate premium structure. Premiums were altered to reflect at least some portion of exposure given to the insurance company.

The law also changed other rules that could reduce future claims to the PBGC. For example, liens now arise when firms do not pay required contributions, and the law changed the criteria in Chapter 11 bankruptcy proceedings (reorganization). To make a claim on the PBGC in Chapter 11, the bankruptcy court must find that in the absence of a PBGC transfer, the firm will be unable to successfully reorganize.

While the new law addresses many problems that have plagued the PBGC, from an insurance perspective, the solution is not ideal. Chapter 6 discusses pricing solutions that would reduce cross-subsidies in the system much more dramatically than the solution enacted into law. Chapter 8 discusses gaming potential still in the system and areas

---

[4]One of the new funding rules [the deficit reduction contribution rule in the Internal Revenue Code, Section 412(L)] does not apply to plans with fewer than 100 participants.

where the new, stricter rules may be less effective than Congress envisioned.

Ironically, though the new law was intended to affect underfunded pension plans, perhaps its biggest impact was felt by the best-funded plans. A separate section of the Omnibus Budget Reconciliation Act enacted new *maximum* funding laws that were much stricter than those specified in ERISA (and subsequent amendments). In the past, the Internal Revenue Code permitted full funding of ongoing pension benefits. The new law restricts trust assets to no more than 150 percent of termination liabilities. (Ongoing and termination liabilities are discussed at length in Chapter 2.)

The new maximum funding rule prevents over half of all pension plan sponsors from contributing anything to their plans until their funding levels fall within the new limits.[5] It can be shown that by preventing firms from fully funding their pension plans on an ongoing basis, the new law effectively imposes a special tax on many defined benefit plans that easily can amount to 5 to 10 percent of benefits paid.

EFFICIENCY ASPECTS OF THE NEW LAWS

Chapter 9 discusses the efficiency aspects of various pension insurance systems. In this section, the economic efficiency implications of the Pension Protection Act (PPA) are evaluated and compared to alternative reform ideas. The potential distortions created by the new maximum funding rules in the Omnibus Budget Reconciliation Act (OBRA) are also considered in some detail. Because this tax change attaches an extra corporate tax assessment against defined benefit plans, a tax bias is created in favor of defined contribution plans.

Under prior law, a minority of firms were taking advantage of the lack of insurance principles in Title IV of ERISA, thereby imposing a small but growing burden on other defined benefit plan participants. The PPA restricted many of these distortions. At the same time, the law itself imposes new distortions. For example, the law works in the direction of reducing pension plan underfunding regardless of the risk of default. This may impose inefficiencies on financially sound firms for which underfunding may be optimal.

Chapter 9 shows that in addition to (or perhaps partly in place of) past reform, the problems created by the lack of insurance principles enacted under ERISA could be greatly reduced by taking two modest actions: (1) reducing the guarantee of basic pension benefits to a level not exceeding the average of all insureds, payable beginning at age 62;

[5]Some of these firms might also have been constrained by the old funding limits as well. This cannot be determined from information provided in the Form 5500 annual reports.

and (2) introducing meaningful pricing reform that reflects exposure and risk posed by insureds, subject to a "reasonable" maximum price (say, in the range of $200 per participant per year). In combination, these changes would greatly reduce the subsidies inherent in the current scheme and therefore reduce the resource cost imposed by efforts to control losses.

In light of the problems that have plagued the insurance system and the ever-growing distortions that the system (and attempts to fix it) has imposed, it is interesting to step back to rethink the entire structure of pension insurance. The last chapter of the book goes through this exercise, taking advantage of all the information accumulated to date. This exercise takes the form of a proposal for an entirely new insurance system.

The proposal incorporates many of the insurance principles discussed throughout the book. The policy incorporates two congressional mandates: that any insurance reform retain the mandatory nature of pension insurance and that premiums be constrained by some maximum permissible charge.

In a nutshell, the insurance proposal is characterized by free market prices, except an assigned risk pool would be available for all plans that could not find protection for less than some predetermined maximum allowable premium charge. Once in the pool, special procedures would go into effect, including the reduction of benefit levels to the average of the defined benefit universe, payable in full no earlier than age 62. The details of the proposal are discussed in Chapter 10.

CHARACTERISTICS OF THE VOLUME

Before proceeding to Chapter 2, it is useful to describe a few characteristics and assumptions in the volume. First, except by way of illustrating comparisons for reform, the book deals with the single-employer (private-sector) defined benefit universe. Multiemployer defined benefit plans, which are insured through a separate program characterized by different rules, generally have not exhibited deficits.

Defined contribution plans are fully funded by definition and hence are not subject to the insurance provisions (Title IV) under ERISA. Finally, plans administered by federal, state, and municipal governments are not subject to ERISA and therefore are not discussed in the volume.

The book generally presents data through 1986, which means that the termination of the pension plans sponsored by the LTV Corporation in 1986 are reflected in much of the data. In fact, the PBGC restored these plans in 1987. That is, in 1986, LTV filed for Chapter 11 bankruptcy. Owing to a failure to meet the minimum funding standards, the PBGC initiated termination of four of LTV's plans, which resulted in a claim in excess of $2 billion.[6] Essentially, the plans were "restored," or given back to LTV, because: (1) LTV created a "follow-on" plan that virtually offset the losses in the terminated plans and (2) LTV became profitable during bankruptcy proceedings and thus was able to resume contributions to its plans. At the time this book went to press, these matters were still in litigation.

I could have rewritten the book to excise these LTV restorations from the data. My primary reason for retaining these 1986 events is that they played a role in the debate and, ultimately, the new legislation enacted in 1987. This claim manifested the reality that the PBGC "problem" could become much larger if a few large claims were made. Its inclusion in the data is representative of large claims that could be accepted by the PBGC in the future, and therefore it helps us understand more visually why reform efforts have been focused on the PBGC.

Finally, the book often presumes some knowledge of the PBGC and surrounding insurance and pension data. To make this information available without interrupting the natural flow of the discussion, several appendixes to the book are included. These include various statistical tables (Appendix A); methods to adjust liabilities in common interest rates (Appendix B); description of the method used to generate PBGC interest rates (Appendix C); description of the largest PBGC claims, including LTV (Appendix D); and a listing of the provisions of the Pension Protection Act of 1987 (Appendix E). Complete citations for references used in the book are found in Appendix F. Thus, a reference to VanDerhei (1988) in the text has a full citation in this appendix.

---

[6]Under certain circumstances, the PBGC is authorized to initiate termination rather than await the filing of a claim by the plan sponsor. See Section 4042(a) and (c) of ERISA.

CHAPTER 2

Insuring a Defined Benefit Contract

Before issues surrounding federal pension insurance can be addressed, it first is necessary to understand the contract that is the subject of insurance: the defined benefit pension. This chapter will discuss the implications of this contract for the development of sound insurance principles, including those related to the nature of the insurance contract and to asset allocation. The degree of protection offered workers who are covered by the insurance is also studied. These principles lay the groundwork for evaluating the federal pension insurance program administered by the Pension Benefit Guaranty Corporation (PBGC).

THE DEFINED BENEFIT CONTRACT

A *defined benefit pension* is a promise by a firm[1] to pay workers an annuity at retirement age. Usually the benefit is proportional to years of service and to some measure of final pay (e.g., the average of the highest three annual salaries).[2] Some pensions offer flat benefits (pensions dependent on years of service, not salary), but the economic implications of flat benefit plans do not differ from so-called final pay formulas. This is because flat benefits usually are increased on a regular basis in relation to wage growth. Hence the discussion can be restricted to a stylized final pay plan without sacrificing our ability to generalize from the results.

---

[1]Technically, the promise is made by the pension plan. The firm, in turn, is held responsible for satisfying the minimum funding laws.

[2]A good summary of different types of defined benefit plan formulas is U.S. Department of Labor, 1983. A sample of actual formulas can be found in Banker's Trust, 1980. Full citations are found in book Appendix F.

Defined benefit plans are not the same as defined contribution plans. In the latter, the firm contributes a portion of the wage package each period to a separate account for each worker. After a short vesting period (usually five but not more than seven years), the account belongs to the workers, even if they leave the firm. The account accumulates interest and dividends until retirement. The annuity that can be purchased depends on the value of the account at retirement; benefit levels are not guaranteed, only contributions are.

Federal pension insurance covers only defined benefit plans. Thus, from this point onward unless otherwise specified, references to pensions mean defined benefit varieties.

Pension Formula

For analytical ease, suppose the worker's age is set to zero when he starts work in the firm. Then his age and service are always the same; denote this variable by a. The expressions are also simplified if we assume a lump sum is paid at retirement instead of an annuity. In a final pay formula, a worker's pension at age of retirement is denoted by the following benefit formula:

$$P_R = bRW_R \qquad (2\text{–}1)$$

where

P_R = lump-sum pension at retirement age R
W_R = worker's wage during the last year of work
b = measure of generosity in the pension plan

Recall that age in the formula starts at zero at the time the worker begins employment with the firm. If the worker starts with the firm at age 35 and retires at 65, the value of R is 30. The worker gets a benefit based on 30 years of service, proportionate to his final wage, W_R. If W_R is \$20,000, and b equals .15,[3] the value of this worker's pension is $30 \times \$20{,}000 \times .15 = \$90{,}000$.

We now want to determine the value of this promised pension—not at the age of retirement, but at the worker's *current* age, a. At his current age, the worker does not have R years of service; he has a years of service. But the promised pension is still indexed to final wage at retirement, W_R, not current wage. For illustration, assume the chances of death or quitting the firm (or the firm failing) prior to retirement are zero. Thus, the value of the pension to the worker of age (and service level) a is

---

[3]This amount reflects the average generosity of private pension plans. A distribution of these parameters is found in McCarthy, 1985.

$$P_a = baW_R e^{-i(R - a)} \tag{2–2}$$

where

i = long-term rate of interest.

The formula in Equation (2–2) is the same as Equation (2–1) except the formula reflects a years of service, not R, and the value of the pension is discounted to current age, not retirement age. The interest rate incorporates a real interest component (roughly 2 percent) plus some reflection of expected inflation (if the interest rate is 8 percent, expected inflation might be in the range of 6 percent). It is convenient to rewrite Equation (2–2) in terms of *current* wage, not wage at retirement:

$$P_a = baW_a e^{(g - i)(R - a)} \tag{2–3}$$

where

g = rate of expected wage growth

For simplicity, I can reasonably assume that expected wage growth is roughly the same as the interest rate. That is, wages are expected to grow at the expected rate of inflation (in the above example, 6 percent), plus some factor that reflects growing seniority in the firm plus overall productivity growth in the economy [which, taken together, are in the range 2 percent—see Ippolito (1986)]. With this simplification ($g = i$), Equation (2–3) becomes

$$P_a = baW_a \tag{2–4}$$

Equation (2–4) says that the value of the pension promise is proportional to current service and current wage. Thus, if current wage is \$20,000 and current service is 10 years (and recall that $b = .15$), the value of a pension promise that is indexed to final wage is \$20,000 × 10 × .15 = \$30,000.

Who Pays for the Pension?

In the example above, it can be reasonably inferred that the \$30,000 pension value is not a gift from the firm. Over the worker's 10 years of service, this amounts to roughly a \$2,700 contribution per year of service in real terms (\$2,709 per year accumulated at a continuously compounded 2 percent real interest rate over 10 years equals \$30,000). This amounts to almost 15 percent of the wage. If this firm gave 15 percent "extra" to workers, it would not be able to compete with firms who paid the same wage but offered no pension. In equilibrium in our example, it must be true that the no-pension firm pays a cash wage of roughly \$23,000, and the pension firm pays approximately \$20,000 plus a pension worth roughly $3,000. Total compensation in each firm is approximately the same.

The issue of who pays for a pension, and how much, has been the subject of much study. This evidence shows that workers pay for pensions through lower cash wages (e.g., Ehrenberg, 1980; Schiller and Weiss, 1980b; and Smith, 1981) and that they pay for pensions as if they expect to receive them at retirement, that is, as if their pensions will be indexed to their final wage (Ippolito, 1985; Clark and McDermed, 1986; and Mitchell and Pozzenbon, 1986). If workers expect and pay (through lower cash wages) for the value of the pension depicted in Equation (2–4), then, in our example, the worker earning $20,000 with 10 years of service views his $30,000 pension value as an asset, just as he would view the equity value of his house. Like the investment in his house, however, his pension wealth is not a risk-free asset.

PENSION CAPITAL LOSSES

Losses upon Quitting

If everything goes as planned, the worker will receive his $30,000 value at retirement (plus the equivalent of all future service accruals plus interest). But if events are different than expected, he may absorb capital losses on his pension wealth. To develop this notion it is useful to consider the consequences of the worker quitting the firm. Later the same concept will be applied to the major event of concern to this book: failure of the firm and termination of the pension.

What happens if the worker just described quits the firm after five years of service? With inconsequential exceptions, the law requires all workers to vest after five years, and thus the first tendency may be to think that the worker who quits loses nothing. But this is not correct. On quitting the firm, a vested worker loses much (and in many cases, most) of his pension wealth. The reason is that the firm is not required to pay workers a pension indexed to final wage, unless the worker actually stays until retirement. If the worker quits early, the firm is legally required to pay a pension at retirement age R, but the pension value is indexed to the wage at the time the worker leaves the firm, not the wage that would have prevailed had he stayed until retirement.

Intuitively, the reason the pension loses value on quitting is that the pension accumulated to date is eroded in real terms due to inflation during the period between current age and retirement age (and because the worker forgoes any real interest accumulation on his pension savings as well). If the vested worker in our example leaves after 10 years, his pension value is calculated as $30,000, but he will literally receive this $30,000 lump sum at retirement age R, not $30,000 indexed to wage growth.

TABLE 2–1 Capital Losses from Quitting

Interest Rate	*Age at Time of Quit* 30	40	50
2%	39.3%	25.9%	9.5%
5	71.3	52.7	22.1
10	91.8	77.6	39.3

NOTE: This table assumes retirement with full benefits occurs at age 55. Numbers expressed as a percent of ongoing liabilities at the time the worker quits the firm. See Equation (2–6).

If time to retirement age is 20 years (retirement age is 55, and age at the time he quits is 35), then the present value of $30,000 received 20 years from now, discounted at 8 percent, is $6,054. If the worker stays until age 55, his pension based on his first 10 years of service has a present value of $30,000. Thus, on quitting the firm, the worker absorbs a capital loss equal to $23,946 ($30,000 – $6,054), or 80 percent of his pension wealth.

In general, this loss can be represented by reconsidering Equation (2–3). The pension value on quitting is represented by setting the rate of wage growth to zero. Doing this, we can rewrite Equation (2–3) in the special case of quitting the firm:

$$P_a^* = baW_a e^{-i(R - a)} \qquad (2\text{–}5)$$

If the worker in our example quits, the value of P_a^* in Equation (2–5) is $6,054. If he stays, his pension value is P_a as given by Equation (2–4), or $30,000.

In general, the *capital pension loss* from quitting is the difference between the ongoing and termination-value pensions, P_a and P_a^*. Expressed as a percent of his pension wealth, P_a, we have

$$CL_a = (P_a - P_a^*)/P_a = [1 - e^{-i(R - a)}] \qquad (2\text{–}6)$$

The solutions to Equation (2–6) for various interest rates and ages of quits (assuming a retirement age R of 55) are shown in Table 2–1. It is apparent from the table that even though workers get their vested benefits on quitting, they can lose large portions of their accumulated wealth. If the interest rate is 5 percent, a 40-year-old worker with 15 years of service loses half his accumulated pension value. At a 10 percent interest rate, he loses more than three fourths of his benefits.[4]

[4]In view of the large cost of quitting a pension firm, it is not surprising that a large body of literature shows that workers covered by pensions quit less frequently than those not covered by pensions (e.g., Bartel and Borjas, 1977; Mitchell, 1982; Schiller and Weiss, 1980a). This is not necessarily undesirable: long-term employment may enhance productivity in the firm. Presumably one advantage of defined benefit pensions is that they give firms the opportunity to provide incentives for workers not to quit the firm.

The calculations in the table demonstrate an important principle for pension insurance: *Even though termination-value pensions are insured, the loss of an ongoing plan is costly to workers.* This feature will come into play as a coinsurance feature later on, and it will be critical to an understanding of the debate surrounding so-called follow-on plans.

Losses upon Plan Termination

Quit costs are important for this book because they exactly describe the capital losses imposed on workers when their pension plan is terminated. On termination, the firm owes workers nominal benefits, not benefits indexed to wages at retirement age. If a termination occurs without sufficient assets in the pension plan to pay legal benefits, then the Pension Benefit Guaranty Corporation pays only the *nominal*, or *legal*, pension benefit.

Related Issues: Coinsurance and Follow-On Plans

The issue of *coinsurance* is demonstrated in Table 2–1. Suppose a pension plan is terminated with no assets (and the net worth of the sponsor is zero). Thus, federal insurance must cover the entire legal pension value. If the interest rate is 10 percent, the age-40 worker absorbs 77.6 percent of his pension losses; the PBGC picks up the remaining 22.4 percent. The age-50 worker loses 39.3 percent of his pension; the PBGC picks up 60.7 percent of its value. In other words, given the large pension losses absorbed by workers on termination, workers are essentially brought in as coinsurers. In general, workers will not prefer to see pension plans terminated. This preference gives the insurance company a major ally in the battle against moral hazard.

The basic presumption behind the coinsurance notion is that a firm will be reluctant to terminate its pension plan and thereby impose large losses on workers. If workers believe the firm could continue as a viable entity without a pension termination, then these workers and the labor market as a whole will be distrustful of the firm in the future. This distrust translates into a risk premium the firm will be required to pay workers that will not be required of competing firms. Presumably this explains why healthy firms terminating pension plans to obtain reversions almost always structure the transaction to offset all capital losses.[5]

When firms are truly in financial difficulty, however, it is assumed that workers will be willing to participate in the firm's revival, which may require them to accept at least temporary reductions in compensa-

[5]See Hay-Huggins Company, 1986.

tion to secure their jobs. The coinsurance feature rides off this implied contract—that pension plan termination is an unavoidable solution to a serious market problem and thus is less likely to reflect a firm's taking advantage of the insurance carrier.

This coinsurance is destroyed if, subsequent to the insurable event—say, termination in Chapter 11 of the Bankruptcy Code (Chapter 11 permits reorganization and continuation of the firm as an ongoing entity)—the firm is permitted to set workers' losses to zero. If the firm were able to restructure a *follow-on* plan after reorganization in a way that eliminated worker losses from termination, the insurer essentially would lose its coinsurer.

One way worker losses can be eliminated is to reestablish a new plan following termination that is identical to the old plan. On termination, the PBGC promises to pay the worker the value of the pension equal to P_a^* in Equation (2–5). But suppose that after the termination, the firm sets up a new plan that is exactly like the old plan and awards past service credit. That is, the firm promises to pay the amount on retirement:

$$P_R = bRW_R \qquad (2\text{–}7)$$

To prevent double payments for the first a years of service (the value P_a^* is already being paid by the insurance company), the firm *offsets* the value P_R by the amount of the insurance guarantee, P_a^*. In this way, the firm and workers obtain the insurance payments without requiring workers to absorb any coinsurance loss.

This description of plan *reestablishment* is exactly what is done in most terminations for reversion.[6] That is, healthy plans can terminate, pay off legal liabilities, and take back any excess assets beyond this amount in the pension plan. So as not to impose losses on workers, they reestablish the old plan with past service credit and offset the plan by the amount given to workers on termination.

When healthy firms engage in reestablishment, the transaction merely reflects a rearrangement of assets from the pension trust to elsewhere in the firm. When a firm does this following a termination that involves an insurance claim, it eliminates all worker incentives against terminations and thus increases the potential for moral hazard problems.

Age Distribution of Coinsurers

Before leaving this issue, it is important to recognize that all workers in the firm do not share alike in the coinsurance. This can be important because if some pension plans have age distributions concentrated

[6]A study of terminations for reversion is found in Hay-Huggins Company, 1986. Also see Ippolito, 1986.

among those who absorb only small losses on termination, the coinsurance feature is diluted.

To illustrate, it is important to go beyond the capital losses depicted in Table 2–1. In that table, workers at older ages lose a smaller portion of their pension wealth. What the table does not reflect is the larger absolute level of pension wealth that characterizes older workers. A better way to show the amount of coinsurance across ages is to calculate capital losses from termination as a percent of wage:

$$(P_a - P_a^*)/W_a = ba[1 - e^{-i(R - a)}] \tag{2–8}$$

The values from this equation are shown in Table 2–2 for interest rates equal to 2, 5, and 10 percent. It is apparent that workers far from retirement and those close to retirement lose less from termination than those in the middle of the age-service distribution. For example, when the interest rate is 5 percent, those workers between the ages of 35 and 45, with 10 to 20 years of service, absorb pension losses between 95 and 118 percent of their annual wage. Those aged 30 with 5 years of service or age 54 with 29 years of service lose the equivalent of 53 and 21 percent, respectively, of their annual wage. Clearly, the value of coinsurance depends on the age and service distributions in the firm.

The capital loss calculations shown in Tables 2–1 and 2–2 implicitly assume that postretirement inflation adjustments are zero. By using an example where a lump sum is paid at retirement, I have assumed away this issue. Thus, a 55-year-old worker eligible for full benefits in my example would be indifferent to a termination, assuming he would normally retire at age 55.

For most plans, the pension is paid in the form of an annuity. Most pension plans, especially large plans, also periodically enhance service benefits to reflect inflation erosion during retirement. Allen, Clark, and Sumner (1983) have shown that these adjustments accounted for at least one half of the inflation rate during the 1970s. For example,

TABLE 2–2 Pension Losses from Termination, by Age

		Interest Rate		
Age	*Tenure*	*2 Percent*	*5 Percent*	*10 Percent*
25	0	0.00%	0.00%	0.00%
30	5	.29	.53	.68
35	10	.49	.95	1.29
40	15	.58	1.19	1.74
45	20	.54	1.18	1.90
50	25	.36	.83	1.47
54	29	.09	.21	.41
55	30	0.00	0.00	0.00

NOTE: Numbers express pension losses as a percent of salary at the time of the termination. The illustration assumes a worker started the job at age 25 and retires with full benefits at age 55. The lump-sum pension equals 15 percent times years of service times wage. See Equation (2–8).

suppose the inflation rate is 5 percent and the real interest rate is zero. If the plan is ongoing, suppose it will periodically increase benefits for retirees on average 2.5 percent per year. If the retiree dies with certainty at age 80 and the interest rate is 5 percent, the present value of a pension annuity that starts out at $5,000 per year is worth $92,948 at age 55. If the plan is terminated when the worker is age 55, the federal insurer will not award inflation adjustments, and hence the annuity is discounted at the full 5 percent. This yields a value of $71,350 at age 55.

Thus, in general, even workers close to retirement have some stake in plan terminations. As long as they expect to lose some inflation adjustments during retirement, termination will be a costly event. Of course, firms most likely to terminate may be the least likely to award any postretirement adjustments even absent termination. If so, older workers are effectively lost from the coinsurance pool.

These calculations suggest that once a pension plan becomes dominated by older workers and retirees (which might be expected in dying firms), the value of coinsurance is diminished. One way for the insurer to retain coinsurance even in this case is to guarantee something less than 100 percent of nominal pensions to retirees. In fact, in a world in which expected inflation becomes very low, the latter solution is the *only* way to retain a coinsurance feature.

ROLE OF THE INTEREST RATE

If interest rates are high, the insurance carrier can earn higher nominal returns from investing in long-term bonds, which lowers the cost of paying off fixed pension obligations. From the workers' perspective, because long-term nominal interest rates primarily reflect market expectations of future inflation rates, high interest rates imply substantial erosion of their real benefits if they leave the firm or if the firm terminates the pension plan. Thus, when the insurance carrier views the cost of a termination as "low," workers tend to view the cost as "high" (and vice versa when interest rates are low).

Levels of Claims

The discussion above hints at the large role played by long-term nominal interest rates in the cost of insuring termination-value pensions. This point is made forcibly in Table 2–3. The table depicts a 40-year-old worker with 15 years of service in a plan that pays a lump-sum pension at retirement equal to 15 percent per year of service multiplied by final wage. The funding ratio in the plan is zero.

Columns 2 and 3 in the table show the shares of pension losses on termination to the worker and insurer. [See Equation (2–6).] When the

TABLE 2–3 Role of Interest Rate in Pension Insurance

Interest Rate	Claim as Portion of Current Wage* (1)	Percent Real Pension: Paid by Insurer† (2)	Percent Real Pension: Percent Not Covered‡ (3)
2%	1.66	74.1%	25.9%
5	1.06	47.3	52.7
10	.50	22.4	77.6

NOTE: Example assumes pension has one participant aged 40 with 15 years of service; retirement with full benefits at age 55; pension generosity is 15 percent [$b = .15$ in Equation (2–1)]. The funding ratio in the plan is assumed to be zero.

* Solution to Equation (2–5) divided by the wage level W_a.

† 100 percent minus worker's share of loss in column 3.

‡ Solution to Equation (2–6).

interest rate is 10 percent, the worker absorbs 77.6 percent of the pension losses from termination, and the insurer pays the remaining 22.4 percent. If the interest rate is 2 percent, however, the shares essentially are reversed: the individual pays only 25.9 percent of the loss, and the insurer pays 74.1 percent (see Figure 2–1).

The claims implications of these share distributions are shown in column 1 in Table 2–3. At a 10 percent interest rate, the insurer faces a

FIGURE 2–1 Insured and Uninsured Losses on Termination

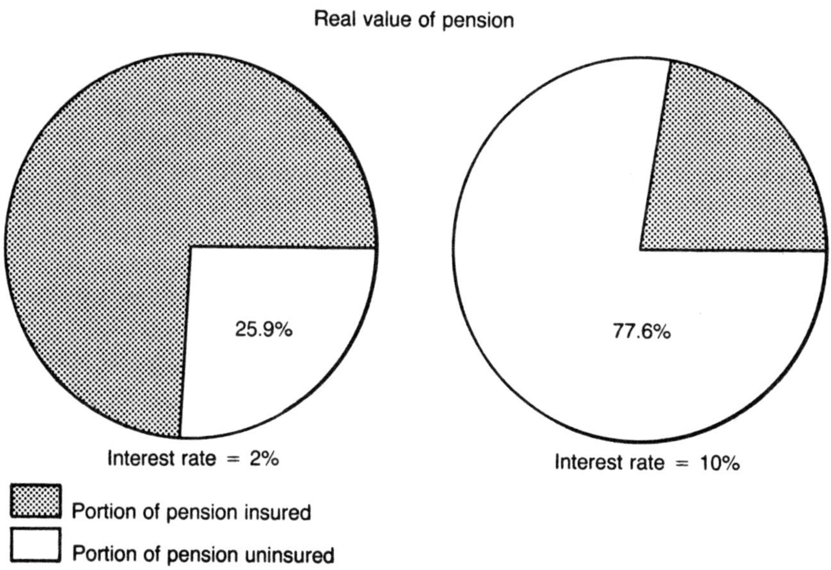

claim equal to 50 percent of this worker's wage on termination of the pension plan; at a 2 percent interest rate, the value of this claim increases more than threefold, to 1.66 times current wage. If the worker's wage is $10,000, the insurer's obligation increases from $5,000 to $16,600, depending on whether the interest rate is 10 percent or 2 percent.

In general, the sensitivity of claims to interest rates depends on the age and service distributions in the plan. But, in general, the numbers in Table 2–3 make it clear that any rational premium scheme to cover such claims must take current interest rates into account. The numbers in the table, however, do not tell the whole story.

Reconsider the distribution of losses between the insurer and the insured. When the interest rate is 10 percent, the worker has a 77.6 percent stake in the loss; at 2 percent, he has only a 25.9 percent stake. Because the coinsurance amount falls with lower interest rates, there is more potential for moral hazard problems. Put another way, when interest rates are lower, employers can impose a larger portion of the burden of termination on the PBGC (as opposed to on workers), and thus more terminations are expected. This factor tends to aggravate the cycle of higher claims likely to occur when interest rates fall.

Figure 2–2 gives some idea of the variation in the coinsurance shares if the PBGC insurance policy had been in effect in 1950. The

FIGURE 2–2 Coinsurance, 1950–1987

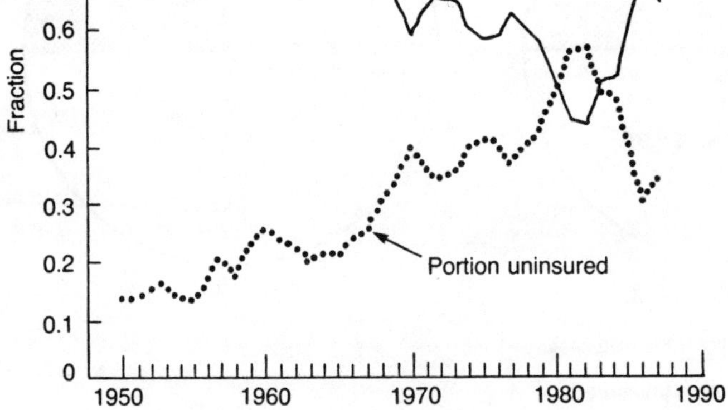

numbers in the figure are based on the ratio of termination to ongoing liabilities for the entire defined benefit pension system; thus, the numbers depict the portion of pension value that would have been preserved if the "typical" pension terminated during each period. The coinsurance share is also denoted.

Over the entire period depicted, the portion of pension wealth guaranteed would have decreased substantially. There also has been great variation in these shares during the ERISA period. The illustration makes it clear that if interest rates revert to levels that prevailed in the 1950s, the cost of providing PBGC insurance would escalate dramatically.

Investment Implications: The Principle of Immunization

Interest rate volatility can introduce large uncertainties into the value of pension liabilities at termination. It is possible, however, to offset much of this risk by choosing appropriate investments on the asset side. Choosing assets that offset liability risk is known as *portfolio immunization*. This complex topic would take us far beyond the scope of this book, and thus only the essence of the idea is presented here.[7]

To make this illustration, suppose a plan sponsor wishes to eliminate the risk that it will not be able to pay its pension liabilities in the event of a termination. Consider the same example used above (only one worker, who is age 40 and has 15 years of service). Assume the sponsor's obligation is to provide a lump sum at the time of termination. The pension obligation of the firm on termination of the pension is given by Equation (2–5). This obligation is rewritten here:

$$P_a{}^* = baW_a e^{-i(R-a)} \qquad (2\text{–}9)$$

where

a = current age (and service)
R = retirement age, when the lump-sum equivalent must be given to the worker

Now suppose the plan sponsor contributes an amount to the pension plan equal to $A = P_a{}^*$, so that the pension plan is fully funded in a termination sense. And suppose the firm wants to insure against having the funding ratio fall below 100 percent. First, consider a strategy that will not work. Suppose the firm buys all Treasury bills. This portfolio certainly does not eliminate volatility. If long-term interest rates fall from 10 percent to 2 percent in the next instant,

[7]A good introduction to the notion of immunization is found in Lebowitz, 1986a, 1986b.

termination liabilities in Equation (2–9) increase by over 200 percent (see Table 2–3). Because the value of T-bills is virtually unaffected by changes in interest rate, asset values do not change. In this case, a large difference would arise between insured liabilities and assets backing the insurance.

Suppose, instead, that the pension plan buys either a noncallable, zero-coupon bond or a "stripped" bond with a maturity equal to $R - a$ years.[8] These bonds guarantee a stated rate of interest for the entire investment period. The firm purchases bonds equal in value to termination liabilities:

$$B(i, R - a) = P_a^* \qquad (2\text{–}10)$$

where

$B(i, R - a)$ = amount of the bond investment that pays the interest, i, payable in $R - a$ years

If the interest rate changes from i to zero a moment after the bond is purchased, the funding ratio will remain 100 percent. This is because when the interest rate falls to zero, the liability value increases by the factor $e^{i(R-a)}$. But the value of assets must increase by the same factor; that is, if the interest rate falls to zero, the market value of a bond B paying an interest rate i over $R - a$ years increases by the factor $e^{i(R-a)}$.

Consider a 40-year-old worker with 15 years of service. Retirement normally occurs at age 55. If his wage is $10,000 and the interest rate equals 10 percent (recall that $b = .15$), his pension wealth on termination is 50 percent of his wage, or $5,000 (see Table 2–3). Assume a $5,000 noncallable, zero-coupon bond that pays 10 percent per annum is purchased. If the interest rate falls to zero in the next instant, the termination pension wealth increases to $22,500.[9] But the market value of the bond also increases to $22,500. That is, if the interest rate decreases from 10 percent to zero percent, a noncallable, zero-coupon bond yielding a continuously compounded interest rate equal to 10 percent will appreciate by the entire amount of interest over the 15-year life of the bond: $22,500 = $5,000 accumulated over 15 years at a 10 percent interest rate.

This example illustrates the principle of immunization: assets are matched against liabilities. Real increases in termination benefit obligations are offset by real increases in matched asset values.

---

[8]A zero-coupon bond pays no interest during the period it is outstanding. All interest is accumulated at the stated rate of interest on the bond. A "stripped" bond is one where all coupons have been clipped from the bond and sold; proceeds represent an implicit constant rate of interest over the period the bond is held. In both these cases, there is no interest rate risk: The rate of interest stated on the bond is guaranteed over its life.

[9]This is equivalent to the pension formula of 15 percent per year times 15 years of service times current wage ($10,000) with no discount.

The insurer can apply the same principle. First, it can protect itself from changes in liability values for any obligations it purchases by exactly matching a bond portfolio against liabilities. Second, the insurance company can invest all premiums (minus administrative expenses) into a "matched" asset pool, where the maturity of the portfolio is based on the age/service distribution of the insured plans. If this matching is followed over several periods, terminated obligations will tend to be offset by matched asset pools.

MARKET FOR INSURANCE

The discussion of the principles of pensions and insurance raises several interesting questions. The most important is whether a market would develop without government involvement to insure against pension losses, and, if so, whether it necessarily would insure termination-value pensions.

Insurance for Termination-Value Pensions

Consider the second issue first. One attraction of providing insurance against termination-value liabilities is that through careful management of a bond portfolio, the liabilities can be immunized. The agent guaranteeing payment (the pension plan or the insurer) and the insureds both know in advance that the promise to pay can be made credibly because insured promises are backed by an appropriately selected matched portfolio.

The problems with insurance against termination-value pensions are apparent in Table 2–3. From the workers' perspective, the amount of protection against loss of pension wealth varies greatly with the interest rate. From the insurer's perspective, the amount of coinsurance, and therefore the potential for moral hazard problems, also varies greatly with the interest rate. These problems are addressed by an insurance contract written for ongoing benefits.

Insurance against Ongoing-Value Pensions

The question arises whether insurance for ongoing benefits requires the insurance carrier to abandon the notion of portfolio immunization. The answer is no. It is also possible to choose assets that largely offset the risk of insuring against ongoing-value pensions. In this case, however, assets must be chosen so that their values are not affected substantially by unanticipated inflation.

Cost of ongoing versus termination insurance. Consider the example above. A 40-year-old worker with 15 years' service has a current annual wage of $10,000. The pension generosity parameter is

15 percent ($b = .15$). Using Equation (2–4), which assumes wage growth will approximate the interest rate, the ongoing value of this pension is $22,500:

$$P_a = .15 \times 15 \text{ years} \times \$10{,}000 = \$22{,}500 \qquad (2\text{–}11)$$

A termination pension is worth much less than an ongoing pension. For example, if the nominal interest rate is 10 percent and retirement occurs in 15 years, the termination value of the pension is worth only $5,000:

$$P_a{}^* = .15 \times 15 \text{ years} \times \$10{,}000 \times .223 = \$5{,}020 \qquad (2\text{–}12)$$

where

.223 = discount factor representing the present value of one dollar payable at age 55 discounted to age 40 using a 10 percent interest rate

This discount factor is what distinguishes termination from ongoing liabilities. It is omitted from the ongoing calculation in Equation (2–11) because wage growth exactly offsets the discount effect.[10]

Cost of an actual ongoing contract. A real insurance contract, however, does not necessarily cover the full value of the ongoing pension. First, instead of insuring a pension indexed to wages, the contract may insure pensions indexed to prices (prices generally increase at a rate 1 to 2 percent lower than wages—see book Appendix A, Table A–1). Second, a coinsurance factor may be used guaranteeing some portion of the real value of the pension.

The value of the insured pension could be written in the following general terms:

$$P_a{}' = I\, baW_a e^{(k - i)(R - a)} \qquad (2\text{–}13)$$

where

I = portion of the pension insured
k = the inflation rate

Because the interest rate equals the inflation rate plus a real interest rate component (that is, $k - i = -r$, where r is the real interest rate), Equation (2–13) can be written as:

$$P_a{}' = I\, baW_a e^{-r(R - a)} \qquad (2\text{–}14)$$

In the above example, the value of b is .15, current wage is $10,000 per year, and time to retirement is 15 years ($R - a = 15$). If the

[10]In my model, I assume the expected wage growth rate equals the interest rate. If this is not the case, the wage growth and discounting effects would not be exactly offsetting. Qualitatively, however, the results would be the same as those depicted by the simpler model demonstrated above.

insurance pays 67.7 percent of this amount ($I = .677$) and the real interest rate is 2 percent ($r = .02$), the amount of the insured pension P_a' equals approximately $11,300:

$$P_a' = .677 \times .15 \times 15 \text{ years} \times \$10{,}000 \times .74 = \$11{,}272 \quad (2\text{–}15)$$

where

.74 = present value of $1 discounted 15 years at 2 percent

Comparing the insured amount in Equation (2–15) with ongoing benefits in Equation (2–11), it is apparent that the "real" pension insurance contract in this example protects roughly half of the ongoing value of the pension ($22,500). Put another way, the coinsurance factor is 50 percent.

The advantage of a contract stated in real terms is that the value of the insurance is not affected by changes in unexpected inflation, and therefore: (*a*) the coinsurance factor (in this case, 50 percent) is stable; (*b*) the insureds know exactly the real value of their pension guarantee long before they attain retirement age; and (*c*) the insurer does not need to reassess the real price for the insurance each period, as the long-term interest rate changes.

Immunizing a Real Pension Insurance Contract

Can this contract be immunized or hedged on the asset side? The answer is yes. The insurer can match its liabilities (P_a') against a 100 percent short-term T-bill portfolio. Over a long period of time, T-bills are expected to yield a small, risk-free real rate of interest (r) plus the rate of inflation. To be conservative, the insurer could write the contract assuming r equals zero and offer a "bonus" at retirement in the event r is positive over time.

In this type of portfolio, assets grow with inflation (plus r) and indexed pensions also grow with inflation. The covariance between changes in asset and liability values is expected to be positive and large. Federal government-issued indexed bonds would be even better candidates for a real pension liability match because they are long term and explicitly pay a real interest rate plus the inflation rate.[11] In this case, no hedge on the real interest rate needs to be incorporated in prices.

Examples of immunization strategies are shown in Table 2–4 for

[11]Unlike some countries like England and Israel, the United States does not issue indexed bonds. Some such bonds are available through private issuers. For example, the Fidelity Fund offers instruments indexed to the CPI plus a real rate in the vicinity of 3 percent. Maturities, however, are limited to 10 years. I am indebted to Zvi Bodie for alerting me to the existence of these securities.

TABLE 2–4 Immunization Strategies

Insurance Contract	Current Value	Value in 15 Years* $i = 0$	$i = .1$	$i = .2$
Termination-value liability (evaluated at $i = .10$)	$ 5,020	$22,500	$22,500	$ 22,500
Noncallable, zero-coupon, 20-year bond, $i = .10$	5,020	22,500	22,500	22,500
Real-value liability (67% of price-indexed pension)	11,300	11,300	50,643	226,966
T-bills (assumed to pay inflation rate)	11,300	11,300	50,643	226,966

Assumptions: Worker has 15 years of service, is 15 years from retirement, has a salary of $10,000, and a lump-sum pension that pays 15 percent of wage ($b = .15$). See text.

* It is assumed that the *actual* interest rate becomes effective the day after the insurance contract is signed, is equal for short- and long-term bonds, and is constant over the entire period. It is also assumed that expected and actual real wage growth and the real interest rate are zero.

both the termination and real insurance contracts discussed in the example above. Consider the termination-value contract. Suppose the insurer locks into a noncallable, zero-coupon bond of the same maturity as the liability (15 years, in the example). If the bond pays the same interest rate used to discount the pension (10 percent), assets will be sufficient to pay the nominal benefit on the date it becomes payable. In the example, a bond valued at $5,020 will pay off the stated liability regardless of subsequent changes in interest rates.

In the case of a real-value pension, as long as T-bills do not pay negative real interest rates, they will accumulate sufficient funds to pay off price-indexed pensions.[12] Table 2–4 assumes that T-bills pay a zero real rate of interest (thus, the interest rate is the inflation rate). If the interest (inflation) rate suddenly falls to zero, liabilities *and* assets retain their value of $11,300 in 15 years. If the interest (inflation) rate increases from 10 to 20 percent, the value of assets *and* liabilities will both grow to $226,966 in year 15.

Why Any Insurance?

Technically, either termination-value or real-value pensions can be insured in a free market. The question is whether a market in pension insurance *would* develop. That is, why would not all pension plan

[12]To protect itself against the possibility of negative real returns, the insurer could write the contract to index pensions to the T-bill rate or to the inflation rate, whichever is lower.

sponsors self-insure? Why would not all firms merely invest an amount in matched bonds sufficient to cover liabilities in the event of plan termination?

In the event the firm continues in operation, it will face pension obligations substantially higher than those payable on termination [compare the value of ongoing benefits (P_a) in Equation (2–4) with either termination benefits (P_a*) in Equation (2–5) or insured real benefits (P_a′) in Equation (2–14)]. The firm could match these liabilities by investing in either long-term bonds in the case of termination-value insurance or T-bills (or indexed bonds if available) in the case of real-value insurance. Additional liabilities could be funded with securities that will more likely keep pace with obligations indexed to wages (stock, real estate, etc.).

One reason might be *information* problems. Without regulation, it is difficult for workers to monitor the firm's actions and, in particular, to know that assets are held in a separate trust and properly matched against termination liabilities. This is not a problem in many large firms with valued reputations; but in many smaller firms, it is less clear that sufficient trust exists for workers to accept a pension promise without at least some guarantee from a third party. In these cases, by requiring an insurance contract, workers in essence hire an agent whose self-interest will act to guarantee that at least the insured portion of a pension will be paid. That is, the insurance firm will attach conditions to the contract to ensure that a fully funded trust matches either termination-value or some portion of real-value pension liabilities, whichever is promised in the contract. A third-party insurer makes defined benefit pension plans more feasible in some firms. In this case, the insurer acts as a *quality-assurer:* it guarantees the "quality" of the insured portion of the pension.

Another answer is related to *leverage*. Suppose workers prefer a larger pension and are willing to gamble with more volatile securities, say, 100 percent growth stocks. But they want some guaranteed pension if the firm must terminate the pension (say, because the firm encounters financial difficulties). Suppose 1 plan in 100 will terminate per year at random, regardless of funding levels in the plan; and suppose, because of market volatility, funding ratios in all plans are either 50 percent or 150 percent in any given year. In this example, only one all-bond portfolio is needed to insure nominal benefits for the single termination expected every two years. Without an insurer, *all* plans must hold the amount P_a* in bonds to offer the same insurance protection. With an insurer, all firms can invest in riskier but higher-return stocks and still protect workers against termination.

A special case occurs when the firm underfunds its plan. In effect, the plan is holding its assets in the plan sponsor's stock. If many firms underfund in this way, the same leverage argument holds.

When these firms combine to find insurance, the insurable event is the confluence of two events: the plan becomes underfunded *and* the firm encounters severe financial difficulties. In the case discussed above where firms maintain underfunding, the first condition always prevails. When firms have a target funding ratio of 100 percent but are invested in a diversified portfolio, underfunding occurs when the market value of securities falls markedly. When this happens *and* some firms fail, an insurable event occurs.

This kind of insurance is akin to life insurance, where "death" is the failure of the firm. In life insurance, accidental insurance can be purchased on a term basis, but death from health problems must be sold on a term/renewal basis. Otherwise, the insurer could drop insureds as soon as, say, cancer is diagnosed. Because most firms fail slowly, we could think of these contracts as renewable, term contracts. Some agreement can be made in advance about the amount of insurance paid at the time of the insurable event.

Though there is some reason to believe in the possibility of a market for pension insurance, at least one serious problem could prevent its development. In reality, markets generally do not rise and fall in predictable patterns. In the above example, assets may fall by 50 percent and remain there for several years. Moreover, when investment returns are low, the evidence suggests that firms terminate plans in "clusters" because of the burden that higher contribution levels (to offset reduced asset values) placed on them (Ippolito, 1986). The occasional years in which large amounts of underfunding develop, and lots of terminations occur, generate "bunching" of claims over time, or catastrophic risk.

Catastrophic risk poses solvency problems for insurance firms. If large claims are taken after the first year of operation, the insurance company may be unable to honor its promises (unless it can find events to insure that are negatively correlated with pension losses). The problem is especially severe if the size of the insured plan population is skewed. If a few large plans randomly terminate soon after the insurance begins, the insurance company can easily be overwhelmed. This is a rationale for participation of an industry group or government in some type of reinsurance scheme.

CONCLUSION

The discussion in this chapter laid the groundwork for understanding why a demand for pension insurance might exist; how these insurance contracts might look; and why a private market might not arise to meet this demand. The starting point is understanding the nature of the pension promise between the firm and its workers. Workers in effect give up a portion of cash wages in exchange for a promised pension at retirement. This pension is essentially indexed to final wages at retirement (and, in effect, at least partially indexed to prices during retirement). If the firm survives, the workers will receive the value of the "ongoing" pension.

Insurance contracts could be written to protect termination-value or real-value pensions. The contract, however, must guarantee something less than ongoing pensions so that workers are included as coinsureds. The carrier must hold a portfolio that immunizes the value of the guarantee; this immunization could involve an all-bond portfolio or an all-T-bill portfolio, depending on the nature of the guarantee. Real-value contracts are more stable because all parties know in advance the real value of the guaranteed pension, the real price of the insurance, and the amount of coinsurance.

Insurance firms can play two roles in a pension market. First, they can act as *quality-assurers*, ensuring that firms not entirely "trustworthy" can credibly promise to pay termination-value or partially guaranteed real-value pensions. The self-preservation interests of the insurers guarantee that they will act as agents for workers in protecting at least insured benefits.

Second, insurance firms could permit *leverage* by firms and workers who want a riskier but higher expected pension amount but also desire some minimum insurable pension in the event the firm fails. In this case, instead of all insureds holding a requisite bond or T-bill portfolio that guarantees at least a partial pension to workers, the insurer holds a much smaller bond or T-bill portfolio that actually will be used by the few insureds who need it.

One problem with private insurers offering pension insurance is the expected bunching of claims over time. Funding levels tend to fluctuate together for all insureds, and pension plan terminations tend to occur in clusters. Nonrandomness in claims makes it difficult for the private sector to offer credible insurance. This will be the starting point for the next chapter, which adopts this rationale for public insurance and begins the process of deriving insurance principles that would exist in a private insurance market.

CHAPTER 3

Insurance Principles and the PBGC

There are two theories why the Pension Benefit Guaranty Corporation exists: first, to provide insurance coverage that cannot be offered in the private sector because of poor information or the possibility of catastrophic claims; and second, to transfer monies from workers in the majority of sound pension plans to participants in poorly funded plans in dying industries.

I will not enter this debate in this book.[1] Instead, I simply assume that the first theory is correct—that the intent of Congress is for the PBGC to establish sound insurance principles much like the private sector would if it could feasibly insure pensions in the long run. This assumption does not determine the content of the book, just the "handle" that I use to collect and discuss pension insurance principles. If the second theory is correct—that Congress intends to maintain a transfer system rather than an insurance system—then the book can be viewed as an explanation of how transfers are effected through violation of sound insurance principles.

I assume that a demand for pension insurance existed prior to 1974. This does not mean insurance in a quality-assurance sense. The private market could have acted as an agent of sorts to guarantee workers that the firm could pay termination-value benefits in the event of firm failure. Instead, it means a demand for insurance against firm failure when pension plans are not fully funded and/or are characterized by portfolios that are not matched against pension liabilities. It is assumed that no market arose to meet the latter demand primarily because of the possibility of catastrophic events.

[1]Lengthy discussions of these matters can be found in Ippolito, October 1985, and April 1988. Full citations are found in Appendix F to this book.

In addition, a reasonable argument could be made that no insurance company wanted to be the first to market a new line of insurance. In the absence of any information about the size of claims, and any experience with moral hazard and selection problems, the first firm in this market would be an innovator of sorts, a collector of statistics, and a developer of solutions to problems. Everyone has an incentive to free ride on the first entrant, that is, to copy the product of the first entrant's research, thus making it difficult for the first firm to recoup its development cost. In this sense, the PBGC can fulfill a role: it can collect and disseminate statistics on the frequency and magnitude of the insurable event and can identify moral hazard problems that need to be addressed, together with some attempted solutions.

In this chapter as well as the next two, I will discuss the experience of the PBGC from 1974 to 1986. This experience provides a basis to (1) understand reform efforts, including legislation enacted in 1987 (the subject of Chapters 6 and 8) and (2) formulate ideas for economically rational insurance schemes (the subject of Chapters 9 and 10).

DEVELOPING POLICY AT THE PBGC

The previous chapter's discussion centered around insurance principles that likely would characterize pension insurance in the private sector. Assuming the PBGC's ultimate goal is to mimic a private-sector solution, it is interesting to create a scorecard of sorts comparing its actual policy against these principles.

Benefit Guarantee

The PBGC guarantees nominal pension benefits. This guarantee introduces two sound principles into the insurance system: coinsurance with workers and the ability to immunize obligations. It has also pursued a vigorous policy to preserve the coinsurance feature by opposing new plans designed to offset worker losses following insufficient terminations.

ERISA is also written to control some moral hazard prior to termination. It does this by applying a five-year phase-in rule (20 percent per year) for newly enacted benefit increases. There is also an overall maximum benefit payment of $1,909 in 1988 dollars, indexed to the social security wage base.

While these rules work to control the amount of the guarantee, the PBGC, through regulation, has made decisions that have greatly expanded the nature of the guaranteed amount. These decisions include a regulation that pays benefits prior to normal retirement ages (usually age 62 or 65), *not* at actuarially reduced amounts but at amounts as high as those available at normal retirement. Thus, if a plan has a normal retirement age of 62 but permits full benefits at age 55 with 30 years' service, the PBGC guarantees the full amount to anyone with 30 years' service (subject to the actuarially reduced maximum benefit at age 65). The PBGC could have guaranteed benefits beginning only at age 62 or paid benefits prior to age 62 at actuarially reduced rates, but it chose not to effect this policy.

In addition, the PBGC issued a benefit payments regulation[2] that later was interpreted by the PBGC to include the payment of pretermination *shutdown benefits*.[3] This means that if a plan has a provision to pay, for example, full unreduced benefits to all workers with 30 years' service on plant shutdown, a worker age 48 would be guaranteed full benefits at the PBGC (subject to the maximum benefits limit). In comparison to a rule that could have been consistent with the social security system (full benefits at age 65), the PBGC agreement to pay shutdown benefits to a 48-year-old worker is equivalent to paying unemployment benefits for 17 years and retirement benefits thereafter.

In addition, because the PBGC insures nominal benefits, there is great variation in the coinsurance value of the contract and a strong sensitivity of the PBGC's financial condition to variations in the long-term interest rate. The mirror of these problems is that workers are uncertain about what portion of their pension actually is insured in real terms. For much of this book, the character of this PBGC contract simply is accepted, but discussion of real-value insurance alternatives will take place later.

Pricing

These benefit-guarantee decisions would not be so problematic if a pricing scheme had been developed that set premiums in relation to risk and exposure. Until 1988, there was only one per-participant premium charge. The premium was not higher for plans that had higher benefit levels, lower funding ratios, more generous early retirement benefits, shutdown provisions, or higher risks of default. A small range of prices was introduced in 1988, but the range is so limited that it is economically indistinguishable from a flat premium pricing system (see Chapter 6).

In view of the inflexible pricing system, it might have been more logical to expect the PBGC and Congress to define a more homogeneous insurance policy. For example, until more information was obtained through experience, the policy could have been written to pay annual benefits not to exceed the "typical" pension plan benefit (say, 1

---

[2]See 29 CFR 2621.4.

[3]Special benefits triggered by plant shutdowns that occur after termination of the pension plan are not guaranteed by the PBGC.

percent, times service, times the average of the highest-three wage years, to commence at age 62). This policy still would not rationalize a one-price policy because it ignores differential funding ratios and risks of default, but at least it would have substantially reduced the magnitude of the cross-subsidies that characterize the existing system.

There is also no provision for the premium to change even if overall exposure changes substantially. If the interest rate falls from 10 percent to 2 percent, PBGC exposure is increased greatly. Until 1988, there was no provision for premium levels to increase to reflect this reality. Since then, premiums can change somewhat but not by amounts sufficient to cover the higher expected claims amounts.

Control of Funding

The discussion of insurance principles in the previous chapter suggests the possibility that insurers could rationally provide insurance for plans that maintained either full funding or less-than-full funding. In the former case, claims would be made only when failures occurred *and* prices of trust securities fell below existing levels. In the latter case, the insurable event occurs on firm failure, even if asset prices remain unchanged from existing levels. Of course, the price of insurance in the former case would be much lower than in the latter case. PBGC insurance clearly falls in the second category.

Though full funding is not required under law, ERISA took some steps in the direction of controlling funding. For example, it precluded firms from holding their own stock or bonds in the plan beyond 10 percent of the portfolio. In addition, the *minimum funding rules* instituted were ostensibly designed to reduce underfunded pensions over time. It is apparent that these funding rules were not very constraining. When Allis-Chalmer's United Auto Workers pension plan terminated in July 1985, its funding ratio was less than 2 percent; the firm never received a funding waiver and never violated ERISA's funding rules.

On top of ineffective funding rules, ERISA permitted firms in distress to obtain contribution *waivers* in up to 5 of every 15 years. This policy permitted firms to defund their pension plans if they were in financial difficulty. Control over the waiver policy was given to the Internal Revenue Service rather than to the PBGC. If the IRS granted waivers, their tax revenue would tend to increase because of lower pension contributions; it is not obvious that increased exposure given to the PBGC always was recognized or given major consideration.

The institution of waivers, the inadequacy of minimum funding standards, and the lack of control over guaranteed benefits give firms enormous control over the magnitude and timing of the insurance claim. It is inconceivable that private-sector insurance firms would provide protection to events so much in the control of the insured. This policy could be defensible if the PBGC had a high priority in bankruptcy because it essentially would be equivalent to setting market prices for insurance. For example, suppose bankruptcy rules were altered to create a new top-priority claim for pension obligations, so that up to 75 percent of these obligations were paid before all other claims, including secured claims. Then, in most cases, regardless of the moral hazard affiliated with defunding the pension prior to failure, the PBGC at most could absorb 25 percent of the promised benefits; the effective funding ratios would have a floor of 75 percent.[4]

The effect of such a rule could be that other creditors, including secured creditors, would have a strong incentive to set credit prices to reflect the firm's funding condition. That is, the higher the level of exposure and risk, the higher the interest rate that would be set by creditors to the plan sponsor. This is akin to the imposition of a risk-and-exposure–related premium structure enforced by the private sector.

The substitution of private-sector enforcement for government enforcement did not occur. PBGC claims are included in those of unsecured creditors, and they recoup very little of their claims on firm failure (historical recoveries are in the range of 10 percent).[5]

In 1988, changes made in ERISA's minimum funding rules required stricter standards on firms that maintained underfunded pension plans and reduced the amount of defunding prior to termination. Owing to transitional rules (especially favorable to large integrated steel firms), it will be some time before the impact of these rules can be measured. The legislation, however, did not change the level of benefit guarantees; nor did it eliminate all the potential for defunding prior to termination. Thus, the possibility remains that these rules alone will not solve the so-called PBGC problem. Chapter 8 deals with these issues in detail.

The Insurable Event

When ERISA was enacted the insureds had much control over the insurable event. The firm could terminate a pension plan in exchange for 30 percent of its net worth at any time. This meant that firms were not required to enter bankruptcy proceedings or even evince financial distress in order to "put" their claim to the PBGC.

---

[4]The floor would be lower in cases in which firms had insufficient assets to pay off unfunded pension liabilities. But because pensions would be at the top of the queue of creditors (including secured creditors), this would presumably be a rare event.

[5]PBGC claims are treated as priority claims (like unpaid taxes) up to 30 percent of the company's net worth. The problem is that many firms in bankruptcy proceedings arguably have little net worth.

In 1986, Congress enacted the Single-Employer Pension Plan Amendments Act of 1986 (SEPPAA), which redefined the insurable event. Essentially, it precluded the possibility that healthy firms could dump pension plans on the PBGC. As a practical matter, the law made financial "distress" the insurable event.

CONSEQUENCES OF CURRENT POLICY

The policies pursued at the PBGC represent serious violations of fundamental insurance principles. The pricing system makes no attempt to require insureds to face the cost of the insurance, and moral hazard is seemingly encouraged. Before considering reform ideas for the institution, which will be the subject of later chapters, it is useful first to review the experience of the PBGC under past policies, beginning with its pricing and claims history. In 1974, ERISA set a single-employer premium equal to $1 per participant per year; this was increased to $2.60 in 1978 and to $8.50 in 1986. These rates, however, proved insufficient to cover claims. The amount of the deficit is shown in Table 3–1.

What started as a small shortfall ($47 million in 1975) grew rapidly.

TABLE 3–1 PBGC Net Claims and Deficit ($ 1986)

Year	*Net Claims**	*Deficit†*	*Premium per Participant*
1975	$ 56	$ 47	$1.00
1976	31	71	1.00
1977	37	153	1.00
1978	109	207	2.60
1979	62	202	2.60
1980	110	123	2.60
1981	87	226	2.60
1982	300	380	2.60
1983	199	568	2.60
1984	36	481	2.60
1985	190	1,378	2.60
1986	2,895	3,826	8.50‡
Total	$4,112		

Note: Deficit is calculated as of September 30. Numbers for 1986 include LTV terminations.

* Losses for plans pending termination as of fiscal year-end are included in the deficit as of the end of the fiscal year in which the pending reserve is established. Net claims subsequently incurred for those plans are included above in the fiscal year in which the plan terminated, with the exception of fiscal 1986. Estimated claims for plans pending termination as of 9/30/86 are included above in net claims for fiscal year 1986.

† Deficit is as reported in PBGC's financial statements at fiscal year end (Annual Reports, various years), indexed to 1986 dollars.

‡ Effective in 1988, the base premium was increased to $16. In addition, an exposure-related charge is assessed against underfunded plans. The maximum premium is set at $50 (see Chapter 6).

Despite the premium increases, the deficit increased to $226 million in 1981, then to $481 million in 1984, and then to $3.8 billion in 1986. The data in this table provide the information to begin developing a rational insurance policy. The effort to control the increasing deficit has forced the PBGC and Congress to begin rethinking issues, including the insurable event, moral hazard, and pricing.

The data in the table make two things clear. First, the stickiness of the premium charges suggests the PBGC and Congress have been reluctant to believe that growing claims are a permanent fixture of the insurance system. Second, the data confirm the variance in claims over time: the annual claims amounts vary from less than 10 percent of the average annual claims amount to over 12 times the average. This variance is attributed to two factors. First, most of the PBGC's deficit is attributable to a handful of large claims. This is made evident in Table 3–2, which lists the 12 largest claims against the PBGC through 1986. These events account for fully 76 percent of the PBGC's claims through 1986. Second, the underlying possibility of plan termination is not independent across plans. A common factor responsible for much of the deficit at the PBGC is the decline of a single industry, steel. The data in Table 3–3 show that terminations from the steel industry account for

TABLE 3–2 The Twelve Largest Claims against PBGC as of 1986 (dollars in millions)

Number of Plans	*Plan Sponsor*	*Fiscal Year Termination Occurred*	*Event Resulting in Termination*	*Net Claim in 1986 Dollars*	*Percentage of Total PBGC Net Claims*
4	LTV	1986*	Chapter 11	$2,038	49.7
9	Wheeling-Pittsburgh	1986	Chapter 11	384	9.4
1	Allis-Chalmers	1985	Other†	145	3.7
10	Allis-Chalmers	1986	Other†	7	.2
8	White Motors	1982	Chapter 11	74	1.8
3	Rath Packing	1982	Other‡	68	1.7
3	Continental Steel	1986	Chapter 7	59	1.4
2	Wisconsin Steel	1980	Chapter 11	75	1.8
2	McLouth Steel	1983	Chapter 11	62	1.5
3	Braniff Airlines	1982	Chapter 11	58	1.4
4	White Farm Equipment	1982	Chapter 11	55	1.3
3	Phoenix Steel	1983	Chapter 11	45	1.1
2	Alan Wood Steel	1978	Chapter 11	60	1.4
	Total			$3,130	76.4†

Note: A list of the largest 100 insufficient pension plan terminations ranked by underfunding amount at termination is found in Appendix A, Table A–13.

* Three of LTV's plans actually terminated in early FY87. They are shown here as FY86 terminations due to their inclusion as pending terminations as of 9/30/86 in PBGC's financial statement.

† Allis-Chalmers underwent a reorganization with its creditors that was outside of the bankruptcy chapters.

‡ Rath Packing terminated its plans due to adverse business conditions while still an ongoing firm not in bankruptcy.

TABLE 3–3 PBGC Claims from Steel Industry (in millions, adjusted to $ 1986)

Year	*Steel Claims*	*All Claims*	*Percentage*
1975	$ 2	$ 56	3.5
1976	7	31	22.5
1977	21	47	56.7
1978	66	109	60.5
1979	18	62	29.0
1980	84	110	76.3
1981	13	87	14.3
1982	10	300	3.3
1983	155	199	77.8
1984	8	36	22.2
1985	10	190	5.5
1986	2,827	2,895	97.6
Total	$3,221	$4,112	78.3

SOURCE: Nominal claims are taken from the PBGC Annual Report, 1986, and adjusted to 1986 dollars using the Bureau of Labor Statistics nonagricultural wage index (see Appendix A, Table A–1). Steel claims are based on a separate analysis of the Case Processing File.

almost 80 percent of all PBGC claims. A list of 50 large steel industry pension plan terminations (not including the three restored LTV plans) is given in Table 3–4.

Because the steel claims are heavily weighted by the LTV terminations, it is useful to depict the distribution of claims prior to this event. Table 3–5 shows this distribution as of June 1986 (prior to the LTV event) based on the largest 100 insufficient plan terminations through that date.[6] Fully 43 percent of claims came from the steel industry and another 20 percent from the auto industry. These two industries accounted for over three fifths of the PBGC claims. Equally interesting, virtually all claims have come from pension plans covering unionized workers (almost 95 percent).[7]

In addition, the interest rate has played an important role in the economic condition of the PBGC. Over the 1975–87 period, the PBGC immediate close-out rate at the end of the fiscal year varied from 6.75 percent in 1977 to 10.50 percent in 1982 to 7.75 percent in 1986. The highest close-out rate over the entire period was 11 percent. Had the interest rate been 11 percent over the entire period, total claims over the history of the PBGC would have been roughly two thirds of actual amounts (see Table 3–6).

---

[6]Industry and union codes were taken from the case processing files, supplemented by cross-matches with the U.S. Department of Labor's so-called EBS–1 tapes.

[7]Plans covering unionized workers are dramatically underfunded compared to plans covering nonunionized workers. See Ippolito, 1986.

TABLE 3–4 Steel Plan Terminations, 50 Largest Claims (excluding LTV terminations)

	Date of Termination	Plan Underfunding
WPSC-Ohio Valley Pension Plan*	11/08/85	$255.6
Republic Steel	09/30/86	219.2
Kaiser Steel Hourly	07/28/87	201.0
WPSC-Mon Valley Pension Plan*	11/08/85	161.4
WPSC Retirement Income Pension Plan*	11/08/85	93.5
Wisconsin Steel Works	05/16/80	55.3
Alan Wood Steel Co. Hourly	11/01/77	34.8
Continental Steel Corp	02/14/86	34.2
Mesta Machine Hourly	06/16/83	34.1
Kaiser Steel Salaried	02/28/87	31.5
Century Brass Products, Inc.	12/02/85	29.7
LTV—Reserve Mining Hourly	05/24/87	28.7
McLouth Steel Corp. Hourly	11/30/82	27.1
Phoenix Steel Corp. Claymont	08/22/83	22.8
Phoenix Steel Corp. Phoenixville	08/22/83	17.9
McLouth Steel Corp. Salaried	11/30/82	15.0
Heppenstall Co. Hourly	05/31/79	13.9
Mackintosh-Hemphill	01/31/87	13.6
Chase Brass and Copper Co.	06/28/76	13.3
Washburn Wire Company	10/31/76	13.2
Continental Steel Corp. Plan B	02/14/86	12.4
LTV—Continental EMSCO**	04/30/88	8.4
WPSC RR Mon Valley*	11/08/85	8.4
Donner Hanna Coke Hourly	12/01/87	7.5
LTV—Reserve Mining-Salaried**	03/25/87	7.4
Lebanon Steel Foundry Hourly	07/31/83	6.8
Washburn Wire Co.	10/01/79	6.4
Volco Steelworkers	10/22/85	5.8
Central Foundry Co. Molders	05/18/81	5.8
Alan Wood Steel Co. Salaried	11/01/77	5.7
Johnson Steel and Wire Co.	09/13/82	5.7
Mid-Vale Heppenstall Company	04/30/76	5.1
Kaiser Steel Fabricating	07/28/87	4.7
Kaiser Steel Napa	08/03/87	4.2
Continental Steel Corp. Joliet	02/14/86	4.1
Ironton Coke Corp. Hourly	05/06/82	4.0
The Union Metal Manufacturing	05/15/85	3.9
McKeesport Steel Casting	04/13/84	3.9
New Jersey Zinc Co.	01/01/83	3.6
Adirondack Foundries Hourly	12/31/87	3.6
Van Huffel Tube Corp.	11/30/85	3.5
Lebanon Steel Foundry	06/30/83	3.2
Universal Foundry Co.	04/08/85	3.1
Standard Tube of Detroit	12/30/83	2.7
Van Huffel Tube Corp.	11/30/85	2.7
Ashtabula Forge, Inc.	08/31/83	2.4
Superior Steel Casting Co.	08/11/78	2.4
Newman-Crosby Steel, Inc.	05/30/83	2.3
Adirondack Foundries Salaried	12/31/87	2.3
Mesta Machine Co. Salaried	06/16/83	2.2

Note: Plan underfunding differs from the net claim against the premium system. It excludes recoveries for unpaid contributions and employer liability. Claims are usually 20 percent lower than total underfunding at termination.

Duplicate entries denote multiple plan terminations by the same plan sponsor.

* Wheeling-Pittsburgh Steel Company.

** Not one of the four LTV terminations in 1986 (see chap. 1).

TABLE 3–5 Claims by Union Status, June 1986

Union Status of Terminated Underfunded Pension Plan		*Percent of Claims*
Nonunion		5.4%
Union		
Steel workers	43.0%	
Auto workers	20.0	
Others	31.6	
Total		94.6
Grand total		100.0%

NOTE: Numbers exclude LTV terminations; otherwise, they are based on the largest 100 insufficient plan terminations through June 1986.

SOURCE: PBGC Case Processing File, supplemented by the U.S. Department of Labor, EBS–1 tape.

Another way to see the importance of the interest rate is to calculate exposure levels facing the PBGC over time. Table 3–7 and Figure 3–1 show the exposure presented to the PBGC from all single-employer defined benefit plans from 1978 to 1986 (estimated). The funding ratios are calculated from Form 5500 Annual Pension Plan Reports and adjusted to 1986 dollars and the size of the defined benefit

TABLE 3–6 Sensitivity of Net Claims to Interest Rates (dollars in millions)

Fiscal Year	*PBGC Close-Out Rate*	*Net Claims in Nominal Dollars*	*Net Claims in 1986 Dollars*	*Net Claims, 1986 Dollars, Assuming a Close-Out Rate of 11 percent for All Years*
1975	8.00%	$ 30	$ 56	$ 35
1976	7.00	18	31	16
1977	6.75	23	37	23
1978	7.25	73	109	63
1979	7.75	45	62	39
1980	9.00	85	110	73
1981	10.25	73	87	67
1982	10.50	263	300	297
1983	9.50	183	199	165
1984	10.50	35	36	31
1985	9.25	177	190	148
1986*	7.75	2,895	2,895	1,704
Total	8.62%	$3,900	$4,112	$2,661

Note: The method used to adjust liabilities to a common interest rate is described in book Appendix B.

* Net claims figures for fiscal year 1986 include estimated claims for plans pending termination as of 9/30/86.

FIGURE 3–1 Termination Underfunding, 1978–1986

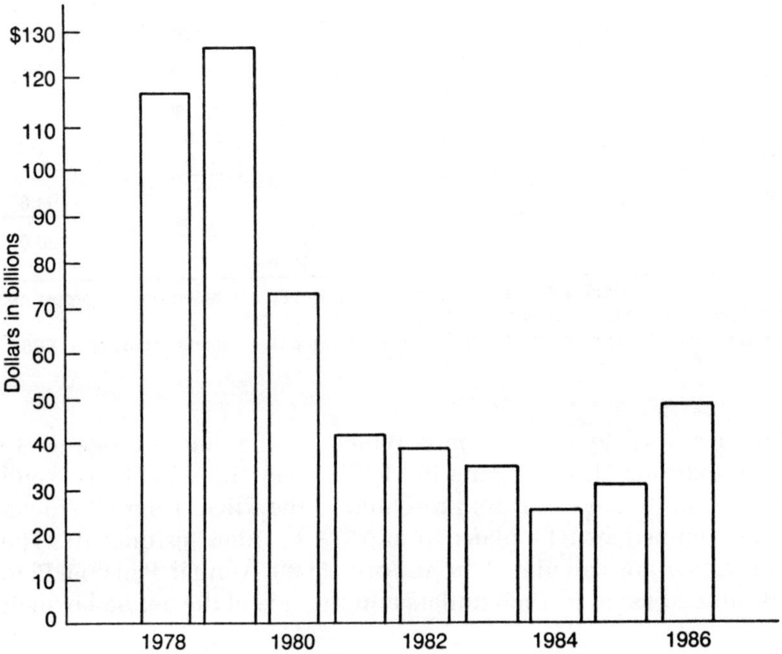

TABLE 3–7 Exposure Levels Facing the PBGC (dollars in billions)

Year	*PBGC Close-Out Rate*	*Funding Ratios Average*	*Exposure ($ 1986)*
1978	7.25%	92.9%	$116.7
1979	7.75	88.5	126.0
1980	9.00	107.2	73.0
1981	10.25	128.8	42.1
1982	10.50	130.9	39.5
1983	9.50	139.2	35.8
1984	10.50	153.9	25.9
1985	9.25	145.6	31.8
1986	7.75	128.5	49.2
Average	9.08%	123.9%	$ 59.9

Note: Exposure is adjusted to 1986 dollars and size of pension universe. Real funding ratios are calculated for each year using a constant 2 percent discount rate. Assets in year *t* are then set equal to assets in 1986 times the real funding ratio in year *t* divided by the same ratio in 1986. Liabilities in year *t* are set equal to those in 1986 but adjusted to the PBGC immediate rate in year *t* shown in the table.

SOURCE: Form 5500 Annual Pension Plan Reports.

universe in 1986. Thus, exposure does not reflect increases attributable to inflation or real growth in the system over time. Liabilities are converted to the PBGC immediate annuity rates shown in Table 3–7.

The variance in exposure is dramatic. It has varied from as little as $25 billion to over $126 billion in real terms over a period of only five years. Though some of this variation is attributable to overall movements in securities markets, most of it is attributable to changes in long-term nominal interest rates. This relationship is demonstrated in Table 3–8 and Figure 3–2, which show total underfunding in all defined benefit plans on an ongoing basis (also adjusted to net out inflationary growth and overall real growth in the system).

Ongoing liabilities are calculated using a common 2 percent interest rate for all years, reflecting pension promises to index pensions to wages until retirement (and to at least partially index pensions to prices beyond retirement). Variation in ongoing funding ratios as shown in Table 3–8 is not attributable to interest rate changes but instead to volatility in asset values. Because of increasing asset prices over the period, ongoing underfunding in defined benefit plans has decreased from $343 billion in 1978 to $187 billion in 1984.

Figure 3–3 visually compares the variation in ongoing and termination underfunding. In both cases, I have indexed underfunding relative to 1982 amounts. There is less variation in the ongoing underfunding compared to termination underfunding. The latter variable is a function of asset values and nominal long-term interest rates; the former variable varies with asset values but not with long-term interest rates.

The absolute amount of underfunding in an ongoing sense, however, is larger than in a termination sense owing to the much larger

TABLE 3–8 Pension Underfunding on an Ongoing Basis (dollars in billions)

Year	*Funding Ratios Average*	*Underfunding ($ 1986)*
1978	65.3%	$343.0
1979	60.3	387.5
1980	67.3	325.8
1981	74.4	268.5
1982	74.1	272.4
1983	84.3	203.5
1984	87.5	187.6
1985	86.5	191.3
1986	87.2	189.3
Average	76.4%	$262.8

Note: Underfunding is adjusted to 1986 dollars and size of pension universe. The adjustment procedure is same as described in the notes to Table 3–7, except liabilities in all years are fixed at 1986 levels, evaluated at a common 2 percent interest rate.

SOURCE: From 5500 Annual Pension Plan Reports.

FIGURE 3–2 Ongoing Underfunding, 1978–1986

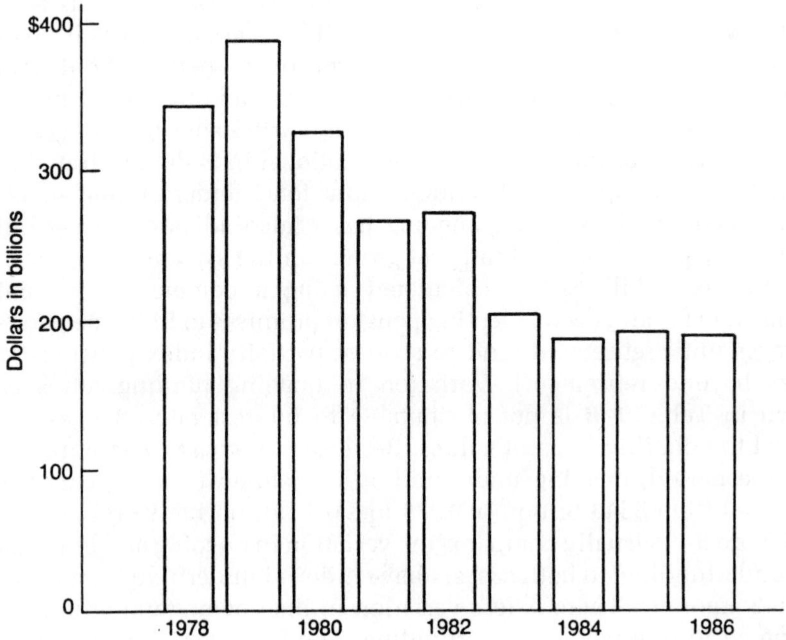

liabilities in the former. A comparison of Tables 3–7 and 3–8 shows that if PBGC insurance covered full expected pension benefits, instead of termination benefits, exposure levels would be over four times higher (and the coinsurance factor would be zero).

CONCLUSION

In this chapter, an attempt was made to summarize the insurance contract written by the Pension Benefit Guaranty Corporation. The system adopts a pension concept (termination-value pensions) that is insurable. And some rules were instituted by ERISA to protect the insurance system from obvious abuse. But many policies that violate sound insurance principles have been, and are, followed.

Much of the problem facing the PBGC is attributable to two factors: first, a lack of knowledge about the true extent of expected claims and the determinants of these claims; and second, a lack of a pricing system that allocates costs to expected claims. Notwithstanding the information problem, it is obvious that some pension features in some plans are costly relative to the average plan. If premium pricing is inflexible (as it apparently is, owing to congressional constraints), it is peculiar that the

FIGURE 3–3 Variation in Funding, 1978–1986 (relative to 1982 funding ratio)

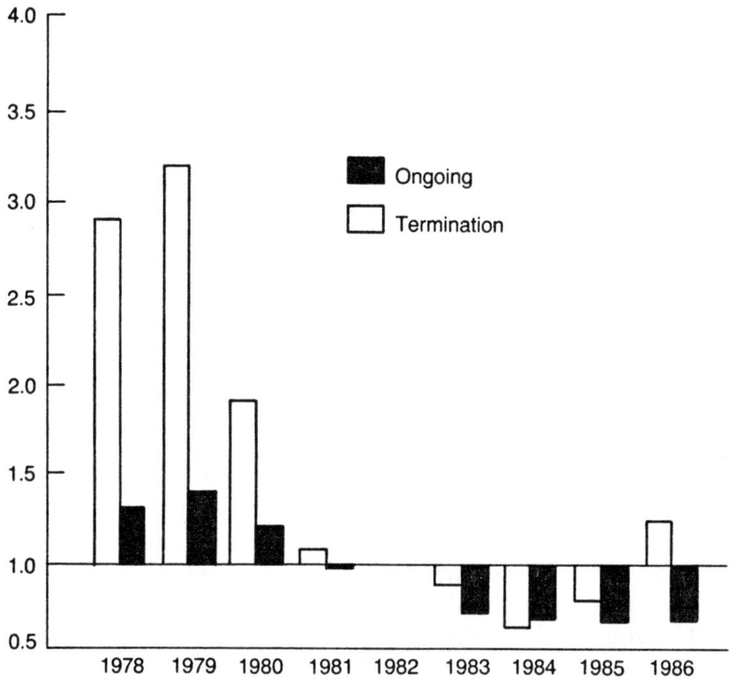

PBGC issued regulations guaranteeing unreduced (instead of actuarially reduced) benefits to early retirees, including "very" early retirees eligible for shutdown benefits.

Moreover, owing to ineffective funding rules, partial coverage of enhanced pension benefits prior to termination, and inexplicable provisions (such as contribution waivers, which are outside the control of the PBGC), the moral hazard problems facing the PBGC are very large. The combination of operating an insurance company in violation of fundamental insurance principles, especially the absence of a rational pricing policy, has led to extraordinary economic problems at the PBGC.

The data also provide some evidence as to why private insurers may be reluctant to accept a brand new line of insurance. It is still not clear what claims levels can be expected, even after 13 years of experience. Claims are dominated by a few large terminations, mostly in the same industry. This discussion will be continued in Chapter 4, which traces the history of PBGC claims.

CHAPTER 4

Revenue Implications of Claims Experience

The previous chapters indicate there is much room for reform in the insurance policies practiced by the Pension Benefit Guaranty Corporation. Whatever its policy, however, any insurance company must determine the revenue needs implied by the contract it writes. The problem of trying to set the premium level implied by expected claims has plagued Congress and the PBGC since ERISA was enacted. In this chapter, past experience is summarized, the results of past exposure and premium studies are reviewed, and an attempt is made to use available information to characterize the magnitude of expected claims facing the PBGC under the law existing in 1987. These estimates provide a basis to discuss the likely impact of new legislation enacted in 1987 (see Chapter 8).

EVOLUTION OF CLAIMS EXPECTATIONS

Evidence from the Early Years

The first study of termination pension losses was done by the Departments of Treasury and Labor. Their report, entitled *Study of Pension Plan Terminations, 1972*, was published in August 1973. The study assumed that (1) termination activity during the year 1972 was representative of pre-ERISA experience and (2) benefit losses incurred in 1972 would be a good index of activity after the enactment of ERISA.

The first assumption was accurate. In fact, the evidence suggests 1972 witnessed an unusually high number of terminations (Ippolito, 1986). Moreover, the interest rate in 1972 was certainly no higher than the range of interest rates after ERISA. (Moody's Aaa bond rate in 1972 averaged 7.2 percent—see Appendix A to book, Table A–17. Compare this to the PBGC close-out rates from 1975 through 1986, which ranged from 6.75 percent to 10.50 percent—see Table 3–6.) Thus, calculations of termination-value benefits should not have been unrealistically low. The second assumption, we shall see, was not met.

Some of the characteristics of the insufficient terminations included in the study are shown in Table 4–1. Most of the terminated plans with losses had experienced economic problems, as evinced by the significant decline of participants in the five years prior to termination: 55 percent of the plans (weighted by participants) had at least a 25 percent reduction in participants. The funding ratios in these plans averaged 47 percent; and, as would be true of later experience, the results were dominated by a few plans (two plans accounted for fully one third of all losses in 1972).

The implied pension losses from these events (evaluated on a termination basis) are summarized in Table 4–2. There were roughly 19,400 participants in terminated plans that incurred losses; 8,500 were vested prior to termination. ERISA initially required vesting to occur within 10 years. During the period of the study, however, vesting usually occurred much later, often only at retirement age. Thus, many of the unvested losses prior to ERISA would be vested under ERISA rules and therefore subject to PBGC coverage.

Total benefit losses (liabilities minus assets in the pension plans) amounted to $48.6 million; losses to vested participants were $34.4 million. Because ERISA vesting standards would be more liberal than pre-ERISA standards in most plans and because the PBGC would insure only vested benefits, it is reasonable to infer from this experience that post-ERISA losses facing the PBGC would be in the range of $40 million.

The roughly 23 million participants in the single-employer pension plan universe suggest that a premium equal to $1.75 should have been established. Congress chose to be optimistic and set the rate at $1. As it

TABLE 4–1 Characteristics of Insufficient Plans, 1972

Category	*Quantity*
Percent with participant decline over 5 years (weighted by participants)	
At least 25% decline	55.7%
With some decline	96.7
Percent losses attributable to 2 largest plans (out of 546 plans with losses)	33.0
Funding ratio (including unvested benefits)	47.0

SOURCE: U.S. Departments of Treasury and Labor, *Study of Pension Plan Terminations, 1972,* (Washington, D.C.: U.S. Government Printing Office, August 1973).

TABLE 4–2 Losses from Terminated Plans, 1972

Category	*Quantity*
Participants	
Total	42,000
With losses	19,400
Vested with losses	8,500
Losses*	
Total	$48.6 million
Vested	34.4 million
Participants in all single employer plans	23 million
Participants with losses (19,400/23 million)	.08 %

* Losses are defined as termination-value liabilities minus the sum of trust assets and 30 percent of the plan sponsor's equity.

SOURCE: U.S. Departments of Treasury and Labor, *Study of Pension Plan Terminations, 1972*, (Washington, D.C.: U.S. Government Printing Office, August 1973), Tables 3–1 and 3–5A.

turned out, the $1.75 number would have been almost precisely what was needed to ensure a zero deficit at the end of the second fiscal year (September 30, 1976).

In 1977, the PBGC released the results of its first premium study. Data from the study are shown in column 1 of Table 4–3. The data show that based on the $1 premium, a $41 million deficit had been accumulated. To remedy this, the study recommended a premium

TABLE 4–3 The PBGC Deficit, 1976 and 1981 (dollars in millions)

	Cumulative Amount from Inception	
Category	*9/30/76*	*9/30/81*
Revenues		
Premiums	$48.2	$336.6
Investment income	5.0	55.8
Total revenues	53.2	392.4
Expenses		
Net claims from termination	59.3	429.8
Actuarial adjustment*	7.7	56.5
Pending terminations	15.0	—
Administrative expenses	12.2	94.9
Total expenses	94.2	581.2
Net deficit	($41.0)	($188.8)

* The actuarial adjustment reflects (1) charges caused by the passage of time that shortens the discount period before benefit payments are scheduled to be paid and (2) charges due to changes in the interest rate between the date of plan termination and the financial statement date. Assets and liabilities are reported on a market-value basis.

SOURCE: PBGC, *Premium Requirements for the Single-Employer Basic Benefits Insurance Program*, 1977 and May 1982.

increase to $2.25, which was roughly consistent with the original Treasury/Labor study, except a provision now was required to amortize the deficit and to account for inflation. Congress took the conservative route and enacted a premium of $2.60 effective January 1, 1978.

By 1981, this premium was obviously insufficient. Part of the problem was that the premium was not indexed to benefit levels. For example, wages (to which most pensions are explicitly or implicitly indexed) increased by 50 percent in the five-year period from 1976 to 1981 (see Appendix A, Table A–1). The other part was that claims rose at an ever-increasing rate even after adjusting for wages. Annual claims during the first two years of operation averaged $25 million; claims in the next five years increased by 140 percent in real terms, averaging over $60 million.

In 1982, the PBGC released its second premium study. The financial statement presented in the study is shown in the second column of Table 4–3. By the end of 1981, the deficit was $188 million. Based on this study, the PBGC asked for a premium increase to $6 effective January 1, 1983. Otherwise, the deficit, based on recent claims experience, would increase to $470 million by year-end 1986. Congress did not enact a premium increase.

Reappraisal of Claims and Policy: The 1982–1983 Experience

Though claims had increased to approximately $60 million per year during the five-year period ending in 1981, this still represented a problem of small magnitude. With defined benefit plan participation approaching 30 million, a flow of $60 million in claims could be financed by a premium of $2 per participant. Amortization of the deficit (over five years) and administrative expenses could also be accommodated by a $6 premium, which was the recommendation of the 1982 PBGC study.

In addition, interest rates in 1982 were historically high. Moody's Aaa in 1982 averaged 16.1 percent (see Appendix A, Table A–17); the PBGC immediate close-out rates averaged 10.7 percent (Appendix C, Table C–2). As discussed in previous chapters, high interest rates reduce the current deficit and reduce expected claims (benefit obligations are discounted at higher rates). In short, given the experience of the previous five years and the existence of high interest rates, the PBGC had every reason to expect that a $6 premium (perhaps with some inflation adjustments) would make the institution solvent.

This institutional confidence had another subtle effect. As long as the policy of the PBGC implied a "small" numbers problem (that is, if claims resulting from a cavalier insurance policy implied a small premium), it was not necessary to reconsider the adequacy of insurance principles practiced by the institution.

This collective attitude, shared by the PBGC and Congress, began to change during 1982. Prior to this time, the PBGC had accepted two extraordinary claims: $40 million resulting from Alan Wood Steel Company in 1978, and $58 million from Wisconsin Steel in 1980. After completing its 1982 premium study, however, the PBGC received four large claims: White Motors (truck manufacturer), Rath Packing (meat packer), Braniff (airline), and White Farm (farm machinery manufacturer). These claims totaled $223 million. All claims in 1982 amounted to $280 million. This rate of claims exceeded the prior five-year annual experience by over 300 percent.

The extraordinary 1982 experience was followed in fiscal 1983 with several additional steel terminations, beginning with McLouth Steel's $57 million claim, followed by Phoenix Steel and Mesta Machine with over $70 million in combined claims. Total claims in 1983 amounted to $174 million. The deficits on September 30 were $332 million in 1982 and $523 million in 1983, in comparison to $188 million in 1981.

The claims experience of 1982 and 1983 caused great concern at the PBGC. The sheer magnitude of the claims that lay behind this experience, however, created a tendency to treat them as aberrations. Congress shared this attitude. Despite the huge additional claims beyond those that justified the $6 premium request, Congress did nothing to augment PBGC's revenues. The ensuing experience in 1984 appeared to justify this wait-and-see attitude: claims during 1984 were only $27 million.

The 1982–83 activity, however, began a process of reassessing both the magnitude of claims that might characterize the insurance program and the policies followed by the institution. First, among the four large terminations in 1982, only one had a guaranteed funding ratio (assets divided by PBGC guaranteed benefits) greater than 33 percent (Braniff's funding ratio was 46 percent). Rath had a funding ratio of 16 percent. And recall that these funding ratios are evaluated at historically high interest rates.

The reasons underlying these funding situations gradually became apparent. Waivers from required contributions were found to be an important contributing factor. This became obvious in 1982 when Rath Packing terminated its plans. As Table 4–4 shows, Rath had received waivers for the maximum five years from 1977 to 1982 before it terminated in 1982 with a claim of $59.8 million. Accumulated unpaid waivers (unadjusted for interest) amounted to $29.5 million, approximately half of the claims amount.

The PBGC also began to appreciate the true cost of regulations issued early in the program to guarantee full benefits prior to normal retirement age, including shutdown benefits (see Chapter 5). In essence, auto and steel unions, among others, had retirement provisions

TABLE 4–4 Waivers Example—Rath Packing (numbers in millions)

Year	*Amounts*
1977	$ 4.9
1978	5.1
1980	6.3
1981 and 1982 combined*	13.2
Total†	$29.5
Claims (September 1982)	59.8
Waivers as portion of claims	49.3%

* Figures not separately available for each year.

† At time of termination, Rath had repaid roughly $1.8 million of its cumulative waivers to the plan.

SOURCE: PBGC Termination Case File. Because I did not have access to Internal Revenue Service documents (which are not publicly available), the data in the above table should be considered estimates.

that paid full benefits at age 55 with 30 years' service, 10 years prior to normal retirement age. In addition, they had contract provisions that made full unreduced benefits available to most middle-aged workers after a plant shutdown even though they otherwise did not qualify for full pension benefits. Thus, on a plant shutdown, benefits might be payable to an individual at age 45 with 20 years' service. Because shutdowns tended to be concentrated shortly before termination dates, huge unfunded new benefits were imposed on the PBGC.

An early example of this was the Alan Wood Steel termination for hourly workers in 1977. Table 4–5 summarizes the data describing the plan and the nature of the claim. The plan had a "30-and-out" requirement for full benefits (after age 55) and full benefits on shut-

TABLE 4–5 The Alan Wood Steel (Hourly) Termination

Category	*Descriptions/Amounts*	
Facts of the case		
Date of terminations	November 1977	
Normal retirement age	Age 65	
Full benefits rule	30 and out at age 55	
Shutdown provision	Age 55 with 15 years, or when the sum of age and service is 80	
Number of participants	1,955	
Breakdown of the claim		
Amount of claim ($ millions)	$34.8	100%
Shutdown benefits	3.6	10.3
Other early full benefits	5.9	16.9
Total early supplements	$ 9.5	27.2%

down to all workers age 55 with 15 years' service or a combined age-and-service total of 80 (for example, a 50-year-old worker with 30 years' service). Of 1,955 participants in the plan, 354 were collecting shutdown benefits.

Of the total claim of $34.8 million, $3.6 million was attributable to PBGC guarantees to pay shutdown benefits until normal retirement age, and $5.9 million was attributable to guarantees to pay full benefits prior to age 65 (normal retirement age in the plan). Fully 27.2 percent of the claims were attributable to PBGC guarantees to pay unreduced benefits prior to normal retirement age.

Escalation of Activity: 1985–1986

The reduction in claims activity in 1984 turned out to be short lived. In 1985, the flow of large terminations resumed. Allis-Chalmers (farm implements) made a claim of $142 million. In 1986, further steel terminations occurred, including Wheeling-Pittsburg's claim of $383 million. Also in 1986, however, the event that PBGC had hoped would not occur did occur. Previous large threatened terminations involving Chrysler Corporation and International Harvester never occurred (though the Wisconsin Steel termination was a spinoff of International Harvester). LTV Corporation entered Chapter 11 of the Bankruptcy Code, and the PBGC terminated four of its pension plans, resulting in a claim of over $2 billion. The deficit at the PBGC doubled to almost $4 billion.

These claims together with the post-1981 experience ultimately conveyed the notion that the cost implications of the pension insurance program would be much greater than the one-dollar-per-participant premium that Congress originally envisioned. As a consequence, policies that had been established in the ERISA legislation began to be reevaluated.

The Allis-Chalmers termination provided an illustration of the ineffectiveness of minimum funding standards enacted under ERISA. This firm's terminated plans had an overall funding ratio of 19 percent. One plan for its unionized workers terminated with enough assets to pay two months of benefits to existing retirees: This occurred even though the plan sponsor never received a waiver and never violated the minimum funding requirement.

The problem occurred for two reasons. First, the plan had a "flat dollar" benefit (dollars per year of service). Even though the union and firm renegotiate the flat benefit each three years to reflect inflation (it essentially mimics a final pay plan), the Internal Revenue Code does not recognize that the flat benefit will increase regularly over time. Thus, if a firm uses a flat benefit plan, it receives a license of sorts to underfund persistently.

Second, the existence of underfunding is permitted to be amortized over as long as 30 years. In a dying firm like Allis-Chalmers, the participants are dominated by older workers and retirees. The amortization period is much longer than the average life of plan participants.

Exposure Measurements

To augment the paucity of historical data, the PBGC developed a system to measure its exposure beginning in 1981. The first exposure calculations, however, were done outside the PBGC. The first post-ERISA study I am aware of was included in a book published in 1976 by Jack Treynor and colleagues, *The Financial Reality of Pension Funding under ERISA*. That book reported the results of a survey done by the authors of 40 large pension plans. They found that in 1974, only one fourth of the plans were fully funded (using actuarial interest rates). They ranked underfunded vested benefits (UVB) as a proportion of total assets in the firms. The average firm had UVB equal to 9 percent of firm assets. Interestingly, of the 14 firms with pension burdens higher than this (up to 25 percent of asset value), 4 were automobile companies, 1 was a farm equipment manufacturer, 2 were automobile-related tire firms, and 4 were steel firms.

During the same year, *Business Week* reported the results of a survey by Investor's Management Sciences, Inc. (IMS—a subsidiary of Standard & Poor's Corporation) of 1,644 large firms in 1976. *Business Week* listed the amount of underfunding for the 74 largest firms. This report was noticed by the PBGC, and a staff analysis of the data was made on an industry basis. Apparently no formal report was ever made, but I found a handwritten note dated August 3, 1977. The note, reproduced in Figure 4–1, reports an alarming amount of systematic underfunding in one industry, steel (amounting to almost $1 billion in 1976 dollars), and warns of pending catastrophe at the PBGC "if the steel industry (goes) sour."

Subsequent to the issuance of a rule by the Financial Accounting Standards Board requiring firms to report underfunded pension liabilities and assumed interest rates (*FASB 36*), the PBGC began a systematic evaluation of its exposure. It calculated unfunded vested pension liabilities from the Compustat, Inc., database and applied various measures of firms' financial stability available from the financial literature. An algorithm for classifying firms as "very high risk," "high risk," and "moderate risk" was employed.

Firms in these risk categories were listed with calculations of their unfunded vested pension liabilities. Firms with at least $5 million in underfunded benefits were analyzed. A summary of these exposure calculations is shown in Table 4–6. Exposure in the two highest risk classes amounted to approximately $2 billion in all years except 1987,

FIGURE 4–1 Observation on Underfunding, 1977

JOHN –

OUT OF 1644 FIRMS STUDIED BY IMS INC., 1321 REPORTED DATA ON UNFUNDED VESTED BENEFITS. OF THESE, 43 HAD UNFUNDED VESTED BENEFITS IN EXCESS OF 30% OF NET WORTH. OF THESE, 11 ARE IN THE STEEL INDUSTRY. APPARENTLY, THIS IS THE ONLY INDUSTRY TO FOLLOW THE PRACTICE VIRTUALLY ACROSS THE BOARD OF POOR FUNDING OF PENSION BENEFITS. THESE 11 COMPANIES HAVE A COMBINED EXPOSURE TO PBGC OF $964.9 MILLION. IF WE WERE TO HAVE A CATASTROPHE RESERVE, THE EVENT WHICH WOULD BE A MAJOR CATASTROPHE FOR PBGC WOULD BE IF THE STEEL INDUSTRY WENT SOUR.

BOB
8-3-77

SOURCE: Note from Robert Klein to John Hirschmann

when the number increased to roughly $3 billion.[1] Adjusted to 1986 dollars and interest rates, however, and adding exposure in the LTV restored plans (not reflected in the 1987 study database), these numbers are closer to $5 billion in most years (see the last column in Table 4–6).

[1]The data in Table 4–6 reflect *FASB 36* rules for reporting underfunding on the balance sheet. It permits firms to combine all pension plans for purposes of calculating underfunding. Because the PBGC is liable for underfunding in insufficient plans but has no claim to excess assets in overfunded plans, the true PBGC exposure in risky firms is greater than shown in the table.

TABLE 4–6 Risk Exposure to the PBGC (numbers in billions)

	Amount of Underfunding			
*Year of Study**	*Very High Risk*	*High Risk*	*Total*	*Adjusted†*
1982	$1.6	$.1	$1.7	$4.3
1983	1.2	.4	1.6	5.5
1984	1.5	.1	1.6	3.6
1985	1.4	.5	1.9	5.4
1986	N/A	N/A	N/A	N/A
1987	2.6	.8	3.4	5.0

* Data for each study pertain to the year prior to the study date. Thus, the 1982 exposure data relate to the 1981 reporting year. Data for 1981 are not presented on a basis consistent with other years. Also, see footnote 1 in text.

† Numbers in this column are adjusted to the same PBGC interest rate and price level that characterize the numbers reported in the 1987 study. The 1987 results were adjusted to include LTV, which otherwise was excluded from the database.

SOURCE: PBGC exposure measurements, various years.

Virtually all large claims absorbed by the PBGC after 1981 have been "flagged" by the exposure calculations. Table 4–7 lists the 10 largest terminations after 1981. All appeared as very high risks in exposure lists prepared in previous years.

The major shortcoming of using exposure lists is that no probability

TABLE 4–7 Risk Categories of 10 Largest Terminations after 1981

		Category of Risk Reflected in PBGC Exposure Calculations 1981–1985		
Plan Sponsor	*Year Terminated*	*Very High Risk*	*High Risk*	*Moderate Risk*
LTV	1986	84, 85	81, 83	82
Wheeling-Pittsburgh*	1986	82, 84	83	81
Allis-Chalmers*	1985–86	84	83	—
White Motors	1982	81	83	—
Rath Packing	1982	81	—	—
Continental Steel*	1986	82, 83, 84	—	—
McLouth Steel	1983	82	—	81
Braniff	1982	81	—	—
White Farm Equipment†	1982	81	—	—
Phoenix Steel	1983	81, 82, 83	—	—

* Not included in 1985 for following reasons: Wheeling-Pittsburgh (pending termination); Allis-Chalmers (terminated subsequent to the 1984 plan year); Continental Steel (in process of involuntary termination).

† White Farm was a subsidiary of White Motors and therefore was included with the figures for White Motors in 1981.

SOURCE: PBGC exposure measurements, various years.

of failure is attached to firms in various categories, and presumably these probabilities are not constant within each class. If better probability estimates could be developed, the beginnings of a usable forecast model would be at hand at the PBGC. (One such model is presented in Chapter 6 in the context of an estimated risk and exposure pricing model.) Notwithstanding their shortcomings, however, these measurements have been successful in identifying a population of plans that are clear candidates for claims in ensuing years; and together with claims experience, the data help formulate expectations about future claims activity.

CALCULATION OF AN ECONOMIC PREMIUM

Magnitude of Expected Claims

The discussion in this chapter essentially includes all the information available to reassess the magnitude of expected claims. As discussed above, a predictive model to pension default risk has not been implemented at the PBGC. Nevertheless, estimates of exposure and default can be based on past experience on the assumption that sufficient time has passed to permit a fair representation of long-term experience.

This section reports the results of the most recent PBGC premium study, *Pension Promises at Risk* (1987). This study based its projections solely on historical claims received during the PBGC's first 12 years. In some sense, it updates the U.S. Departments of Treasury and Labor study, which was based on one year of data, 1972.

The first step taken in the study was the recalculation of historical claims in 1986 dollars. Claims variation attributable to variation in interest rates was not eliminated from the data; thus, there was an implicit assumption that interest rates over the period were representative of future experience. This claims experience is presented in column 2 of Table 4–8. For the sake of comparison, I adjusted these numbers to a common 7.25 percent interest rate, which was the average of the 1986 PBGC close-out rates. These numbers are shown in column 3 of Table 4–8 and are shown separately in Figure 4–2.

The data show that claims have been increasing steadily over time. Two alternate claims assumptions were made. First, a 12-year average was used. This assumes historical claims exhibit a cyclic pattern with some high-claims years and some low-claims years and 12 years is sufficient, in some sense, to characterize average expected claims experience. Second, the experience of the latest five years was used. This approach assumes that the early years of the insurance are not useful indicators of the future, that firms have since learned how to take

TABLE 4–8 Claims Experience, Adjusted for Interest Rates (numbers in millions)

Year	*Actual*	*$1986*	*7.25 Percent Interest Rate ($1986)*
	(1)	*(2)*	*(3)*
1975	$ 30	$ 56	$ 62
1976	18	31	33
1977	23	37	35
1978	73	109	103
1979	45	62	65
1980	85	110	136
1981	73	87	134
1982	263	300	487
1983	183	199	316
1984	35	36	52
1985	177	190	233
1986	2,895	2,895	3,226
Total	$3,900	$4,112	$4,882
Average			
12 years	325	341	406
5 years	710	724	862
5 and 12 years	518	532	634

Note: 1986 numbers reflect LTV terminations.

advantage of the PBGC, and therefore that more recent experience is more predictive of future experience.

In the study, both claims projections were used independently for sensitivity tests (see below). But for the so-called baseline forecast, the two numbers were averaged: essentially all 12 years of experience were incorporated into the expectation of future claims, but extra weight was given to the most recent five years of data. This resulted in a claims expectation of $532 million in 1986 dollars. The 12 and 5 years' numbers are also shown in Table 4–8.

Translating Claims to Premiums

The study presumed Congress would enact a premium formula that would yield a high (but unspecified) probability that the PBGC would not need to return to Congress for 30 years. Because the claims numbers are based on a weighted average interest rate in the vicinity of 8.25 percent, the forecast could be susceptible to reductions in the interest rate. As the numbers in Table 4–8 illustrate, if the interest rate is 7.25 percent, claims would be almost 20 percent higher.

Because the structure was to last 30 years, Congress would not be able to adjust the premium for inflation, and thus a model was designed

FIGURE 4–2 PBGC Claims, 1975–1986 (adjusted for prices and interest rates)

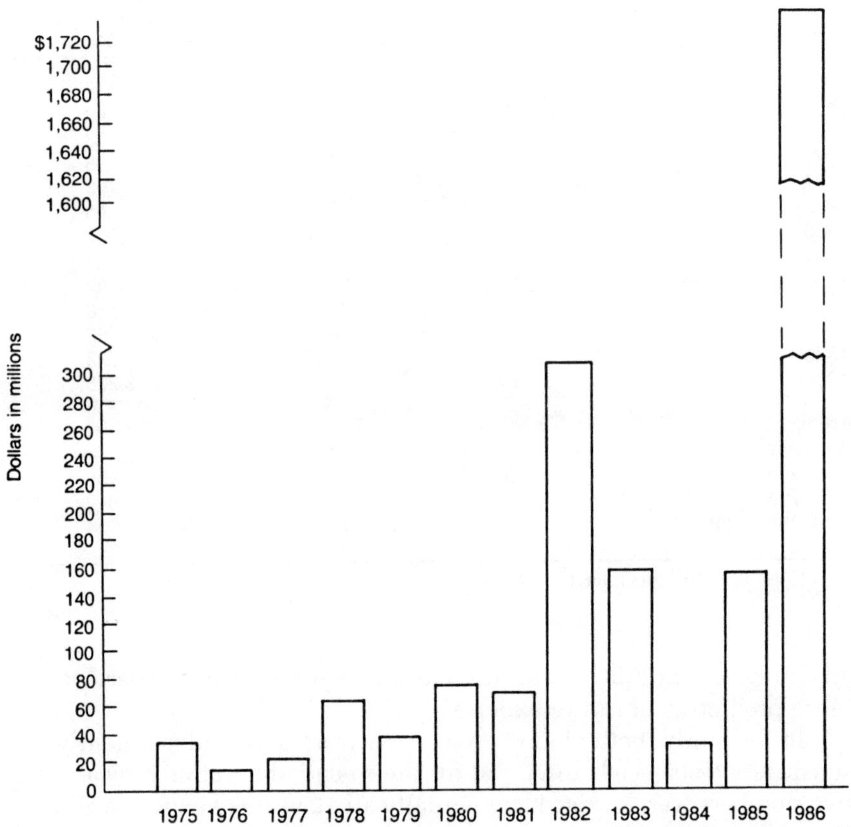

to calculate a premium per participant in 1986 dollars, which, if indexed to wages, would amortize the existing $4 billion deficit and finance claims over the next 30 years. The wage index was used because pensions are either directly or indirectly tied to wages.

A model was used to simulate the financial impact of future claims on the PBGC. It was assumed that wages would increase at the rate of 6.25 percent per year and that the number of defined benefit participants would increase at the rate 1.5 percent (consistent with employment growth over the past 30 years—see Appendix A, Table A–1). The discount rate was set at 7.25 percent. Claims per participant were expected to increase at the same rate as wages (6.25 percent). Funding ratios of terminated plans were assumed to remain at the average of recent experience, 41 percent. These assumptions are listed in Table 4–9.

TABLE 4–9 Economic Premium: Baseline Model

Premium (per participant)	
Indexed	$25.64
Flat	$54.05
Claims ($1986)	$532 million
Claims growth	7.75%
Interest rate	7.25%
Wage growth	6.25%
Participant growth	1.5%
Funding ratio at termination	41%

Note: Except for the last entry, all numbers are expressed on a per annum basis.

SOURCE: PBGC, *Pension Promises at Risk* (Washington, D.C.: Pension Benefit Guaranty Corporation, 1987).

Solving this model over 30 years yielded a required premium of $25.64 in 1986, indexed to wages. If Congress enacted a flat premium instead (one not indexed to wages), it would have to set the rate equal to $54.05. This rate is higher because in a flat premium scheme, the PBGC must collect "too much" money early to offset the inflation erosion of the premium in later years. These price schemes in real terms are shown in Figure 4–3.

FIGURE 4–3 Indexed versus Flat Premiums

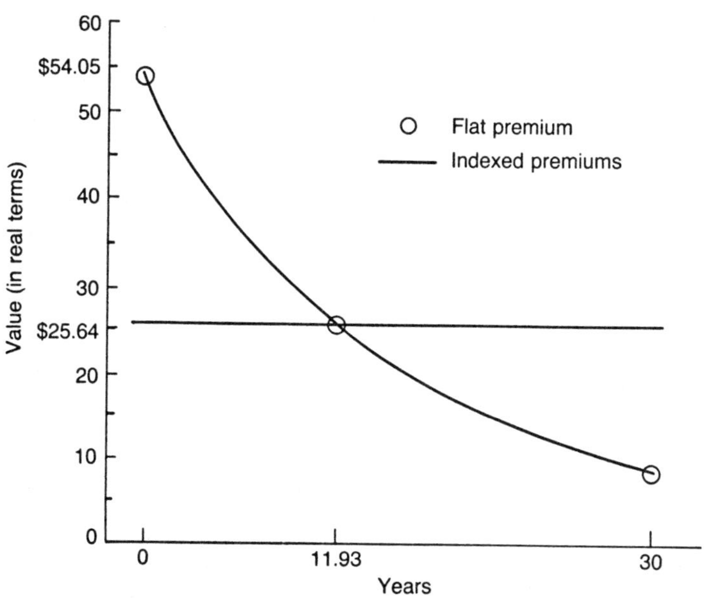

Sensitivity Tests

The next question posed by the study was the sensitivity of the premium requirement to the assumptions in the baseline model. Thus numerous additional scenarios were simulated. A representative selection of these scenarios is shown in Table 4–10. Scenario 1 is the baseline forecast. Scenarios 2 and 3 portray the 12- and five-year claims assumptions independently. Using the 12-year average, the economic premium is $18.56; using the five-year range, the premium is $32.73.

In scenario 4, the assumption that growth in defined benefit participants will continue to increase in approximate proportion to overall employment is replaced with the assumption that participant growth will be zero but claims will continue to increase at the 7.75 percent rate. Thus the number of premium payers evince a reduction in growth but not claims. This scenario results in a premium of $32.18. If participant growth remains at 1.5 percent but future funding ratios at termination fall in half to 20 percent, the economic premium is $33.48.

If the last three scenarios are combined, arguably a worst-case scenario is portrayed (scenario 6 in the table): the higher claims forecast prevails over 30 years; there is no growth in premium payers; and funding ratios at termination fall to 20 percent. This combination of events generates a required premium equal to $54.61, indexed to wages.

The last two scenarios (7 and 8) assume that interest rates will permanently increase or decrease by five percentage points in 1997. It is assumed that assets are all in bonds and matched to liabilities, which eliminates most of the effect on the balance sheet in 1997. Instead, it affects the amount of claims in the last 20 years of the horizon. The results show that if interest rates increase, the problems facing the PBGC will diminish. This is manifested by the need for a premium

TABLE 4–10 Economic Premium: Sensitivity Tests

Scenario	*Change in Assumptions*	*Premium (Indexed)*
1.	Baseline (see Table 4–8)	$25.64
2.	Lower claims: 12-year average ($341M)	18.56
3.	Higher claims: 5-year average ($710M)	32.73
4.	No growth in DB participants	32.18
5.	Lower funding ratios (20%)	33.48
6.	Combine 3, 4, and 5	54.61
7.	Higher interest rates* (12.25% beginning in 1997)	18.45
8.	Lower interest rates* (2.25% beginning in 1997)	39.11

* Assumes its entire asset/portfolio is in matching long-term bonds.

SOURCE: PBGC, *Pension Promises at Risk* (Washington, D.C.: Pension Benefit Guaranty Corporation, 1987).

equal to $18.45 indexed over the entire 30-year period. If the interest rate decreases to 2.25 percent (expected inflation is roughly zero), the economic premium is $39.11 over the period. In this scenario, the PBGC essentially insures real pensions after 1997 (see Chapter 2).

The model, including all sensitivity tests, tends to bound the economic premium at roughly $50, indexed to wages. The "best guess" in the study is roughly $25, but various plausible scenarios suggest this number could easily be in the range of $35, indexed to wages.

CONCLUSION

More than 15 years have passed since the first estimates of pension claims were made. Twelve years of claims and a series of risk and exposure studies are now in hand. These data demonstrate that the pre-ERISA estimates of claims were too low. Expected required premiums based on information available through 1986 turned out to be 25 to 50 times greater than originally expected.

The data also demonstrate the nonrandomness of the insurance events, evinced by large variation in claims over time. In addition, notwithstanding the continual reform efforts discussed in the next chapter, insureds may not have learned optimal gaming strategies against the PBGC. These two factors suggest that 12 years of data still may be insufficient to reliably estimate the true cost of the existing insurance contract; but we at least have a better ballpark estimate of the magnitude of claims. We also have confirmation of the nonrandomness of the events that make pensions a more difficult contract for the private sector to insure.

Current information also has implications for pricing. When pension insurance involved a cost of one dollar, devotion of resources toward control of moral hazard and development of proper pricing rules may have been uneconomic. Given that the problem is much greater than this, efforts toward reform are more rational. If the flow of claims is roughly $600 million per year, indexed to wages, and the real interest rate is 2 percent, approximately $13.5 billion (in 1986 dollars) will be transferred through the insurance system over a 30-year horizon.

PART TWO

Efforts to Reform Program

CHAPTER 5

Reform Efforts through 1987

There is an obvious wedge between sound insurance principles and the actual administration of federal pension insurance. This does not mean, however, that the PBGC and Congress have not worked in the direction of a better, albeit still imperfect, program. In this chapter, I will discuss important reforms implemented through 1987. The next step, which will comprise subsequent chapters, is to build on these ideas toward the development of a true economic insurance program. Table 5–1 provides a summary of the regulations, litigation, and legislation discussed in the chapter.

REGULATORY AND LITIGATION EFFORTS

In this section, I will discuss the internal policy decisions that have been the most significant in controlling insurance losses. These are (1) opposition to establishment of follow-on plans after an insufficient termination; (2) vigorous efforts to enforce ERISA safeguards to include the entire control group in the 30 percent net worth employer liability clause; and (3) a conservative interpretation of ERISA language to impose a full actuarial reduction of the maximum benefit for retirement ages earlier than 65.

Follow-On Plans

A basic principle of any insurance contract is coinsurance; and because ERISA was written to insure terminated (not ongoing) benefits, a pension plan termination by definition imposes large coinsurance losses on workers. As discussed in Chapter 2, depending on the interest rate and age distribution of workers, these losses can reasonably be

TABLE 5–1 Important Steps toward Reform

Issue	*Policy Decision*	*Litigation/Regulation/Legislation*	*Year*
Follow-on plans	Prevent replacement of noninsured losses	*PBGC* v. *Wheeling-Pittsburgh*	1985
		PBGC v. *Alloytek*	1979
		PBGC v. *LTV*	1987
		PBGC v. *Facet*	1980
Control groups	Enforce 30 percent net worth rule to control group	*PBGC* v. *Ouimet*	*1979*
		PBGC v. *International Harvester*	*1980*
Maximum benefit	Actuarial reduction for retirement prior to age 65	Limitation on guaranteed benefit (29 CFR 2621.4)	1976
Insurable event	Limit claims event to firms in financial distress	SEPPAA	1986
Multiemployer reform	Limitation of guaranteed benefits and other rules	MPPAA	1980
Pricing and funding	Exposure-related premiums and stricter funding standards	Pension Protection Act	1987

expected to amount to 25 percent to 75 percent of ongoing pension values. If firms can find ways to eliminate this coinsurance, the potential for moral hazard for the PBGC becomes much greater because firms can take advantage of the insurance policy without adversely affecting their workers and thus their reputations in the labor market.

For example, if after an insufficient termination a new plan is created that not only provides future service accruals but also offsets capital losses suffered by workers on termination, then the coinsurance feature is eliminated. Attempts to create these types of follow-on plans have occurred throughout PBGC's history. Through the litigation of various cases, the PBGC has established a policy against the formation of some types of follow-on plans, though it is unclear at this point whether the courts will ultimately ratify the policy.

The PBGC's position on follow-on plans is set forth in Opinion Letters 81–11 and 86–27 and in papers filed by the PBGC in cases involving Wheeling-Pittsburgh and LTV.[1] An excerpt from Opinion Letter 81–11 is given in the appendix to this chapter.

In four cases the PBGC has publicly contested the right of an employer who terminated a plan with insufficient assets to establish a follow-on plan: AlloyTek, Facet, Wheeling-Pittsburgh, and LTV. AlloyTek and Facet have been settled; as of fall 1988, follow-on plan

[1] See *In Re: Chateaugay Corp., Reomar, Inc., The LTV Corporation, et al.*, SDNY, Case No. 06-B-11273 BRL through 86-B-11334 BRL inclusive; and *United Steelworkers of America, Wheeling-Pittsburgh Steel Corp., et. al.* v. *Pension Benefit Guaranty Corporation*, WDPa, Civil Action No. 87-0355.

issues in Wheeling-Pittsburgh and LTV were in litigation. In these four cases (and others), the PBGC opposed establishment of follow-on plans that, when added to the benefits paid by the PBGC, would provide participants with benefits substantially equal to the benefits that would have been provided by the terminated plan if it had continued.

AlloyTek. AlloyTek was the first case involving the follow-on plan issue. AlloyTek filed a notice of intent to terminate its defined benefit pension plan covering hourly employees, which was subject to a collective bargaining agreement between AlloyTek and the United Auto Workers, in October 1979. The plan's assets were approximately $4 million less than guaranteed benefits, and, according to information submitted with the notice, AlloyTek had little net worth and thus would have little employer liability.

AlloyTek and the union had agreed to establish a target benefit plan (an individual account plan not covered by Title IV) and various other plans to allow benefits that were provided under the plan to be terminated. In addition, AlloyTek and the union also agreed that AlloyTek would make up the difference between what an employee would have received if no termination had occurred and what is provided under the combination of new plans. The PBGC rejected this arrangement as a continuation of the original plan.

AlloyTek eventually agreed it would not establish a defined benefit plan or a target benefit plan for hourly employees prior to September 1, 1986. As a result of this agreement, the PBGC accepted the termination of the hourly plan.

Facet. The Facet case was similar to AlloyTek. It involved the proposed termination of a defined benefit plan and the establishment of a follow-on target benefit plan and other supplementary benefit arrangements. The PBGC originally opposed the termination, as it did in the case of AlloyTek, but subsequently withdrew its opposition when Facet agreed to pay the PBGC employer liability nearly equal to the asset insufficiency of the terminated plan, which was approximately $21 million.

Wheeling-Pittsburgh. Wheeling-Pittsburgh filed a notice of intent to terminate its hourly and salaried pension plans on October 29, 1985, with a proposed termination date of November 8, 1985. At the time of the filing, the firm and seven of its subsidiaries were in a Chapter 11 bankruptcy proceeding. The plans were underfunded by approximately $360 million.

Wheeling-Pittsburgh and its union had signed an agreement for a "pensioners' relief program" to provide payments to current and future retirees in the event the hourly plans were terminated. A similar program was adopted for salaried employees. The programs, in the PBGC's view, appeared to provide substantially the same benefits as the terminating plans; as a result, the PBGC did not initially recognize the termination notices, and it refused to assume trusteeship of the plans.

Following negotiations between the PBGC, Wheeling-Pittsburgh, and the Steelworkers, agreements were entered under which the PBGC agreed to accept the termination of the plans, and the company agreed to cancel the relief programs and not to implement any other follow-on program without PBGC approval or a court order. The PBGC reserved its right to withhold its agreement

> if the proposed follow-on program or any successor, companion, or substitute therefore (*a*) seeks to effect a continuation or restoration of the plans terminated under this agreement, (*b*) consists of . . . a plan covered under Title IV of ERISA . . . , (*c*) consists of an ongoing employee benefit program providing benefits substantially equivalent to those of the hourly plans, (*d*) consists of a qualified or nonqualified defined benefit plan or a target benefit plan for the company's [hourly/salaried] employees proposed prior to the expiration of five years from the date of confirmation of a plan of reorganization of the company, or (*e*) otherwise fails to comply with consistently applied policies of the PBGC under applicable law.[2]

In August 1986, Wheeling-Pittsburgh and the union submitted follow-on plans to the PBGC for its approval. In December 1986, the PBGC disapproved the proposed follow-on plans on the basis that such plans constituted a de facto continuation of the terminated plans. The company and the union subsequently asked the PBGC to recommend acceptable alternatives, which the agency declined to do. On February 9, 1987, Wheeling-Pittsburgh and the union filed suit in district court, seeking an order that they be allowed to establish the proposed follow-on plans and that the PBGC is without authority to restore the assets and liabilities of the terminated plans on the establishment of such follow-on plans. The case was pending as of fall 1988.

The proposed follow-on plans consist of two components: (1) a target benefit plan covering active employees and (2) a supplemental plan covering both active employees and retirees. The proposed supplemental plan is designed to provide retirees with 95 percent of the difference between the benefits they would have received under the terminated plan and the benefits guaranteed by the PBGC.

LTV Corporation. LTV entered Chapter 11 bankruptcy proceedings in 1986; the PBGC initiated termination of four of its pension plans in late 1986 and early 1987. The combined plans covered over 100,000 participants, 60,000 of whom were retired, and had over $2 billion in unfunded guaranteed benefits.

In June 1987, LTV and its union agreed to a collective bargaining

---

[2] Brief of PBGC in *United Steelworkers, Wheeling-Pittsburgh, et al.* v. *Pension Benefit Guaranty Corporation,* No. 87-0355 at 30 (W.D.Pa.).

agreement that included a follow-on plan for hourly workers. A similar follow-on plan was formulated for salaried employees. On July 30, 1987, the bankruptcy court approved the follow-on plans, over the PBGC's objection.

The PBGC restored three of the LTV plans to their pretermination status on September 22, 1987.[3] The bases for the PBGC's decision to restore were

1. The abuse of the termination insurance program caused by LTV's establishment of follow-on plans that, along with the PBGC's guaranteed benefits payments, essentially continued the terminated plans.
2. The improvement in LTV's and LTV Steel's financial conditions.
3. The demonstrated willingness of LTV Steel to fund retirement programs.

LTV opposed the restoration, and the dispute became the subject of a district court case—*Chateaugay Corporation, Reomar, Inc., LTV Corporation, et. al.* Among other rulings, the District Court found insufficient evidence that the follow-on plans were so abusive of the insurance system as to justify restoration. As of fall 1988, the case has been appealed by the PBGC in the U.S. Court of Appeals for the Second Circuit.

Control Groups

Another potential gaming issue is related to the concept of control groups. Suppose a holding company comprises three wholly owned subsidiaries: each has net worth of $100 million, two have fully funded plans, and one has $50 million in underfunding. In the absence of a control group policy, one of these subsidiaries could transfer $50 million in underfunded pensions to the PBGC. In exchange, it would be liable for only 30 percent of its net worth, or $30 million. A $20 million profit would be earned by terminating a single plan and making a claim against the insurance company. Anticipating this problem, ERISA provided for a control group liability concept, which, in the above example, would give the PBGC access to $90 million of the control group's net worth.

The PBGC vigorously pursued the control group concept outlined in ERISA from very early in the program. One prominent case that helped develop this policy was Ouimet Incorporated, a subsidiary of Avon Sole.

---

[3] The other plan was not reinstated because it had insufficient assets to make current benefit payments.

Ouimet (Avon Sole). In 1975, Avon Sole terminated its underfunded pension plan under Title IV of ERISA. The PBGC, pursuant to Sections 4062 and 4001(b) of ERISA, as originally enacted, asserted employer liability against Avon Sole and other members of the same control group. The PBGC's position was that the term *employer* for purposes of employer liability included not only the direct employer of employees covered under the plan but also all trades or businesses under common control of such direct employer.[4]

The bankruptcy court, on March 13, 1977, ruled that only Avon Sole was liable and the other members of the control group were not liable. The PBGC appealed the decision to the district court.[5] The district court reversed the bankruptcy court, holding that Section 4001(b) defines the "employer" for purposes of determining Section 4062 liability and thus "the PBGC may impose liability on each member of a controlled group, whether or not such member contributed to the terminated pension plan."[6] The case went through various appeals, and the PBGC's position was sustained.

International Harvester–Wisconsin Steel. Another way a firm can evade the control test is to sell an about-to-fail division or subsidiary before the division or subsidiary terminates an insufficient plan. Generally, the parent company's net worth would be sufficient to pay off the plan asset insufficiency if plan termination occurred prior to the sale. After the sale, employer liability of the division or subsidiary alone is less likely to be sufficient to offset the underfunding. Thus, after the sale, a greater portion of the underfunding would be transferred to the PBGC. A situation that illustrates the potential of such transfers is the 1977 sale by International Harvester (now known as Navistar) of its Wisconsin Steel Division to subsidiaries of Envirodyne, Inc.

Prior to the sale, Wisconsin Steel had been an unprofitable, capital-intensive operation. To make Wisconsin Steel viable, International Harvester reportedly determined that a large investment was needed. It was unwilling to make that investment. If, however, it were to close Wisconsin Steel and terminate the pension plan, it would be faced with unfunded pension benefits estimated to be $86 million. Instead, the division was sold.

At the time of the sale, Envirodyne was a small, unprofitable company with no experience in steelmaking. It had a net worth of only

---

[4] *Common control* is a tax term and generally requires the same individual or company to own at least 80 percent of outstanding stock or five or fewer owners to hold 80 percent of two or more entities.

[5] *Pension Benefit Guaranty Corporation and United Rubber Workers, et. al.* v. *Ouimet Corporation, Avon Sole Company, et. al.*, 470 F. Supp. 945 (Mass., March 22, 1979).

[6] Ibid., at 954.

$8.5 million. Most of the sale price was financed by notes to International Harvester that were secured by assets of Wisconsin Steel.

In 1980, after Envirodyne defaulted on its note payments, International Harvester seized the assets it held as collateral, thereby triggering Wisconsin Steel's bankruptcy and the termination of its pension plans. Total underfunding of guaranteed benefits in these plans amounted to $55 million.

The PBGC filed employer liability claims against International Harvester as well as Envirodyne. The PBGC held that International Harvester continued to exercise substantial control over Wisconsin Steel and its pension plans following the sale, thus making it an employer maintaining the plan at the time of termination and therefore liable for the unfunded plan benefits. In addition, the PBGC maintained that the principal purpose of the sale was to shift the pension liabilities to the PBGC, which is contrary to the intent of ERISA. As of fall 1988, this case was still pending.

MAXIMUM GUARANTEED BENEFITS

Actuarial Reduction of Maximum Benefits

ERISA constrains the guaranteed monthly benefit. The maximum for a single life annuity at age 65 was $1,909 in 1988. For earlier retirement ages, the maximum is actuarially reduced as shown in column 1 of Table 5–2 (column 2 is discussed below). Except for the five-year phase-in rule, the application of a maximum benefit is virtually the only aspect of ERISA that constrains the benefit guarantees across plans.

Though the maximum is set at relatively high levels for age-65 retirees, the application of an actuarial reduction factor to the maximum may have some significant impact on plans that either have early normal retirement ages or permit retirement with full benefits at very early retirement ages on a plant shutdown. The actuarial reduction, however, establishes much more important principles on which reform can be built: that benefit guarantees should be stated in terms of a common retirement age and benefits collected prior to this age should be reduced for all earlier ages of retirement.

The effectiveness of the guarantee level can be seen in Table 5–3. In 1978, the Department of Labor conducted a survey of pension benefits collected by new retirees in 1977 and 1978. I updated the pension amounts to 1988 dollars using the Bureau of Labor Statistics nonagricultural wage index.

Overall, the average first-year benefit collected by the 1977–78 retiree cohorts was $6,255 in 1988 dollars; the median was $4,505. The

TABLE 5–2 Maximum Benefits for Single Life Annuity, 1988

Age	*Maximum Monthly Benefit: Existing Law (1)*	*Supplemented by Age-65 Full Benefits Limitation* (2)*
65	$1,909	$1,909
64	1,775	1,650
63	1,641	1,410
62	1,508	1,191
61	1,374	988
60	1,240	805
59	1,164	709
58	1,088	620
57	1,011	535
56	935	457
55	859	376
54	820	352
53	782	320
52	744	289
51	706	261
50	668	233
49	630	207
48	591	182

* Numbers in this column assume that amounts in the previous column are payable in full at age 65 and thus subject to actuarial reduction if taken at the age shown in the table. Thus, if a 55-year-old worker was entitled to a full benefit of $859 starting immediately, he would be entitled to only $376 under a rule whereby the full benefit was available only at age 65 and was subject to actuarial reduction on earlier receipt.

TABLE 5–3 Distribution of Retirement Benefits

		Age of Retirement		
Annual Pension	*All*	*Less than 55*	*55–59*	*65*
Less than $4,250	47%	39%	47%	54%
$4,250–6,800	19	22	15	20
$6,800–10,200	16	13	14	13
$10,200–17,000	14	25	20	9
More than $17,000	4	1	4	4
Median	$4,505	$5,320	$ 4,775	$ 3,890
Mean	6,255	6,870	6,495	5,440
Maximum guaranty	—	8,930*	11,810†	22,908

Note: Numbers in table depict distribution of first-year retirees in 1977 and 1978. Pension amount categories have been adjusted to 1988 dollars using the Bureau of Labor Statistics nonagricultural wage index.

* Assumes retirement occurs at age 52.

† Assumes retirement occurs at age 57.

SOURCE: David McCarthy, *Findings from the Survey of Private Pension Benefit Amounts,* U.S. Department of Labor, Office of Pension and Welfare Benefits Programs, 1985, p. 22.

more interesting data, however, are the distributions of benefits across different ages of retirement.

Those retiring at age 65 had a mean annual benefit of $5,440. The maximum annual benefit for a single benefit annuity is $22,908, over 300 percent higher than the mean. Thus, the maximum is constraining for very few highly paid individuals at retirement age 65. Only 4 percent of those retiring at age 65 have pension benefits greater than $17,000 per year. The maximum, however, presents a more meaningful constraint at earlier ages.

For workers retiring between the ages of 55 and 59, the maximum guaranteed annual benefit is between $10,300 and $13,900. Almost one fourth of all retirees over this age range collect benefits in excess of $10,200 per year. For ages 48 to 54, the maximum benefit range is $7,090 to $9,840; almost 40 percent of workers who retire before age 55 (including special early retirements, such as those involved in shutdowns) have pensions in excess of $6,800 per year. Thus, the actuarial reduction of the maximum benefit amount in 1976 apparently has had an impact on a significant portion of the insured population.[7]

Alternate Approach to Maximum Guaranty

Though the full actuarial reduction of the maximum guaranteed benefit does reduce PBGC exposure, the PBGC could have written its benefit guarantee regulations to have a much more dramatic impact on the program's solvency. In particular, early in the program the PBGC decided, through regulation, to interpret ERISA to pay full pension benefits regardless of the age of first receipt. If, for example, full benefits are available in the plan at age 55, the guarantee covers this amount, subject to the maximum amount in column 1 of Table 5–2. If full benefits are available at, say, ages 45 or 50 in the case of a plant shutdown, these too are guaranteed, subject to the same maximum benefit schedule.

An alternative structure consistent with the small, flat premium set by Congress would have been to establish a common normal retirement age for purposes of paying the guarantee. Suppose the social security normal retirement age of 65 was chosen. All full benefits would be payable by the PBGC at age 65, regardless of the plan provisions, actuarially reduced to age of first receipt. The $1,909 maximum in 1988 would remain as the maximum benefit payable at age 65, and thus the schedule in Table 5–2, column 1, would still be binding. But before applying this constraint, all full benefits would be actuarially reduced from age 65.

---

[7] The reduction was permitted by ERISA. But presumably, the PBGC could have interpreted the provision much more liberally than it chose to.

For example, suppose a worker aged 55 was entitled to full monthly benefits equal to $859, which is exactly the maximum benefit amount guaranteed at age 55 under the current PBGC insurance system (see Table 5–2). Thus, if a termination occurred, the PBGC would pay $859 to this worker starting at age 55.

Under an alternative age-65 guarantee rule, the $859 would be payable at age 65, not age 55. That is, even though the plan provided for full benefits at age 55, the guarantee could be redefined to begin at age 65; that is, $859 would be payable at age 65. The worker could still choose to collect benefits at age 55, but, in this case, benefits would be actuarially reduced. For example, if $859 represented full benefits at age 65, then the actuarially reduced amount payable on an age-55 receipt would be $376. In an age-65 guarantee rule, plans that permitted full benefits prior to age 65 would receive the same benefits as retirees from plans that paid full benefits at age 65.[8]

For illustration, a schedule of maximum payments implied by this approach is shown in column 2 of Table 5–2 under the assumption that a worker was entitled to a full benefit exactly equal to the benefit listed in column 1 at the corresponding ages. Thus, the individual previously entitled to a full benefit of $859 at age 55 would be subject to a maximum of $376 under an age-65 normal retirement rule.

The impact of this alternative rule on maximum allowable benefits at various ages is shown visually in Figure 5–1. The numbers depicted by schedule AB are the maximum benefits for various ages currently enforced by the PBGC. The numbers depicted by schedule CB represent the implied maximums resulting from enforcement of a rule setting all normal retirement ages to 65 for purposes of paying guaranteed benefits. We will return to a discussion of this alternative concept in Chapter 10.

Costs of Special Early Benefits

The cost implications of the current PBGC policy of paying unreduced and subsidized benefits prior to age 65 are significant. For example, it is not uncommon for a "rule of 65" to prevail in the event of a plant shutdown: as long as a worker is at least 45 years old with 20 years' service, he is entitled to unreduced benefits commencing immediately. In 1983, the PBGC conducted a study of 18 large terminations that occurred through 1981. The results of the study were contained in a report entitled *Cost of Supplemental Early Retirement Benefits*.

---

[8] In general, benefits collectible by the worker according to his plan's provisions would be adjusted to age 65 using the firm's actuarial rates, then rediscounted back using PBGC actuarial rates. This puts all firms on the same basis, regardless of the subsidy that may be implicit at early retirement.

FIGURE 5–1 Maximum Benefits Alternatives

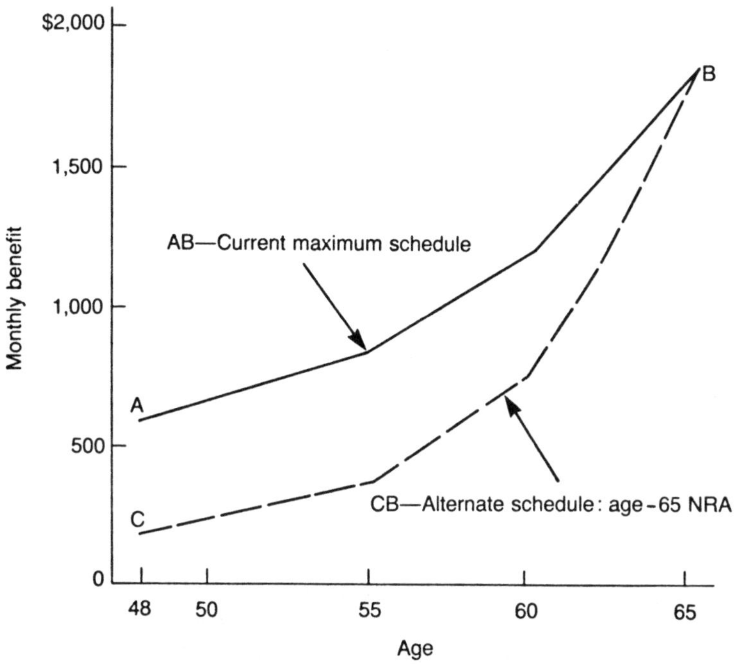

The study calculated the extra liabilities created by providing (1) unreduced full benefits prior to the plan's normal retirement age (this included, for example, the cost of "30-and-out" provisions, which award full benefits as early as age 55); (2) unreduced benefits in the event of plan shutdown (for example, the "rule of 65" cited above); and (3) special supplements to early benefits paid until the normal retirement age (these are often paid until age 62, when social security benefits are available). Benefits actually collected were compared against those payable at the earliest retirement age in the plan, using an actuarial discount factor from the normal retirement age. The normal retirement age in most of these plans was 65.

The study did not calculate the cost imposed by partially subsidized early retirement, only the full benefits available prior to normal retirement age. Nor did the study count extra shutdown payments made to workers prior to the termination as claims costs. It counted only the future flow of these payments as claims costs, even though past payments clearly deteriorated the plan's funding condition.

The results are summarized in Table 5–4. Despite the maximum benefit schedule, special early retirement provisions amounted to 18.4

TABLE 5–4 Costs of Supplemental Early Retirement (SER)

Industry	Plans	Costs of SER (millions)	Percent of Guaranteed Benefits	Percent of Claims
Auto	3	$ .8	5.8%	7.4%
Steel	7	36.2	21.2	28.6
Rubber	4	3.8	11.1	14.6
Cement	2	6.1	21.3	32.3
Glass	2	.2	6.9	8.2
Total	18	$47.1	18.4%	24.9%

Note: Numbers reflect shutdown benefits, unreduced benefits payable prior to normal retirement age, and special supplements payable prior to normal retirement age. They do not include subsidized early retirement benefits or funding deterioration attributable to payment of shutdown benefits prior to termination.

SOURCE: *Cost of Supplemental Early Retirement Benefits*, unpublished PBGC report, 1983.

percent of guaranteed benefit liabilities and 24.9 percent of claims in the sample. This experience suggests PBGC claims could be reduced significantly if either (1) all special early benefits were not guaranteed (that is, all benefits were rediscounted as of some common normal retirement age) or (2) the maximum benefit schedule were sharply reduced. (Data discussed in Chapter 7 suggest that the cost impact of special early benefits has increased significantly since the 1983 study was completed.)

LEGISLATIVE EFFORTS

Three important pieces of legislation after ERISA have worked to reduce the scope of the problems that have emerged in the insurance program: the Single-Employer Pension Plan Amendments Act of 1986 (SEPPAA), the Multiemployer Pension Plan Amendments Act of 1980 (MPPAA), and the Pension Protection Act of 1987.

SEPPAA

At the time ERISA was enacted, any firm—regardless of its financial viability—could exchange its pension plan underfunding for 30 percent of its net worth. Thus, the insurable event was not firm failure or even evidence of firm difficulty. This option became known as *the pension put*. That is, a firm could "put" its underfunded obligation to the PBGC in exchange for 30 percent of its net worth anytime it was advantageous to do so.

SEPPAA redefined the insurable event.[9] A firm could terminate its insufficient pension plan and make a claim against the PBGC in one of four situations: if the firm (1) files for bankruptcy under Chapter 11 of the bankruptcy code (which permits reorganization of the firm as an ongoing entity), and the court approves the termination; (2) files under Chapter 7 of the bankruptcy code (which is essentially a liquidation proceeding); (3) demonstrates that it cannot pay debts and continue in business *unless* the plan is terminated (which means the firm will enter bankruptcy without a PBGC transfer); or (4) demonstrates to the PBGC that its pension costs are "unreasonably burdensome" due solely to a decline in employment covered by a plan.[10] In addition, the 30 percent net worth limitation was increased.[11] In short, the pension put was replaced by a distress criterion: PBGC claims would be valuable only to firms in financial difficulty, thus eliminating the opportunity for gaming by essentially healthy firms.

SEPPAA may have had significant impact on a few large, potential claims by firms that could have taken advantage of the 30 percent net worth limitation. More important, SEPPAA represents the first attempt to constrain the insurable event. Though somewhat vague in its criteria (notably the last two), the law at least tried to limit the insurable event to firms experiencing significant financial difficulties.

As a practical matter, however, it is not obvious that SEPPAA had an important effect on the insurance program. For example, recall from Table 3–2 that of the 12 largest claims paid by the PBGC, fully 10 were in bankruptcy proceedings, and the remaining two (Rath Packing and Allis-Chalmers) might conceivably have qualified under the remaining conditions.[12]

In its 1985 exposure estimates, the PBGC identified firms with at least a $5 million potential claim against the PBGC that could have profited from the pension put; that is, these firms had unfunded pension liabilities exceeding 30 percent of net worth. Of the eight firms identified, seven were already on the very-high-risk list and one was on

---

[9] Technically, the insurable event was still termination of the pension plan, but the *conditions* required to qualify for a PBGC transfer were changed.

[10] Aside from rules covering terminations instituted by the plan sponsor, the PBGC itself is required to involuntarily terminate a plan where plan assets are not available to pay benefits currently due.

[11] In particular, when the 30 percent rule was limiting, the PBGC was entitled to make an additional claim for up to 75 percent of the underfunded amount. Thus, if underfunding was 100 and net worth 30, pre-SEPPAA rules constrained the PBGC claim to 9, or 30 percent of 30. SEPPAA permitted an additional claim in the amount of 68 or a total of 77 percent of 100. The Pension Protection Act of 1987 increased the PBGC's claim to 100 percent of underfunding.

[12] In fact, because Allis-Chalmers essentially had no assets to pay benefits, the PBGC would have been required to involuntarily terminate the plan. See ibid.

the moderate-risk list. Most large firms for which the put option is valuable are in distress, according to measures of firm viability.

MPPAA

Though this book is confined to evaluation of the single-employer insurance program, it is instructive to consider rules that apply to a parallel (but different) program covering multiemployer plans. Provisions in the latter suggest useful reforms for the single-employer program.

Multiemployer plans usually cover union workers in a common pension plan administered by the union and contributing firms. Each employer is responsible for making contributions to the plan each period (usually x number of dollars per hour of each worker's time at that firm). These plans are popular in the construction, trucking, mining, and textile industries.

Until 1980, ERISA provided guaranteed benefits to multiemployer plans at the discretion of the PBGC (though these plans were required to pay premiums). MPPAA instituted mandatory guarantees for these plans and established special rules under which this insurance would apply. The premium for multiemployer plans was only $2.20 per participant in 1988 (increasing to $2.60 in September 1988), and the system is currently showing a surplus.

Several MPPAA provisions are worthy of attention in comparison to single-employer insurance. First, MPPAA incorporates a control group notion that goes beyond individual firms: it requires a type of self-insurance scheme among all contributors to a common multiemployer plan. To illustrate, suppose five trucking firms in a particular area form a multiemployer plan for the members of the Teamsters that they employ. Suppose all firms are the same size, and the plan is underfunded by $20 million. If one firm withdraws from the plan, it carries with it a $4 million liability, its share of the group obligation (a so-called withdrawal liability). If one firm fails, the PBGC does not assume the $4 million liability: it merely passes to the remaining four firms in the plan. As a practical matter, a large portion of participating firms must fail before the PBGC is required to pay benefits. In addition, firms generally are liable to the plan for the entire amount of the underfunding.

Second, the maximum benefit is less generous for multiemployer plans. The PBGC insures benefits up to $16.75 per month per year of service to multiemployer retirees, independent of the age of retirement (the amount is unindexed). Shutdown and other special early retirements are rare events in multiemployer plans, and thus, age 55 is usually the earliest retirement age. With 35 years of service, the maximum benefit a 55-year-old retiree could collect from the PBGC in

1988 is $586, one third less than the $859 in single plans. For 65-year-old retirees, the multiemployer guaranty for a worker with 45 years' service is only 40 percent of the maximum guaranty for single plans.

In addition, instead of having a five-year phase-in for increased benefits, MPPAA establishes five-year cliff vesting. No benefit increases within five years of termination are guaranteed. This substantially reduces the PBGC obligation. In addition, because virtually all multiemployer plans pay flat benefits (x dollars per year of service, instead of percent times service times wage), this guarantees five years of inflation erosion in benefit payments. Not only does this discourage moral hazard (increasing benefits prior to termination), it guarantees a substantial coinsurance payment by workers. The lower guarantee levels and the stricter phase-in rules in multiemployer plans provide a model for our discussion of a basic benefits reform package in Chapter 10.

Pension Protection Act

On December 22, 1987, as part of the 1987 Omnibus Budget Reconciliation Act, the Pension Protection Act was enacted into law. This probably was the most significant piece of single-employer reform legislation during the post-ERISA period. Spurred by the growing deficit at the PBGC and the clear inadequacy of current rules to keep claims consistent with prevailing premium levels, Congress instituted new rules for federal pension insurance dealing with virtually every aspect of the insurance program.

Some of the reforms were more binding than others on current practices, but the package erected a framework that, with further modifications, could lead to a solvent pension insurance program in the long run. In this chapter, I highlight only the major provisions of the law. Chapters 6 through 8 will consider these reforms in more detail. Table 5–5 lists the major reform provisions discussed below.

Pricing. The legislation abandoned a flat one-price policy and instead instituted a two-part premium structure. The first part is a flat charge (increased from $8.50 to $16). The second part is composed of a $6 assessment against each $1,000 of underfunding in the pension plan. While the new price structure represents an important step in the right direction, it is far from a private market price scheme. The risk of default is not incorporated, and, more important, the premium is limited by a maximum of $50. Chapter 6 will demonstrate that the new price structure still incorporates large subsidies to many firms.

Benefits. The new law leaves intact the current policy to pay full benefits at any age, including, for example, ages less than 50 in the event of shutdowns. But it has a provision that prevents plans from awarding increases in benefits without posting security if the plan is

TABLE 5–5 Major Provisions of the Pension Protection Act

Issue	*Reform*
Pricing	Premiums related to underfunding, limited by unindexed maximum of $50
Funding	Reduced amortization periods
Benefits	No increase in (flat) benefits without posting security if funding ratio is less than 60 percent
Insurable event	Chapter 11 distress test requires the bankruptcy court to find that without termination, the plan sponsor will not be able to complete Chapter 11 reorganization
Liens	Liens arise if certain minimum contributions are not made
Waivers	Number reduced from five to three in any 15 years

Note: A more extensive list of the act's provisions is given in Appendix E to the book.

less than 60 percent funded. This is the first time since ERISA that reform has addressed benefit levels.[13] As we will later show, however, because the funding floor is set in terms of termination benefits, the rule might be circumvented in periods when interest rates increase, later leaving large additional underfunding in the event of subsequent decreases in interest rates.

Insurable event. Congress declined to eliminate Chapter 11 as one of the four distress tests under SEPPAA. Doing so would have left Chapter 7 (dissolution) as the only trigger for termination in bankruptcy. Instead, the new law "blends" the first and third distress tests under SEPPAA (see page 81). That is, it permits Chapter 11 (reorganization) terminations but requires the bankruptcy court to find that if the plan is not terminated, the sponsoring company will not be able to complete Chapter 11 reorganization.

Given the subjective nature of the new provision, this requirement may not constrain the Chapter 11 proceeding in a substantial way. If nothing else, however, it lays the groundwork for potentially more constraining legislation in some future period (for example, restriction of the insurable event to Chapter 7 of the bankruptcy code).

Liens and waivers. The new legislation made two changes that, in principle, addressed the pre-claim defunding process. (This phenomenon is addressed in detail in Chapter 7.) The legislation retains the Internal Revenue Service waiver process but reduces the number of permissible waivers from five to three in each 15 years. This would have reduced the claims of some past claimants (for example, Rath

[13] Arguably, the genesis for this provision is found in Section 4243(d) of MPPAA, which triggers stricter funding rules if benefits are increased in seriously underfunded multiemployer plans.

Packing—see Table 4–4). In general, because pre-SEPPAA waivers were not reported to the PBGC, no database is available to measure the importance of this reform. It is unlikely, however, that the typical large claim had more than three waivers prior to termination.

A potentially more important reform is the creation of a lien potential anytime a minimum contribution beyond a certain threshold is not paid on time (except in the case of waivers).[14] As will be shown in Chapter 7, the problem of unpaid contributions is large. The solution's shortcoming is that in order for the lien to be fully effective, the PBGC or a party designated by the PBGC must "perfect" the lien.

Because the firm and creditors know of this possibility in advance, they might be expected to game this reform by "liening up" all available assets before the PBGC can take action. This reaction is not far-fetched, given that other creditors may well discern the firm's troubled status before the PBGC does and will have strong incentives to act as soon as a required contribution is not made.

Funding. The new funding standards are, by far, the most significant changes imposed by the new law. The funding provisions do not go into effect until 1989 and effectively give a five-year exemption to firms in the steel industry. Further, while the law reduces the amortization period for past service credit substantially, the period for existing underfunding in 1988 is reduced only from 30 to 18 years. (How past service credits create underfunding is discussed in Chapter 7.) These transitional rules suggest substantial underfunding may well be retained in the system for at least a decade.

The longer-term prognosis is better. For example, for underfunded plans, future past service credits are amortized over much shorter periods (see Chapter 8). Shutdown benefits, once triggered, are amortized over no more than 7 (instead of the current 15) years. Waivers are amortized over 5 (instead of 15) years, and experience and actuarial gains and losses over 5 and 10 (instead of 15) years. These new rules hold significant potential for reducing underfunding in the pension system. It will be shown later, however, that although the new restrictions will likely increase average funding for the worse-funded plans, the new system does not necessarily prevent rapid defunding prior to termination.

CONCLUSION

Though Congress and the PBGC have violated many insurance principles during the short history of the pension insurance program, and amassed a large deficit as a result, they have taken some significant

---

[14] The size threshold is met when unpaid contributions amount to $1 million.

steps toward correcting the problem. The value of the pension put has been reduced significantly, and the gaming potential in general has been reduced through a strong emphasis on retaining workers as coinsurers and treating groups of related firms as single entities. Some progress has been made toward narrowing the gap between the benefits and costs of the insurance system.

Nevertheless, the cross-subsidies remaining in the insurance system are great, and moral hazard potential is still sizable. No private insurance firm would willingly operate the pension insurance system under the current inadequate, albeit reformed, rules and prices. The next two chapters will attempt to quantify the nature of the two largest problems in the system—inappropriate prices and inadequate funding provisions—and to discuss the impact of the 1987 legislation in more detail.

APPENDIX
Excerpt from Opinion Letter 81–11—Follow-On Plans

"The termination insurance program of Title IV was not intended to subsidize an employer's ongoing retirement program. Accordingly, we believe that a purported termination of one plan, contrived in concert with the establishment of new retirement arrangements which are designed to provide substantially the same benefits for the future, should not be treated as a termination within the statutory contemplation so as to require the payment of PBGC guarantees.

"If PBGC guarantees were to be paid under such circumstances, then any company whose unfunded liabilities under a defined benefit pension plan exceed 30 percent of its net worth could find it advantageous to establish similar arrangements to secure PBGC's payment of the major portion of its costs of an ongoing retirement program. Such a result would have extremely adverse cost consequences for this insurance system.

"Our review of available data for major corporations whose pension liabilities are reported by Standard & Poor's Compustat service has readily identified over 20 very large firms whose unfunded pension liabilities substantially exceed 30 percent of their net worth, and whose financial difficulties would undoubtedly make tempting the adoption of arrangements similar to those you are proposing. The combined unfunded pension liabilities of those plans which have been thus identified is approximately $6 billion, and PBGC's potential exposure if they were to terminate, based upon net worth estimates, is some $4.1 billion. Thus, the consequences of our acceptance of the type of proposal you are advancing could be either a huge shift of pension costs to PBGC's premium payers, or the total collapse of the insurance system.

"We do not believe the statute should be read so narrowly as to require PBGC to accept a result so patently at odds with the legislative purpose—which is, after all, to protect the pension expectations of individual retirees and workers, not to provide bail-outs for financially pressed firms—and so inimical to this program's continuing viability.

"For example, Section 4047 of ERISA, 29 U.S.C. 1347, provides PBGC with express authority to limit plan terminations. That section states in pertinent part:

> Whenever the corporation determines that a plan which is to be terminated, or which is in the process of being terminated, under this subtitle, should not be terminated *as a result of such circumstances as the corporation determines to be relevant*, the corporation is authorized to cease any activities undertaken to terminate the plan, and to take whatever action is necessary and within its power to restore the plan to its status prior to the determination that the plan was to be terminated. [emphasis added]

"The breadth of this provision is further reflected in its additional grant of authority to PBGC to restore to its pretermination status, a plan whose termination has already been completed. In addition, under Section 4048 of ERISA, 29 U.S.C. 1348, there is no date of plan termination unless one is agreed to by PBGC (or established by a court)."

CHAPTER 6

Pricing Solutions

There are two basic approaches to reforming the Pension Benefit Guaranty Corporation. The first, and the one addressed in this chapter, is to leave the current insurance contract intact and to simply change the pricing structure to reflect the risk and exposure affiliated with the contract. The second is to alter the terms and conditions of the contract to make its expected costs consistent with the existing price structure. These issues are discussed in Chapters 7 and 8. While the optimal (and politically feasible) reform package likely will combine parts of both approaches, the exposition is facilitated by separate presentations.

To illustrate various pricing ideas, I will discuss the pricing structure actually proposed to Congress by the PBGC in 1987. It provides a framework to compare the pricing scheme actually enacted, which was based in principle on the PBGC proposal, and an opportunity to discuss pricing concepts not incorporated in final legislation. These pricing structures are compared to an estimated risk and exposure pricing scheme that might actually operate in a private insurance market.

INSURANCE PRICING PRINCIPLES

If the pension insurance contract were issued by private insurers, the current fixed price structure would not survive. As in any other area of insurance, a private pension insurer would set prices in relation to risk and exposure. If a house is worth $100,000 and the probability of destruction by fire is 1 percent per year (assume fires are always completely destructive), then the insurance policy will cost $1,000 per year (ignoring the cost of writing insurance, or the load factor).

Pension insurance resembles renewable term life insurance more than fire insurance. If an insured is stricken by cancer and is ill three years prior to death, the price of the renewable term life insurance policy is not increased during these three years. The contract assumes that some warning will often be available prior to death. To raise the price to reflect "higher risks" shortly before death is akin to having no insurance.

In pensions, it is similarly assumed that firms will experience a deterioration of financial health before they fail. Thus, because pension contributions may be more difficult to make during this stage, exposure may be expected to increase prior to firm failure. The control of the amount of defunding prior to failure, and the definitions of failure itself, of course, must be specified in the contract (the subject of Chapter 10).

Presumably, a renewable term contract will be written each year where the premium will depend on a firm's risk classification at the initial date of the contract. This price will vary with the overall pension loss experience of the insurer, but it will not be altered on a firm-specific basis just because some firms begin to experience financial difficulty.

Suppose the probability of termination for all firms is Q and the *relative* termination probability of a particular firm is q. Let L denote guaranteed benefits per worker and F denote the current funding ratio (assets divided by guaranteed benefits). Ignoring the costs of operating the insurance company, the per-participant premium level chosen by the insurance company for a particular firm is

$$P = qQ\,\mathrm{Max}[0, 1 - (F - g)]L \qquad q \geq 0 \tag{6–1}$$

where g is the percentage amount by which the existing funding ratio will deteriorate prior to a failure event (failure events were discussed in Chapter 5). The term qQ represents the *risk factor*; the remaining terms represent *exposure*.

Thus, if the probability of default for this firm, qQ, is 1 percent, the existing funding ratio (F) is .9, and the funding deterioration factor (g) is .2, then exposure equals .3L [that is, $1 - (F - g) = 1 - (.9 - .2) = .3$]. Thus the premium level is .3 of 1 percent times liabilities. If liabilities per participant are $30,000, the annual premium is $90 per participant. If, on the other hand, the funding ratio exceeds 1.2, then exposure (after accounting for defunding) is zero and the premium is zero regardless of the probability of default.

Over time, the premium will vary directly with exposure. Therefore, as the funding level falls, premiums generally will increase because insureds with past exposure will have more exposure, and those previously showing no exposure will more likely fall below the funding threshold (in this example, 1.2). Similarly, as liabilities increase (due to increases in wages and plan maturity), premiums also generally will increase.

The insurance company will vary its overall rates as its overall termination experience (Q) changes. It will not, however, change the initial risk assessment parameter (q) for individual plans (subject perhaps to certain conditions, such as that the insured does not change its nature through merger or acquisition, just as life insurance prices will change if the insured becomes a race driver).

It is useful to obtain some feel for the magnitude of the parameters reflected in premium Equation (6–1).

Probability of default, *Q*. The per annum probability that a worker covered by a defined benefit pension will also be in an insufficient termination is approximately 1.2 per 1,000 based on the first 12 years of the PBGC's history and almost 4.0 per 1,000 based on the experience between 1982 and 1986. Of course, the probability of default is not constant across firms; that is, the values of q in Equation (6–1) are not all equal to unity. Recall from Tables 3–4 and 3–5 that after the LTV termination, 80 percent of the PBGC's liability was attributable to terminated plans from the steel industry; and prior to this event, almost two thirds of claims were attributable to the steel and auto industries. Fully 95 percent of claims were affiliated with plans covering union participants.

Funding deterioration, *q*. Based on a study reported below, the amount of funding deterioration prior to termination, g, is roughly 50 percentage points. This matter is discussed in greater detail in Chapter 7.

Funding ratios, *F*. The distribution of funding ratios (where liabilities are adjusted using PBGC interest rates) is shown in Table 6–1. Almost 80 percent of plans were fully funded in 1986; the average funding ratio was 124 percent. It is apparent from the table that the majority of firms do not impose much exposure to the PBGC.

This distribution, of course, would vary for different years. Table 6–2 shows the portion of participants in overfunded plans from 1978 through 1986. While roughly 80 percent of plans were overfunded from 1983 to 1986, only approximately 50 percent were overfunded in 1978 and 1979.

Liability levels, *L*. Pension liabilities per insured (vested liabilities per vested worker, adjusted to PBGC interest rates) are shown in Table 6–3. The average pension liability per worker is \$35,183, but there is great variance in this distribution. Approximately one in three insureds have benefits less than \$20,000; roughly one in five have benefits in excess of \$50,000 (see column 1). The liability distribution for selected industry groups is also shown in columns 2 through 5.

Average steel industry benefits are \$53,925, and those in the automobile industry are \$48,296. The industry groups with the highest and lowest benefit levels are petroleum (\$60,970) and services

TABLE 6–1 Funding Ratios, 1986

Funding Ratios	*Participants*	*Plans*
0–24%	0.4%	0.2%
25–49	2.9	2.6
50–74	8.4	6.6
75–99	11.8	12.6
100–124	17.9	17.3
125–149	18.6	17.8
150+	39.8	42.9
Total	100.0%	100.0%
Average: 124%		

Note: Numbers in this table depict estimated funding levels in single-employer defined benefit plans in 1986. They are projections based on actual 1984 funding ratio distributions from the 5500 annual reports, adjusted to 1986 using Wyatt Company published numbers for 1985 and 1986, converted to PBGC interest rates, approximated by 7.25 percent.

All numbers reflect vested active participants and retirees only; nonvested workers are not included.

($15,902). Higher benefit levels reflect more generous benefit formulas, earlier ages of retirement with full (or subsidized) benefits, and larger portions of older workers in the plan who have lots of service credits, with payments due soon in the future.

PBGC PROPOSAL FOR PRICING REFORM

In 1986, the PBGC described a new framework for pricing its insurance. The proposal was published in a report entitled *Pension Promises at Risk* and concurrently submitted as legislation to Congress. This proposal became the basis for legislation actually enacted in December

TABLE 6–2 Percent of Participants in Overfunded Plans, 1978–1986

	Funding Ratios		
Year	*100–124%*	*125% or More*	*Total*
1978	25.5%	26.0%	51.5%
1979	25.8	20.9	46.7
1980	22.9	44.1	67.0
1981	14.1	64.2	78.3
1982	14.2	65.6	79.8
1983	13.4	69.9	83.3
1984	10.1	76.0	86.1
1985	11.7	72.9	84.6
1986	16.3	61.7	78.0
Average	17.1	55.7	72.8

Note: Funding ratios are calculated on a termination basis, using PBGC close-out rates.
SOURCE: See Appendix A to book, Table A–7.

TABLE 6–3 Pension Liability per Insured: Selected Industries

Level	*Total* (1)	*Steel* (2)	*Auto* (3)	*Petroleum** (4)	*Services** (5)
Under $10,000	13.7%	2.2%	1.8%	1.2%	37.8%
$10,000–20,000	16.9	2.8	4.3	3.5	42.1
$20,000–30,000	13.6	2.1	2.0	7.0	10.2
$30,000–40,000	17.0	2.8	28.1	8.7	3.9
$40,000–50,000	17.7	12.1	42.1	9.8	3.9
$50,000–60,000	8.0	38.1	4.1	23.5	1.1
$60,000–70,000	5.8	37.6	0.0	20.5	0.2
Over $70,000	7.4	2.4	17.7	25.9	0.9
Average liability per insured	$35,183	$53,925	$48,296	$60,970	$15,902

Note: Numbers are percent vested participants.

* Petroleum and services are the highest and lowest benefits industries, based on industrial groupings with at least $10 billion in vested liabilities. Liabilities are normalized to a 7.25 percent PBGC interest rate.

SOURCE: 1984 Form 5500 Annual Pension Plan Report data, projected to 1986.

1987, described briefly in Chapter 5 and in more detail later in this chapter.

The PBGC proposal did not replicate the premium structure in Equation (6–1). Instead, it proposed the following structure:

$$P^* = \$8.50 + Q^* \text{ Max}[0, 1 - (F - g^*)L$$
$$P^* \leq \$100 \qquad (6\text{–}2)$$

Equation (6–2) differs from (6–1) in two notable ways. First, the PBGC proposal does not account for different probabilities of default among firms; it sets all values of q as equal to unity. Thus, the PBGC proposal is not a risk-related premium but rather an exposure premium.

Second, the PBGC proposal sets a maximum price equal to $100. Because these constraints distort efficient prices, a constant factor $8.50 is added partly to provide subsidies to those paying less than market rates; and the overall default probability (Q) is increased to Q* for the same reason.

More particularly, the constant term $8.50 accommodates roughly a $4.50 contribution to amortize the deficit at the time of the proposal (approximately $4 billion), plus $1 to cover expenses of operating the PBGC. The remaining $3 is a cross-subsidy to firms that provide exposure to the corporation. Chapter 4 indicated that the PBGC's best estimate of future claims, plus amortization of the existing deficit (in real terms over 30 years), required an average premium (P^*) equal to approximately $25, indexed to wages. The value of the funding deterioration parameter (g^*) was not determined empirically but rather was arbitrarily set at .25. This provides all the constraints necessary to determine the value of Q^* in the equation.

The formula was applied across the funding ratios and liability levels reflected in Tables 6–1 and 6–3, subject to the minimum and maximum premiums. The proposal set a 25 percent *cushion* in reported funding levels (liabilities were evaluated at PBGC interest rates); thus all firms with greater than 125 percent funding paid $8.50, and the rest paid $8.50 plus some funding charge. To generate roughly $25 in average premiums, a value of Q^* equal to .006 was required. The assessment on underfunding was $6 per $1,000 of the sum of underfunding plus the cushion amount.

The distribution of premiums generated by this rate structure is shown in Table 6–4. Roughly 60 percent of the plans and participants paid the minimum premium of $8.50; these plans had funding ratios in excess of 125 percent. Roughly 5 percent of the plans representing 8.5 percent of the participants paid the maximum amount, $100. Among the latter group are subsidies from two sources: first, holding risk assessments constant, these firms do not pay premiums in proportion to exposure; and second, like many firms paying some exposure charge, they likely receive another subsidy because differential risks of default are not assessed. (Of course, some firms paying a funding charge are paying too high a premium because their relative default probability (q) might be less than one—more on this below.)

Table 6–5 shows the same distribution when the $100 maximum premium restriction is eliminated. Almost 1 percent of participants would belong to plans assessed a premium of $300 or more. Fully 54 percent of the premium would be paid by those currently facing the maximum amount; when the $100 maximum applies (Table 6–4), this group pays only 39.8 percent of total premiums. In either case,

TABLE 6–4 Schedule of Premiums: PBGC Proposal

Premium Level	*Premiums*	*Participants*	*Plans*
$8.50	20.9%	60.7%	60.4%
$8.51–20.00	7.8	15.0	15.2
$20.01–35.00	6.2	5.7	8.3
$35.01–50.00	8.1	4.2	4.6
$50.01–75.00	8.3	3.5	4.2
$75.01–99.99	8.3	2.3	2.4
$100.00	39.8	8.5	4.7
Average premium	$25.64		

Rate schedule: $6 per $1,000 in underfunded vested liabilities for funding levels below 125 percent; $8.50 minimum and $100 maximum premiums in 1986 dollars.

Numbers depict participants in plans with 100 or more participants.

SOURCE: 1984 Form 5500 Annual Pension Plan Reports, projected to 1986.

TABLE 6–5 Schedule of PBGC Premiums with No Maximum

Premium Level	*Premiums*	*Participants*	*Plans*
$8.50	16.2%	60.7%	60.4%
$8.51–20.00	6.0	15.0	15.2
$20.01–35.00	4.8	5.7	8.3
$35.01–50.00	6.3	4.2	4.6
$50.01–75.00	6.4	3.5	4.2
$75.01–99.99	6.4	2.3	2.4
$100–199.99	22.0	4.5	3.2
$200–299.99	22.5	3.2	.8
$300.00+	9.5	.8	.4
Average premium	$31.30		

Rate schedule: $6 per $1,000 in unfunded vested liabilities for funding levels below 125 percent; $8.50 minimum and no maximum.

SOURCE: 1984 Form 5500 Annual Pension Plan Reports, projected to 1986.

well-funded plans (funding ratio at least 125 percent) pay approximately 20 percent or less of premiums, even though they represent 60 percent of participants.

As a way to move gradually from the distribution in Table 6–4 to the distribution shown in Table 6–5, the proposal indexed the minimum amount to changes in the social security wage base and the maximum amount to 1.5 times these changes. Thus, if wages increase by 5 percent, the maximum premium would increase by 7.5 percent. This ultimately would generate an average real premium approaching $31.30, compared to $25.64 in 1986. Other features of the proposal are reported in the appendix to this chapter.

COMPARISON TO MARKET RATES

The PBGC legislative proposal represented an important step in the direction of matching premiums and exposure. Because the proposal imposed a maximum rate of $100 ($300 in real terms in the long run), the cross-subsidy in a flat rate system would be substantially reduced. This does not mean, however, that the proposal reflected a rate structure that would exist in a private insurance market. In a private scheme, rates would account for default risk and would not be capped.

In an exposure-related scheme, firms having high exposure levels (attributable to low funding ratios and/or generous benefits) and high default risk still receive subsidies. Firms with high exposure but low default risk pay substantial taxes in the scheme.

In a private insurance market, insurance carriers try to estimate risks across classes to more accurately align premiums and risky exposure. Subsequent to the announcement of the proposal, Jack VanDerhei of the Wharton School was asked by the PBGC to do a study of the PBGC's proposed rate structure compared to one that might be freely established in the private market. His results are discussed in a report entitled *An Empirical Analysis of Risk-Related Insurance Premiums for the PBGC*, which was completed in 1988.

Estimation of Market Rate Structure

In essence, the VanDerhei study undertook the task of estimating the parameters in Equation (6–1). To do this, he merged the PBGC database (which incorporated information on all pension terminations from 1981 through 1986) with the Annual Form 5500 Pension Plan Report tapes for the years 1980 through 1984. These, in turn, were matched against Compustat tapes, which incorporated financial information for plan sponsors. These data were used to estimate the probability of termination as a function of plan and financial characteristics. The default model is discussed in more detail in Chapter 10.

To calculate exposure in 1985 (the year for which market rates were applied in this model), the study calculated underfunding using the 1984 Form 5500 Annual Pension Plan Reports and converted liabilities to the PBGC immediate annuity rate. VanDerhei estimated the portion of defunding prior to termination (denoted by the parameter g) by measuring funding deterioration in PBGC-terminated plans with data up to five years prior to termination. His estimate of g was 50 percentage points (more detail on this finding is given in Chapter 7). Thus, any firm with a funding ratio in excess of 150 percent escaped any risk-related charges. The average funding ratio (measured on a termination basis) was approximately 160 percent for the entire sample of defined benefit pension plans.

To derive the premium for each plan in the sample, VanDerhei estimated the probability of termination based on a model that incorporated the firm's financial plan characteristics, its industry affiliation, and union status of its workers. (This model is discussed in Chapter 10.) This default probability was multiplied by the exposure provided by the plan, defined to include underfunding on a termination basis, inclusive of the cushion amount. The estimated premiums do not reflect insurance expenses or amortization of the existing PBGC deficit. Table 6–6 presents the results.

The estimated risk premium is $65.59 for the average participant. Over two thirds of the participants escape a funding charge because their effective exposure to the PBGC is zero. Approximately 20 percent of the participants pay premiums above $100 (rows 1 and 2), but these account for over 95 percent of the aggregate risk premiums (last column, row 3). Participants in plans paying premiums in excess of $100 pay an average premium of $328 (roughly 7 percent of all participants in the sample pay a premium in excess of $200).

TABLE 6–6 Risk- and Exposure-Related Market Premiums, 1985

Category	*Total*	*$0.00*	*$10*	*$25*	*$50*	*$75*	*$100*	*Over $100*
Estimated market prices								
1. Plans	665	62.4%	15.9	4.2	3.4	2.8	1.5	9.6
2. Participants	2.4m	68.1%	6.2	2.5	1.2	2.0	0.6	19.0
3. Premiums	$157.7m	0.0%	0.1	0.6	0.7	2.0	0.9	95.4
4. Exposure*	$4,644	0.0	5,436	2,802	5,196	8,258	13,506	31,603
5. Default risk† per plan	9.8	7.5	3.0	8.7	9.8	14.8	9.6	34.8
6. Default risk† per participant	12.1	10.1	2.8	8.4	7.7	9.7	7.5	23.2
7. Average risk premium	$65.59	0	1.32	16.15	39.75	64.41	89.94	328.99
PBGC proposal								
8. Percent cross-subsidy	0%	N/A‡	−1,718%	−0.5	42.3	52.0	−90.5	18.2

* Per participant; includes a cushion for pre-termination defunding.

† Per 1,000.

‡ Because plans in the zero-risk premium category pay no risk premium, the amount of subsidy, divided by zero, is undefined. The cross-subsidy paid by this group is $10.

SOURCE: Jack VanDerhei, *An Empirical Analysis of Risk-Related Insurance Premiums for the PBGC,* final report submitted to the PBGC, 1988.

The numbers in rows 4 and 6 provide the underlying explanation for the rate structure. Among plans in the lowest rate class (less than $10), exposure per participant is $5,436, and the annual default risk is 2.8 per 1,000 participants. Among plans in the highest rate class (over $100), exposure per participant is $31,603, and default risk is 23.2 per 1,000 participants.

The results are shown visually in Figure 6–1, (*a*) and (*b*).

Comparison to the PBGC Proposal

VanDerhei applied the PBGC's proposed rates to the plans in his sample. In this exercise, he netted out the portion of the $8.50 fixed charge attributable to expenses and amortization of the existing deficit, leaving roughly a flat cross-subsidy $3 assessment per participant. The average premium under the proposal is $65.59 in his model. This is in comparison to the $20.14 ($25.64 minus $5.50 for expenses and amortization) implicit in the PBGC proposal.

The differences in the numbers are dramatic: VanDerhei's average price is over three times the average PBGC-estimated required premium. There are at least two important reasons for this difference. First, VanDerhei estimates that the required cushion to protect against defunding is 50 percentage points; the PBGC made the assumption that a 25-percentage-point cushion was adequate. Using a 50 percent cushion, the PBGC average premium increases over 60 percent.

Second, VanDerhei's default probabilities are derived exclusively from terminations during the 1980s. The PBGC estimate gave some weight to the much smaller probabilities observed during the 1970s. The numbers from the sensitivity analyses of the PBGC premium estimates show that if based solely on experience in the 1980s, the required exposure portion of the premium would have been 40 percent higher.[1]

Adjusting for these factors, VanDerhei's estimate is still 40 percent higher than the PBGC estimate. This could be attributable either to the nature of the sample in the VanDerhei study or to an implicit trend in his underlying bankruptcy variables.[2]

---

[1] Other differences include the following: VanDerhei (1) estimated prices based on 1984 data, not 1986, (2) adjusted liabilities to different PBGC interest rates (owing to different time periods), and (3) performed estimates based on a relatively small sample that is not necessarily representative of all defined benefit plans.

[2] VanDerhei's sample consisted only of pension plans that had sponsors' data reported on the Compustat tapes and thus was relatively small in comparison to the universe of pension plans. In addition, to the extent that financial variables exhibited less financial soundness in 1985 (the year of his pricing exercise), compared to earlier years in the 1980s, his method would produce higher default probabilities than the PBGC model, which took no account of trends.

FIGURE 6–1 VanDerhei Study, Part (*a*) Estimated Market Premiums, 1985

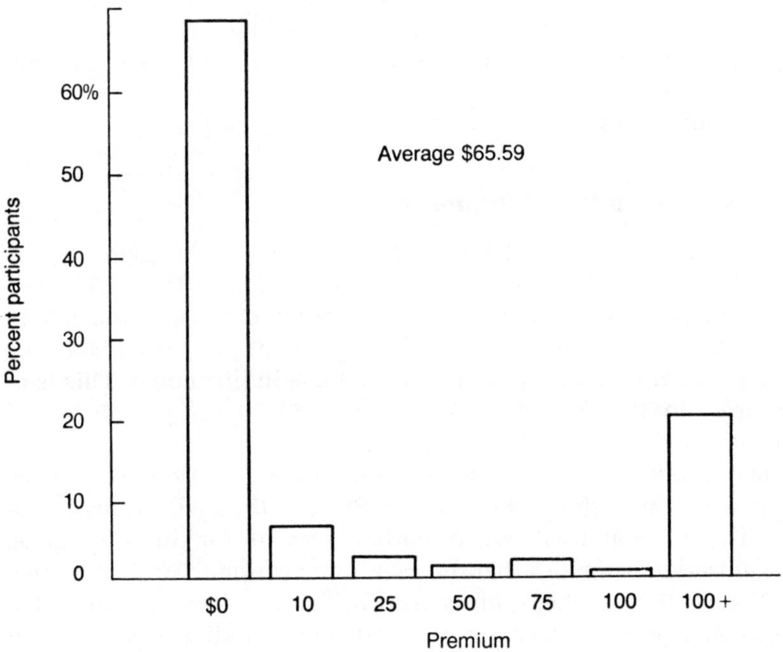

Aside from levels of premiums, the comparison has some interesting findings for the distribution of premiums. This is an important comparison because the PBGC pricing scheme ignores default risk, while VanDerhei's structure does not. Row 8 in the table summarizes these results. To estimate cross-subsidies, VanDerhei assumes the PBGC would increase the minimum and maximum charges as well as the funding charge proportionately so as to generate his $65.59 average premium. Thus, both hypothetical price structures are set up to generate the same revenue. His numbers show that all plans with zero exposure in the estimated market price structure would pay roughly $10 per participant as a subsidy to all other plans (this is in addition to any amount required to cover expenses and retire the existing PBGC deficit).

The remaining numbers in the table show that a PBGC-like proposal that generated $65.59 on average, generally awards a cross-subsidy from plans that otherwise pay a low market price to those that would pay the highest market rates. For example, plans that would pay premiums between $25 and $50 in VanDerhei's pricing structure are awarded a cross-subsidy in the PBGC-like pricing scheme equal to 42 percent of their market rates. For plans that otherwise would pay market rates $0–$10, however, they would be assessed taxes equal to

FIGURE 6–1 VanDerhei Study, Part (*b*) Exposure and Default Risk

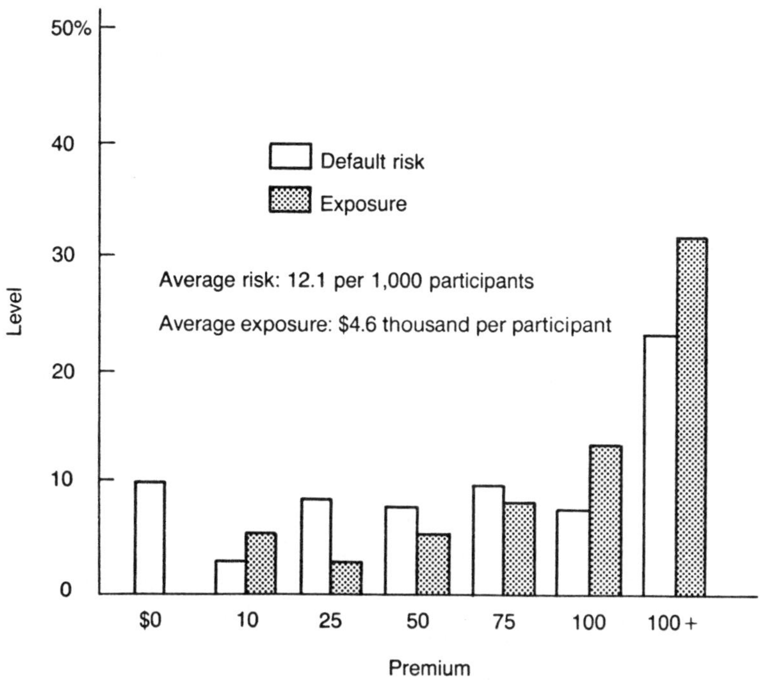

1,700 percent of their market rates. (Oddly $75–$100 plans are also taxed: This is because these plans in general are assessed too much for exposure in relation to the actual risk they pose to the PBGC.)

The biggest gainers from the subsidized rates under the PBGC proposal are those that would pay the highest rates in a private market. While the average market rate in the over-$100 price category is $753 ($328 weighted by all participants in the over-$100 category), the rates for some plans are much higher. A list of the top rate payers in VanDerhei's sample is given in Table 6–7. Rather than identify plan sponsor names, I listed their industry affiliation. Thus five plan sponsors are steelmaking firms, one is an airline, etc. Eleven firms sponsoring 19 plans out of 665 plans priced in the sample (with at least 100 participants) would have paid at least $500 per participant per year in a free market structure. Eight of these plans (five firms) were affiliated with steel and related industries.

The VanDerhei study is merely suggestive. Actual private-sector prices might be based on different risk models. And, while defunding prior to termination was rampant prior to 1987, there is reason to believe that the Pension Protection Act at least will be more successful in restricting this potential in the future (see Chapter 8). The study does

TABLE 6–7 Market Rates for Selected High-Risk Firms

Pension Plan Sponsor Name	*Industry Affiliation of Pension Plan Sponsor*	*Participants*	*Annual Premium* per Participant*
A.	Steel	9,379	$7,068
B.	Steel	730	1,150
C.	Steel	612	1,003
D.	Steel	2,925	701
E.	Steel	847	588
F.	Airlines	110	2,021
G.	Malt breweries	309	958
H.	Sugar refining	167	880
I.	Chemicals	1,861	758
J.	Rubber	2,743	601
K.	Electronic equipment	475	504

* Data for this column taken from Jack VanDerhei, *An Empirical Analysis of Risk-Related Insurance Premiums for the PBGC,* final report submitted to the PBGC, 1988.

show, however, that private-sector prices would likely be markedly different than those in the PBGC proposal.

While a market price structure undoubtedly would be more effective in reducing cross-price subsidies, I will suggest in Chapter 9 that the use of an unrestricted risk model does have some downside potential for overall economic efficiency.

PROVISIONS OF THE 1987 LEGISLATION

The pricing structure actually adopted in the Pension Protection Act of 1987 was modeled after the PBGC proposal, but it turned out to be significantly different in many important respects.

A comparison of the new rate structure and the PBGC proposal is given in Table 6–8. Both rate structures share the $6 funding charge. The new law, however, has no funding cushion (the defunding parameter (g) is set equal to zero). The minimum charge was increased from $8.50 to $16; the maximum was reduced from $100 to $50. There was also no provision for indexing the minimum and maximum rates, no automatic adjustment mechanism to reflect claims experience, and no special surcharges to reflect special unfunded shutdown benefits. In general, the rate structure resembles a flat rate structure more than one related to exposure.[3]

[3] For the sake of comparison to the rate formula given in Equations (6–1) and (6–2), the rate schedule actually enacted is described as follows:

$$P' = \$16 + .006 \text{ Max } [0, 1 - F]L$$
$$P' \leq \$50$$

TABLE 6–8 Comparison of PBGC Proposal and Legislation

Provision	*PBGC Proposal*	*New Law*
Minimum charge	$8.50	$16.00
Maximum charge	$100.00	$50.00
Funding charge (FC)*	$6.00	$6.00
Funding cushion	25%	None
Amount subject to FC before maximum†	$82.3 billion	$32.7 billion
Amount subject to FC after maximum‡	$62.1 billion	$18.4 billion
Indexing of minimum	Yes	No
Indexing of maximum	Yes§	No
Surcharges		
Waivers	Yes	No
Unpaid contributions	Yes	No
Shutdown benefits	Yes	No
Rate adjustment mechanism	Yes	No
Average premium	$25.64	$20.50

* Under the new law, plans can receive discounts up to $15 if they have been funding at the maximum amounts permitted by law.

† The exposure subject to the funding charge is greater under the PBGC proposal because of the 25 percent funding cushion; there is no cushion used in the pricing structure actually enacted.

‡ The imposition of a maximum premium effectively exempts a portion of exposure from the funding charge.

§ Indexed to 1.5 times wage growth.

The premium distribution for the new rate schedule is given in Table 6–9. In the new structure, plans in the minimum-charge category pay 56.6 percent of premiums; those in the $50 category pay 26.2 percent of premiums. In the PBGC proposal, these percentages were essentially reversed (see Table 6–4): those paying the minimum accounted for 20.9 percent of premiums, and those paying $50 or more accounted for 56.4 percent of revenues. Thus, the subsidies in the PBGC proposals are higher in the law actually enacted.

The elimination of the funding cushion in the new law sets up a

TABLE 6–9 Schedule of PBGC Premiums: Pension Protection Act

Premium Level	*Premiums*	*Participants*	*Plans*
$16.00	56.6%	76.2%	77.8%
$16.01–35.00	10.7	9.2	13.1
$35.01–49.99	6.1	3.1	3.5
$50.00	26.2	11.2	5.4
Average premium	$20.50		

SOURCE: 1984 Form 5500 Annual Pension Plan Reports, projected to 1986.

peculiar exposure-related scheme. Because funding levels historically have decreased markedly prior to termination (see the next chapter), the rate scheme in effect imposes a funding charge on part of the plan's exposure and a zero charge on the remaining amount. The effect of this provision (together with the lower maximum premium) is to reduce the amount of exposure subject to a funding charge by approximately 70 percent from $62 billion to $18 billion.

There are no surcharges for shutdown benefits in the plan, waivers, or failure to make minimum contributions;[4] nor is there any provision to adjust rates over time.

In spite of the shortcomings of the price structure actually enacted, it represents an important step toward more market-oriented prices. First, in comparison to a flat rate structure, cross-subsidies are reduced, albeit in a relatively modest way. Second, and more important, the structure represents the potential for more dramatic change in the future. Because the rates are not indexed, inflation alone will almost certainly require Congress to adjust rates in the future. The opportunity will thus be available for Congress to substantially increase the maximum allowable price and perhaps to begin considering risk-related factors as well.

CONCLUSION

In this chapter, an effort was made to illustrate the rate structure that would exist in a private insurance market for pensions. The rates would account for default risk, underfunding, and defunding prior to termination. This structure would recognize that plans with roughly 20 percent of participants account for almost 95 percent of expected claims.

The proposal submitted to Congress by the PBGC in 1987 made allowance for exposure (including defunding prior to termination) but not for default risk. Further, it imposed a $100 premium cap on the annual premium per participant (though it increased to $300 in real terms in the long run). Congress strayed even further from market rates: it excluded any consideration of defunding prior to termination in the exposure base, imposed a maximum premium of $50, and increased charges disproportionately for plans with no effective exposure to the PBGC.

This legislation suggests that, at least in the near term, Congress is not ready to institute significant pension insurance reform through changes in pricing. There is still little relationship between expected claims and premiums paid to the PBGC. This suggests that reform must

---

[4] Some provisions elsewhere in the legislation worked to at least partly reduce the exposure posed by these factors (see Chapter 8).

include changes in the nature of the insurance contract, so that its provisions will more closely reflect the regulated prices imposed by Congress. These reforms are the subjects of the next two chapters.

APPENDIX
Other Features of the PBGC Pricing Proposal

Rate Adjustment

The proposal permitted the PBGC to reassess its rates based on actual versus expected experience. In particular, the actual flow of claims would be compared to projected claims annually. If the three-year cumulative difference between actual and projected claims exceeded 10 percent of the sum of the past three years' projected liabilities, the average premium would be increased by this proportion, subject to a limit of 20 percent.

The excess claims over 20 percent of projected claims would be added to the cumulative actual claims for consideration during the next year. Following an increase of rates due to this adjustment process, projected claims would be increased proportionately, to be consistent with the new, higher average premium. The prospect of unexpected lower claims is treated symmetrically.

The advantage of this approach is that the PBGC would not accumulate large surpluses or deficits. If claims experience were lower than anticipated or if Congress enacted legislation to limit the extent of future claims, then rates will be reduced automatically.

Waiver from Extra Premium Charges

Firms wishing to keep relatively low funding levels could receive a waiver from premium charges above the minimum if either of two conditions was satisfied: the firm annuitized its benefits with commercial insurers or offered security to the PBGC in the amount of the underfunding (inclusive of the cushion amount).

Funding Waiver Surcharge

A surcharge would be levied against firms that failed to make required minimum contributions to the plan or obtained waivers. In the former case, the extra charge is 50 percent of the calculated funding charge for five years; in the case of waivers, the surcharge is scaled down to 40 percent the second year after the waiver is issued, 30 percent in the third year, and so forth. The surcharge is not subject to the $100 maximum. Thus, a plan that otherwise would pay a $100 maximum would instead pay $350 if it missed its minimum contribution for five consecutive years.

Finally, the surcharges would be doubled for firms that had large contingent obligations, primarily related to plant shutdowns. This charge reflects the lack of funding for shutdown benefits. Thus, if a firm missed its minimum contributions for five consecutive years and had shutdown provisions, the plan would pay a rate equal to $600 per participant.

CHAPTER 7

Underfunding Exposure: The Evidence

The last chapter made the assumption that the insurance contract currently enforced by the PBGC would prevail indefinitely. Prices were set either partly or fully to accommodate the resulting risk and exposure. This chapter makes the opposite assumption: that prices for the insurance policy will remain essentially flat across firms. If premiums cannot be reasonably related to risk and exposure, then the contract must in some way be tightened to reduce the potential exposure faced by the PBGC. In this chapter, the exposure experience of the PBGC is described. In the next, various efforts to control exposure (particularly through legislation enacted in 1987) are considered. These discussions lay the framework for developing a rational pension insurance policy, which will be the subject of discussion in Chapters 9 and 10.

OVERALL UNDERFUNDING SINCE ERISA

Impact of ERISA

Prior to ERISA, the most important restrictions imposed by the government on funding levels were in the form of *maximum* contribution limits. Because pension plan contributions accumulate in a tax-exempt trust fund, the Internal Revenue Code has long constrained firms from depositing too much into the pension fund. Firms were required to fund new accruals (normal cost) but could maintain past underfunding forever (except for paying interest on the deficiency). With the passage of ERISA, the government imposed stricter *minimum* contribution requirements. In addition to requirements to fund current accruals (normal cost), firms were required to (1) use reasonable actuarial assumptions in the aggregate; (2) amortize past underfunding over 30 years; and (3) amortize the difference between experience and actuarial assumptions over 15 years.

Apparently Congress felt these standards would reduce overall exposure to levels consistent with the small premium assessed for PBGC insurance. Subsequent evidence supports the opposite conclusion: overall target funding levels were unaffected by ERISA. In fact, target funding levels of the worst-funded plans became even lower after ERISA.

At first, this assertion seems counterintuitive because observed funding levels over the post-ERISA period have generally been increasing. In Figure 7–1, I have plotted termination and economic funding ratios over the 1950–87 period. Termination funding ratios generally increase during the period due to increasing interest rates. Economic liabilities are a better measure of real funding status because they account for higher expected salary growth over time and partial price indexing after retirement. To reflect these realities, economic liabilities in the figure are adjusted to a common 2 percent interest rate for all years.

Figure 7–1 shows that, prior to ERISA, economic funding ratios increased during the 1950s but evinced little trend from 1960 through the early 1970s, though there was considerable volatility. After ERISA, a positive trend is evinced.

Closer examination of the data, however, shows that this "ERISA effect" is more apparent than real. ERISA was passed after a sharp stock market decline: during 1973–74, average economic funding ratios fell by approximately 34 percentage points (see figure). The post-ERISA increases in funding levels reflect moderate increases in stock market prices in the immediate years following its enactment and sharp increases during the 1980s. A model of pension contributions is required to separate market effects from underlying behavioral changes caused by ERISA.

Such a model is developed and estimated in the appendix to this chapter. The results show that ERISA exerted no independent impact on underlying funding ratios in the average private pension plan in the United States. Changes in market rates of return account for all of the increases in funding ratios since ERISA. In fact, the results reveal that the most underfunded plans prior to ERISA became relatively *more underfunded* after ERISA.

The essence of these results can also be glimpsed from the termination funding levels presented in the last chapter, which are reproduced in column 1 of Table 7–1. Column 1 shows the distribution of termination funding ratios in 1986 (calculated using a common 7.25 percent PBGC interest rate). Twelve years after the passage of ERISA, one out of five pension plans (weighted by participants) was less than 100 percent funded, even on a termination basis.

FIGURE 7–1 Funding Ratios, 1950–1987

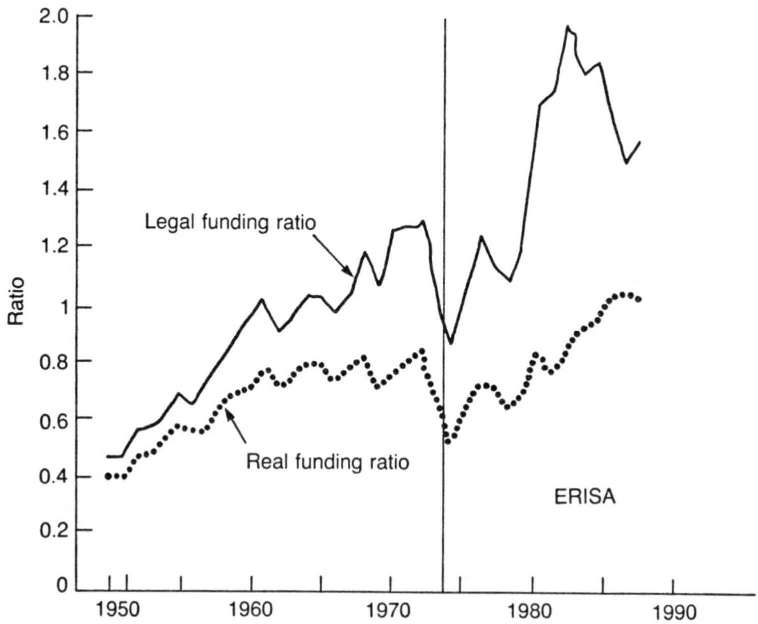

On an ongoing basis, the data in column 2 of the same table reveal that over half of all plans (weighted by participants) were underfunded; one out of four was less than 75 percent funded (ongoing liabilities are estimated by converting liabilities to a common 2 percent discount rate). At the same time, almost one in five participants were in plans more than 125 percent funded on an ongoing basis. Clearly ERISA and Internal Revenue Code funding rules permit a wide distribution of funding levels to persist.[1]

Some Reasons for Persistent Underfunding

A serious gap appears between what was presumably intended by minimum funding rules and what actually happened. There can be several reasons for this, but two in particular are important. First, the

[1] Prior to the Pension Protection Act of 1987, the Internal Revenue Code reduced permissible contribution levels if firms were funded beyond 100 percent of ongoing liabilities. There are two reasons why many plans nevertheless are overfunded on this basis in Table 7–1. First, firms can make assumptions that might be inconsistent with facts. For example, if wage growth was expected to be equal to long-term nominal interest rates, the firm might use a wage growth assumption that exceeded the interest rate assumption, thus generating higher permissible contributions. Second, extraordinary market increases in trust assets could be amortized over 15 years, thereby often permitting continuing contributions even if 100 percent funding had been attained.

TABLE 7–1 Termination versus Ongoing Funding Ratios, 1986

	Distribution of Participants	
Funding Ratio	*Termination Basis** *(1)*	*Ongoing Basis†* *(2)*
0–24%	0.4%	0.8%
25–49	2.9	10.0
50–74	8.4	16.8
75–99	11.8	27.2
100–124	17.9	25.7
124–149	18.6	11.3
150+	39.8	7.9
Average	124.0	87.5

* Evaluated at a common 7.25 percent interest rate.
† Evaluated at a common 2 percent interest rate.
SOURCE: 1984 Form 5500 Annual Pension Plan Reports, projected to 1986.

Internal Revenue Code has an explicit loophole to the funding standards. By choosing a flat (instead of salary-related) pension benefit, the plan is not permitted to fund for ongoing benefits, even if the flat benefit has been, and will continue to be, increased to keep pace with wages.[2] Simply by opting for a flat benefit formula, a firm can ensure that its pension will be perpetually underfunded. Second, the amortization period of 30 years can be dramatically inadequate for a plan composed of retirees and other workers.

Illustrations of problem: Stylized example

Flat benefit. A simple example is adequate to demonstrate these points. Consider a firm that has one worker; the firm will dissolve when this worker retires. The facts of the example are as follows (these assumptions are chosen to make the illustration easy; they do not influence the essence of the results):

- The interest and inflation rates are zero over the entire time horizon.
- The worker is age 45 with 20 years' service and will retire at 55; death is certain at age 80.
- There is no chance that the worker will quit the firm prior to age 55 or that the firm will terminate until the worker retires.
- The pension pays a flat benefit; the annual annuity equals $120 for each year of service.

[2] More particularly, the actuary uses the entry-age (normal) funding method.

- The firm's actuary uses a level contribution method for calculating required contributions.[3]
- The funding ratio is currently 100 percent; the trust fund is 100 percent invested in short-term Treasury bills.

In this example, the pension liability is currently $60,000. The annuity equals $120 times 20 years of service, or $2,400, which is collected from age 55 to age 80 (25 years × $2,400 = $60,000). Assets also equal $60,000. Absent a change in benefits, the firm is required to fund its *normal cost*.

The normal cost is merely the difference in liabilities at retirement age and current age amortized over the remaining years of service. Because liabilities at age 55 will be $90,000 (same calculations as above except substitute 30 years' service for 20 years), normal cost is $3,000; that is, $30,000 ($90,000 minus $60,000 already accumulated in trust) divided by 10 years (the remaining tenure for the worker in the firm). The portfolio in the example is entirely composed of T-bills; therefore, if there are no changes in benefit levels and if normal cost contributions equal to $3,000 are made each year, then the pension fund will remain 100 percent funded until the individual retires.

Suppose, however, that the firm awards a benefit increase: it doubles the benefit to $240 per year of service. The first impact of the benefit increase is to increase the firm's normal cost contribution: it doubles the required contribution from $3,000 to $6,000. This ensures that *future service accruals* are fully funded at retirement.

However, because the higher benefit applies to *all* years of service, including past service, underfunding will be created in the firm. In fact, liabilities attributable to the first 20 years of service increase from $60,000 to $120,000; the funding ratio falls from 100 percent to 50 percent; and $60,000 in underfunding attributable to *past service liability* is created.

Minimum funding rules require this amount to be amortized over *30 years*, thus necessitating an annual contribution of $2,000. Maximum contribution limits would permit a contribution of up to 10 percent of past service underfunding, or $6,000 per annum.

In this example, if a firm paid the maximum allowable contribution, it would be fully funded by the time the individual retires. That is, a $6,000 contribution each year fully amortizes the $60,000 underfunding over 10 years.

If the firm makes the minimum contribution instead, it will have

---

[3] Ibid.

FIGURE 7–2(*a*) Inadequate Funding Rules—Flat Benefit Plan

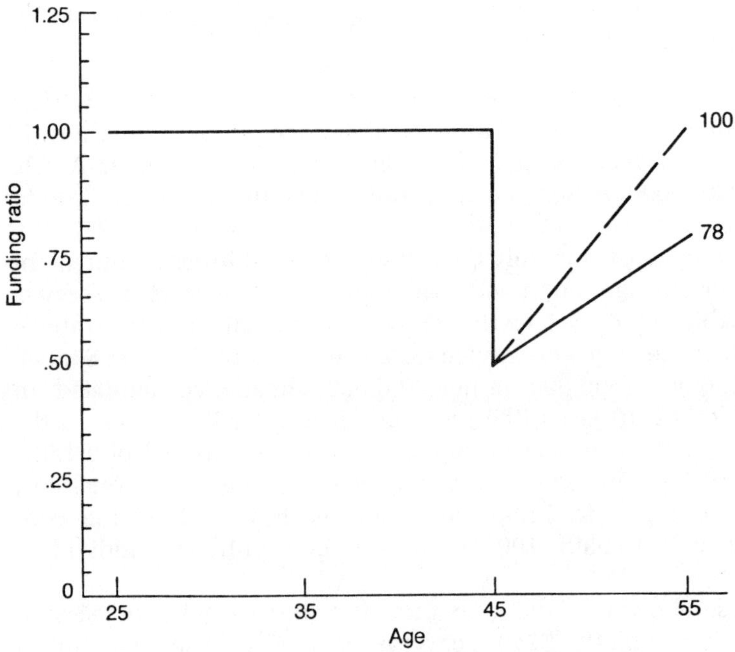

paid off only one third of the past service credit in the ensuing 10 years. If the firm dissolves at the time of the worker's retirement at age 55 (which it will by assumption in the example) and has no net worth at termination, the PBGC will inherit a claim for $40,000, even though the firm satisfied its minimum funding requirement in all years. Liabilities at termination will be $180,000, and assets will equal $140,000; thus the funding ratio will be 78 percent.[4]

Though this example is highly simplified and stylized to demonstrate a point, it illustrates the underfunding problem that can arise when plans with flat benefit formulas increase benefits when the work force is relatively old. The example is visually demonstrated in Figure 7–2(*a*). The broken line in the figure denotes the funding ratio path assuming that the plan sponsor pays the maximum contributions after the benefit increase; the solid line depicts the payment of minimum contributions.

[4] Liabilities at age 55 equal the annual annuity, $240 times 30 years of service, collected for 25 years of retirement: $240 × 30 × 25 = $180,000. Assets equal the $60,000 balance at age 45, plus $60,000 in additional normal cost contributions ($6,000 per year times 10 years), plus $20,000 in past service amortization contributions ($2,000 per year times 10 years).

FIGURE 7–2(*b*) Inadequate Funding Rules—Salary-Related Plan

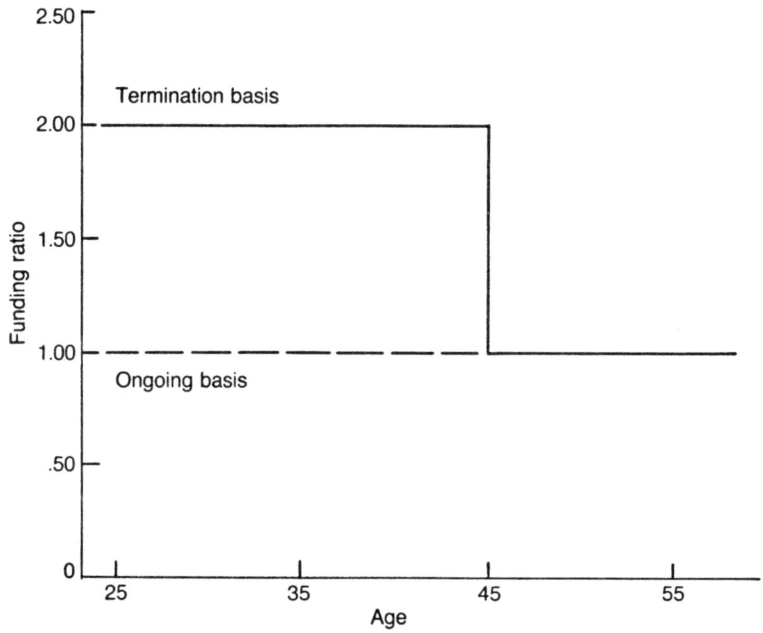

Salary-related benefit. The problem described above generally would not exist in a plan with benefits related to final salary.[5] To illustrate, suppose annuity benefits were 2.4 percent for each year of service, and starting salary was $5,000 (this is equivalent to a benefit of $120 per year of service). In this firm, real salaries generally increase at the rate of 2.3 percent per year, so the ending salary after 30 years will be twice the starting salary, or $10,000.

The Internal Revenue Code *requires* the actuary to take account of higher expected wages at retirement. In fact, if the level contribution method is used, the actuary in year one calculates expected benefits at retirement equal to 2.4 percent times 30 years times *projected* salary at retirement ($10,000); this generates an annuity equal to $7,200, which is valued at $180,000 at retirement (recall the assumption of a zero interest rate).

The normal cost in this plan is $6,000 per year ($180,000 spread over 30 years). If the salary remains at $5,000 through age 45 and then

[5] A similar problem to flat benefit increases arises in a salary plan if, for example, the generosity of the plan is increased midstream. This is different, however, than generating a built-in underfunding feature, merely because benefits increase because of inflation.

FIGURE 7–3(*a*) Adequacy of Minimum Funding Rules, 1975–1985—Flat Benefit Plan

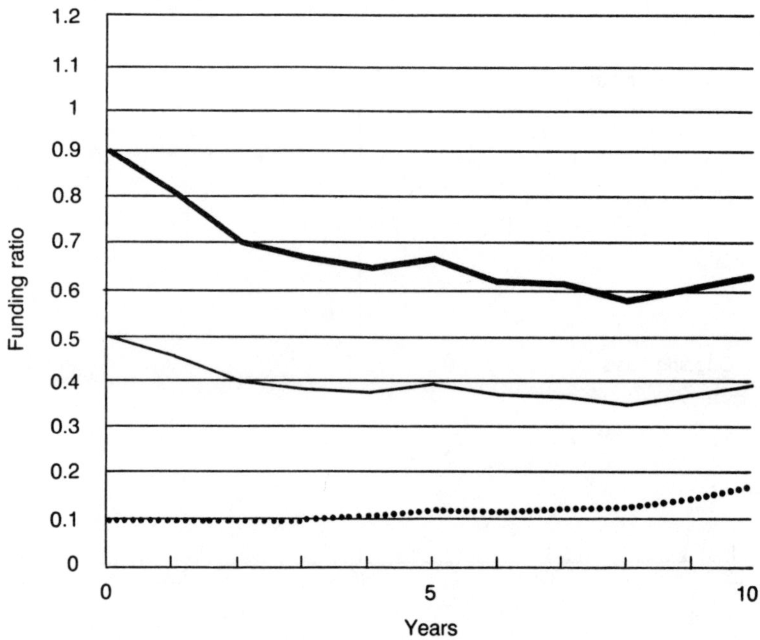

Funding ratio over time for flat benefit plan with periodic plan amendments to bring benefit levels into line with price increases, assuming three different beginning ratios. Participants have high average age and service, with almost half over age 50. The total size of the group is slowly declining.

doubles, the ongoing funding ratio is 100 percent over the entire 30 years of the worker's career (because it recognizes the ending wage from the very beginning of tenure). The termination ratio equals 200 percent until age 45 (because this calculation reflects current, not projected, wages). At age 45, this ratio falls to 100 percent, coincident with the ongoing ratio at this age. This example is demonstrated in Figure 7–2(*b*).[6]

Other illustrations

American Academy of Actuaries plans. The principles developed in the above example also can be demonstrated using a realistic pension plan. In its study, *Pension Promises at Risk,* the PBGC presented the impact of funding requirements in two types of plans

[6] This does not suggest that a firm cannot deliberately underfund a salary-related plan. In the above example, underfunding could be developed by assuming that the final wage would be $7,500 instead of $10,000. Then, at age 45 when the wage was increased to $10,000, a large amount of underfunding would be generated, which would be amortized as an "actuarial loss" over 15 years. Because the plan will terminate in 10 years by definition, underfunding would exist at termination.

FIGURE 7–3(*b*) Adequacy of Minimum Funding Rules, 1975–1985—Salary-Related Plan

Funding ratio over time for a salary-related plan covering a mature and stable group of participants that is expected to grow, assuming three different beginning ratios.

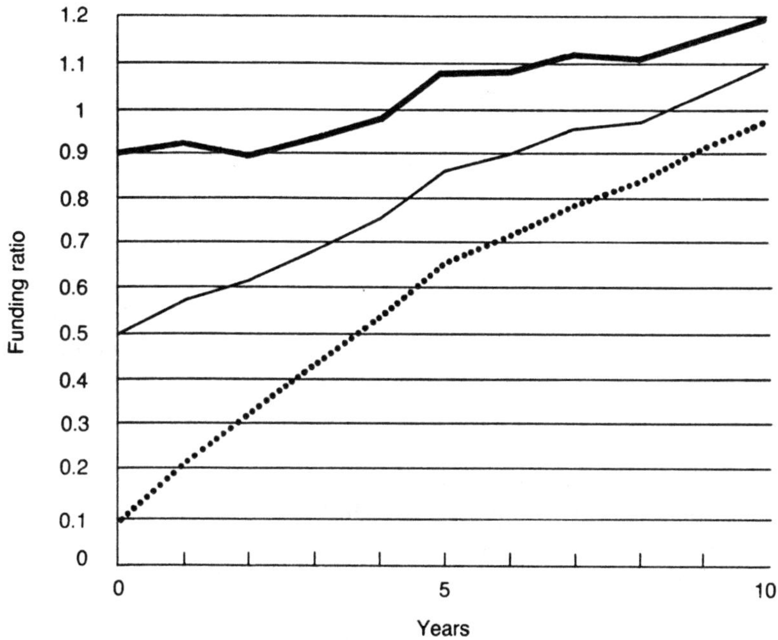

The figures show the dramatically different effect of the current minimum funding standards on two "typical" defined benefit pension plans with differing characteristics. Each figure shows changes in the plan's funded ratio over a 10-year period, assuming the plan sponsor makes all contributions required by the minimum funding standards and that investment returns replicate the first 10 years after the passage of ERISA.

Part *a* of the figure reflects a flat benefit plan with periodic plan amendments to bring benefit levels into line with price increases. Its participants have high average age and service, with almost half over age 50. The total size of the group is slowly declining. These characteristics are currently typical of many plans in troubled, capital-intensive industries, such as steel. The minimum funding standards do not result in any substantial improvement in this plan's funding. Moreover, if funding begins at a relatively sound level, it may decline markedly.

Part *b* of the figure reflects a salary-related plan covering a mature and stable group of participants that is expected to grow over time. The plan and its demographics are typical of many large companies. For this plan, the minimum funding standards work reasonably well. Whatever its initial level of funding, the plan is likely to make significant progress toward full funding.

For a full description of the plan and participants characteristics underlying these figures, see American Academy of Actuaries, Committee on Pension Actuarial Principles and Practices, *Pension Cost Method Analysis,* 1985.

SOURCE: PBGC, *Pension Promises at Risk* (Washington, D.C.: 1987), pp. 29–31.

selected from the American Academy of Actuaries, *Pension Cost Method Analysis (1985)*. Different initial funding ratios were chosen; and market returns on a balanced portfolio were chosen to replicate actual asset volatility over the 1975–85 period. Minimum funding rules were applied in all cases. The results are illustrated in Figure 7–3.

Part (*b*) of the figure shows the results for a salary-related plan that has a relatively young age distribution. Regardless of the initial level of funding, the minimum funding rules lead to relatively high funding levels at the end of the period.

Part (*a*) of the figure shows the results for a flat benefit plan populated by a relatively old work force. Benefits for active workers are increased every two years in the example in amounts equal to the two-year inflation rate. The results are dramatically different: plans that start with very low funding levels maintain virtually the same levels at the end of the period; those with relatively high funding levels show marked deterioration of funding levels. For example, a firm in the latter circumstance that started the post-ERISA period with a funding ratio equal to 90 percent ended with a funding ratio equal to 60 percent.

Allis-Chalmers. These illustrations are not merely theoretical. When the Allis-Chalmers United Auto Workers pension plan terminated in 1985, it had assets equal to $2.3 million and guaranteed liabilities equal to $176 million; the funding ratio was 1.3 percent. The plan used assumptions that were not unusual (for example, it used an assumed interest rate of 7.0 percent, compared to 7.6 percent for all plans in 1985) and met the minimum funding standards throughout the post-ERISA period. The problems in this termination are attributable to a flat benefit formula and a relatively old work force.

The problem is not isolated to one plan. Table 7–2 lists 35 terminated plans that had funding ratios of less than 20 percent at termination. These plans accounted for over $1 billion in underfunding of guaranteed benefits at termination (current dollars).

DEFUNDING PRIOR TO TERMINATION

The above discussion does not adequately describe the extent of the exposure problem facing the PBGC. In addition to ineffective funding rules, funding levels tend to fall quickly during the periods preceding termination. The incentives are apparent: the larger the amount of underfunding at the time of termination, the larger the transfer from the PBGC. Defunding can occur in numerous ways.

Methods of Defunding Prior to Termination

Waivers. Firms in financial difficulty can make a request to the Internal Revenue Service for a waiver from its minimum contribution requirement. Though the IRS generally has accommodated these requests, its policies in awarding waivers have presumably been tightened over time.[7] Prior to the Pension Protection Act (PPA) of 1987, the

[7] Based on admittedly ad hoc evidence (the overall waiver policy of the IRS is not available to study because of the confidential nature of tax records), the IRS appears

TABLE 7–2 Thirty-Five Poorly Funded Terminations

Plan Sponsor	*Date of Termination**	*Underfunding Amount ($ millions)*	*Funding Ratio*
White Motors Co. Auto Car Hourly	11/30/81	$ 6.5	0.0%
Hotel and Restaurant Employees and Bartenders Union	09/30/77	3.7	0.0
Kaiser Steel Salaried	02/28/87	31.5	0.0
Washburn Wire Co. Pension Plan	10/01/79	6.4	0.0
Retail Clerks Union 1357	10/27/80	3.5	0.2
Central Foundry Co. Molders	05/18/81	5.8	0.2
City Stores, Inc.	10/27/80	14.9	0.6
Heppenstall Co. Hourly Employees	05/31/79	13.9	1.1
Bohack Corp. Nonbargaining	10/31/77	2.8	1.2
Williams Press, Inc. Retirement Plan	12/13/85	2.7	1.2
Standard Tube of Detroit	12/30/83	2.7	1.2
Allis-Chalmers Corp. Hourly	07/26/85	173.8	1.3
White Motors Co. Salary	11/30/81	3.2	2.4
Republic Steel	09/30/86	219.2	2.7
Gateway Transportation Co.	06/15/82	4.0	2.9
McKeesport Steel Casting	04/13/84	3.9	5.2
Volco Steelworkers	10/22/85	5.8	5.7
Acme-Hamilton Local 95	05/15/78	5.1	5.8
Washburn Wire Company	10/31/76	13.2	8.1
Rath Packing Co.	09/13/82	55.4	9.1
Mid-Vale Heppenstall Company	04/30/76	5.1	9.2
AlloyTek, Inc. Hourly	10/31/79	4.6	9.7
Ingersoll Products Corp.	12/31/85	10.6	10.2
Kaiser Steel Hourly	07/28/87	201.0	12.2
Diamond REO Trucks, Inc. UAW	05/31/75	9.9	12.6
Mansfield Tire & Rubber Co.	06/30/79	24.0	13.3
White Farm Equipment—Hopkins	09/14/82	6.3	13.4
White Farm Equipment—Hourly	09/14/82	32.7	13.6
Phoenix Steel Corp. Claymont	08/22/83	22.8	14.4
LTV—Continental Emsco	04/30/88	8.4	14.9
Alan Wood Steel Co. Hourly	11/01/77	34.8	16.8
Penn Dixie Cement Division Hourly	05/10/81	19.4	17.4
Century Brass Products, Inc.	12/02/85	29.7	18.7
Chase Brass and Copper Co.	06/28/76	13.3	19.3
White Motors Co. Cleveland Union	11/30/81	45.7	19.9
Total		$1,046.3	7.5%

* Estimated for pending cases.

SOURCE: PBGC Case Processing File.

IRS could approve these waivers in any 5 out of 15 years. (The PPA reduced the number from five to three.)

Chapter 4 discussed the case of Rath Packing. During the period prior to termination, Rath obtained five waivers amounting to almost

over time to be more aggressive in requiring security against its waivers. In the absence of security, the IRS, even before SEPPAA, began requiring as a condition to the waivers that unpaid waivers would be treated as taxes in bankruptcy proceedings.

TABLE 7–3 Waiver Amounts in Relation to Claims (dollars in millions)

	Number	Amount	Number	Amount
Waivers granted 1980 and 1981			115	$622
Claims from this group through 1987	23	$136		
Waivers to subgroup	—	$26.6		$26.6
Percent of claims		19.5%		
Percent of all waivers to claimants through 1987				4.2%
Claims made 1983–1985			321	$840
Waivers awarded to this group, 1981–1984			44	$113
Percent				13.4%

Note: Numbers in this table do not represent the population of all claims and waivers; the numbers are taken from the sample of plans studied by VanDerhei.

SOURCE: Jack VanDerhei, "An Empirical Analysis of Risk-Related Insurance Premiums for the Pension Benefit Guaranty Corporation," final report submitted to the PBGC, 1988.

$30 million. In 1982, it terminated its plan, making a claim in the amount of $60 million. When Continental Steel terminated its plans in 1986, it too had received five consecutive waivers accounting for roughly half of its claims.[8]

Table 7–3 provides more systematic data on this point. In his study, VanDerhei (see Chapter 6) made two calculations reflecting the importance of waivers. First, using Form 5500 data, he calculated all waivers granted during the 1980–81 period. He found 115 waivers in his database amounting to $622 million.

Using the PBGC Case Processing File, he then tracked all waiver recipients through 1987 to find those that became claimants to the PBGC. He found that 23 claims from this group accounted for roughly one in five waivers granted during the 1980–81 period. The claimants, however, tended to be small, accounting for only $26.6 million in waiver amounts, or 4.2 percent of the total amount of waivers granted. Among the waiver recipients that became claimants, however, waivers accounted for 19.5 percent of their total claims. These data are reflected in the top part of Table 7–3.

In short, most waivers granted do not turn out to be bad loans, but

[8] Information on Continental Steel is taken from the PBGC Annual Report, 1986, p. 24.

TABLE 7–4 Unpaid Contributions (amounts in millions)

Years	*Unpaid Contributions (Uncollectible)*	*Claims*	*Percent*
1975–1980	$ 26.4	$147.3	17.9%
1981–1987	154.7	738.3	20.9
Total	$181.1	$885.6	20.4%

Note: Numbers based on a sample of 598 claims from the PBGC Case Processing File. Other cases did not have records sufficiently complete to include in the calculations.

those that do, account for a significant portion of total claims. Data in the bottom part of Table 7–3 provide more information on this point. VanDerhei found that of $840 million in claims paid by the PBGC from 1983 to 1985 for which he had data, fully 13.4 percent was attributable to waivers.

Unpaid contributions. In addition to obtaining legal waivers from the IRS, many firms anticipating a termination simply do not pay minimum contributions to the plan, particularly those firms anticipating filing for Chapter 11 of the Bankruptcy Code. One legal way this can occur is if the firm makes a *request* for a waiver from the IRS. Until the IRS makes a determination (which can take upward of one year), the firm is not required to make a contribution. Or the firm simply may fail to make its required contribution. In this case, the IRS may take more than one year to discover the underfunding (through subsequent 5500 reports); and even then it may take no action.

The IRS is entitled to assess a 100 percent excise tax on a missed contribution, but it has not been successful in enforcing this option. In bankruptcy proceedings, these assessments are treated as penalties, which take on a very low priority. Once in a bankruptcy proceeding, the PBGC has usually recaptured only a small portion of missed minimum funding contributions.

Data in Table 7–4 describe the extent of the problem. A sample of 598 claims that had sufficient data was used to compare claims amounts against due and unpaid contributions to the plan at the time of the termination. The first column in the table lists the amounts uncollectible after settlement of claims. Of $885 million in final claims against the PBGC from this sample, fully $181 million (accounting for 20.4 percent of claims) was attributable to uncollectible, unpaid contributions to the plan.

Shutdown benefits. The principal funding problem affiliated with a shutdown is that new benefits arise only if a plant closes. Actuaries are supposed to attach some probability to this event, particularly when firms encounter financial difficulty. In practice, it is usually treated as a very small probability and therefore essentially ignored. In essence, shutdown benefits are not funded until the event occurs, and until 1987 they were amortized over 15 years.

Recall our above example with one worker in the firm, aged 45 with 20 years of service. The interest rate was zero, and an annual annuity equal to $120 per year of service was paid from age 55 (retirement) to age 80 (death). The firm's current liability was $60,000, which by assumption was equal to assets. If benefits are not increased, then when the worker retires at age 55 with 30 years of service, normal cost contributions would ensure sufficient assets to cover $90,000 in liabilities at that age.

Suppose, however, that the firm closes its plant immediately (when the worker is age 45). The plan has a shutdown benefit "rule of 65"; thus, with his current 20 years' service plus 45 years in age, the worker qualifies for full benefits immediately. Liabilities are no longer equal to an annuity of $120 times 20 years' service times 25 years of retirement ($60,000). Instead, the retirement period increases from 25 years to 35 years, and the plan is immediately underfunded. It has $60,000 in assets, but its liabilities are $84,000 (35/25 times $60,000). On shutdown, the funding ratio falls from 100 percent to 71.4 percent. Because the PBGC guarantees shutdown benefits (assuming the shutdown preceded the plan termination date), it faces a claim in this example equal to approximately 30 percent of the liability amount, even though the firm satisfied all its funding requirements.[9]

As discussed in Chapter 5, shutdown benefits (and other early benefit guarantees) have been responsible for a significant portion of claims made against the PBGC. But terminations during the 1980s have shown that these guarantees are more costly than recognized in the original PBGC study (see Chapter 5). For example, with the termination of LTV Corporation's pension plans in 1986, the agency assumed a claim of $2.3 billion. Of this, rough estimates suggest that fully $600 million to $700 million was attributable to shutdown benefits alone; unreduced early benefits might have accounted for another $400 million to $500 million. Thus, shutdown and unreduced early benefits could have accounted for fully half of the $2.3 billion claim.[10] Similar calculations apply to other steel terminations in the early to mid-1980s.

Changing actuarial assumptions. Actuaries are not supposed to change their assumptions to facilitate defunding of plans prior to termination. If they are accommodating, however, they can help the

---

[9] I chose an example where the monthly full benefit is $200 and therefore fully guaranteed by the PBGC at age 45. More generous benefits might be constrained by the maximum benefits limitation (see Table 5–2).

[10] These estimates account for the erosion of funding attributable to payment of shutdown benefits prior to plan termination. Other estimates presented in Chapter 5 reflected only the post-termination cost of continuing to pay these benefits.

firm increase its expected transfer. For example, recall the one-worker example used above. The yearly pension annuity equals $120 times years of service beginning at age 55 after 30 years of service; death occurs at age 80. Assuming a zero interest rate, the normal cost contribution is $3,000 per year. At age 40, assets equal $45,000 ($3,000 contribution per year times 15 years). The present value of pension benefits at retirement age 55 is $90,000 ($120 per year of service times 30 years, collected from age 55 to age 80).

For the sake of illustration, consider an extreme example. Suppose that when the worker is age 40, the actuary switches to a 5 percent discount rate instead of zero (despite the fact that market interest rates are zero). At 5 percent, the present value of the annuity based on a projection of service to be paid starting at age 55 is valued at age 40 at roughly $25,000. With a zero percent interest rate, the value of the full pension based on 30 years of service evaluated at age 40 is $90,000.

This change in liability valuation at age 40 generates a $65,000 gain from a change in actuarial assumptions ($90,000 minus $25,000). The gain must be amortized and offset against the normal contribution using a 5 percent interest rate and a 30-year amortization period. This yields a $4,183 credit to the funding account, which completely offsets the required $3,000 normal contribution,[11] and thus the net required contribution goes to zero.[12] This game might be even easier to play after 1988, because the Pension Protection Act made amortization periods shorter.[13]

Evidence of accommodating actuarial assumptions is apparent even when cross-section funding ratios are observed. In the top portion of Table 7–5, funding ratios are listed for firms filing Form 5500 Reports in 1984. Funding ratios are normalized to a standard interest rate, 7.25 percent. The distribution of these ratios is compared against the interest rate assumed in the plan. Other things equal, the higher the assumed interest rate, the lower the required contribution.

---

[11] Amortization of $65,000 (like a house) over 30 years using a 5 percent interest rate yields a credit of $4,183.

[12] After three years, the actuary would be required to assess the reasonableness of the 5 percent assumption. Assuming actual interest rates turn out to be zero, he would be required to annuitize the "actuarial loss"; but by the time this occurs, termination may already have occurred. In addition, if an actuary took the extreme step described above, he might be liable to the PBGC for losses attributable to his actions. A smaller change, however, would substantially lessen this possibility and still make a significant difference in required contributions to the plan.

[13] The Pension Protection Act (PPA) changed the amortization period for gains and losses due to changes in assumptions to 10 years. In the context of the example which assumes a 5 percent interest rate, this generates a credit of $8,259, not $4,183. As long as the assumed interest rate is reasonable, the PPA does not preclude opportunistic use of assumptions. In the above example, it might be considered unreasonable if the interest rate were increased from zero to 5 percent. It would be harder to make the case that a 2 percent interest rate assumption was unreasonable.

TABLE 7–5 Relation of Assumed Interest Rates to Type of Plan

Category of Plan	*Assumed Interest Rate*
1984 Funding ratios	
Less than 75%	8.2%
75–125	7.9
More than 125	7.7
1986 Risk categories	
Very-high-risk plans with exposure	8.7
All plans	7.6

Note: Funding ratios are normalized to a 7.25 percent interest rate.
SOURCE: Form 5500 Annual Pension Plan Reports, 1984; and PBGC exposure calculations.

The results in the table suggest that firms with the lowest standardized funding ratios use the highest assumed interest rates. For example, plans that are over 125 percent funded using the PBGC rates use a 7.7 percent assumed interest rate on average; those with less than 75 percent funding use an 8.2 percent rate on average.

Data in the bottom portion of Table 7–5 are even more revealing. The 1987 PBGC exposure measurements identified 14 firms as "very high risk"; these firms hold over $5 billion in exposure for the PBGC (see Chapter 4). On average, these plans used an assumed interest rate equal to 8.7 percent, compared to 7.6 percent for all firms included on the Compustat database.

The VanDerhei study also included information consistent with these findings. He indexed assumed interest rates of PBGC claimants relative to all pension plans over the five-year period prior to termination. He found that interest rates assumed in terminated plans were the same as the pension universe until the plan year prior to termination. In that year, interest rate assumptions increased to 154 percent of the average assumed interest rate (see Table 7–6).

Lump-sum payouts. Another way to increase the PBGC transfer is to pay lump-sum cash-outs prior to termination. ERISA permits pension plans to offer lump sums in defined benefit plans in lieu of an annuity, if the worker agrees. (The firm may unilaterally cash out a worker if the lump-sum benefit is less than $3,500.) The advantage to this method is that a firm anticipating a plan termination can manipulate the PBGC into paying a larger transfer than it otherwise would. The plan can essentially (1) cause the PBGC to pay more than the maximum guaranteed amount and (2) use an interest rate lower than the PBGC rates.

These effects can be illustrated by a simple example. There are only two workers in a firm, both age 55. One just retired on an annuity of

TABLE 7–6 Changing Interest Rate Assumptions

Years to Termination	*As a Percent of Average of All Plans*
5	100%
4	98
3	97
2	103
1	154
0	N/A

SOURCE: Jack VanDerhei, "An Empirical Analysis of Risk-Related Insurance Premiums for the Pension Benefit Guaranty Corporation," final report submitted to the PBGC, 1988.

$1,250 per month; the other is about to retire at the same annuity level. Suppose the PBGC interest rate is 10 percent, and the plan uses this rate to pay lump sums. Assume all retirees die with certainty at age 80 and there is no joint and survivor option in effect. Using a 10 percent discount rate, the present value of the $1,250 monthly annuity for the current retiree is almost $138,000. If the second worker retires on the same annuity, the present value for these two annuities at that instant is twice this amount, or $276,000.

Suppose the plan has $200,000 in assets. If the plan terminates at this time (assuming none of the underfunding is recoverable from the employer), the PBGC would first reduce the annuity to its maximum amount, $859 at age 55 (see Table 5–2). This would reduce its liabilities to approximately $190,000, and thus there would be no claim: there are $190,000 in guaranteed liabilities and $200,000 in plan assets.

If, however, the firm cashes out the second retiree instead of awarding an annuity, it could evade the maximum. That is, the plan would give the retiring worker a lump sum equal to $138,000, leaving $62,000 in assets in the plan. On termination, the PBGC is faced with $95,000 in guaranteed liabilities for the sole existing retiree ($859 monthly from age 55 to age 80, discounted at 10 percent) and $62,000 in assets; it faces a claim of $33,000. In effect, the plan has circumvented the maximum benefits constraint for its about-to-retire worker.

The transfer can be increased yet again if the plan cashes out the new retiree at a lower interest rate than the PBGC close-out rate. Suppose the plan reduces its interest rate assumption from 10 percent to 7.5 percent in anticipation of the impending termination. It would then award a cash-out in the amount of almost $170,000, which leaves $30,000 in assets in the pension plan. The PBGC is still left with a liability of $95,000 for the sole existing annuitant; thus, the claim increases from $33,000 to $65,000. This example is summarized in Table 7–7.

Theoretically, the excess portion of lump sums distributed between

TABLE 7–7 Illustration of Lump-Sum Effects

Plan Variables at Termination	No Lump Sum	Lump Sum	
		i = 10 percent	*i* = 7.5 percent
Assets	$200,000	$62,000	$30,000
Liabilities	190,000	95,000	95,000
Claims	–0–	33,000	65,000

Note: The variable *i* denotes the interest rate used by the plan.

Assumptions: Two workers age 55, one just retired, one about to retire. Annuities of both are $1,250 per month; death occurs at age 80; the PBGC interest rate is 10 percent.

the date of termination and three years prior to termination can be recaptured under Section 4045 of ERISA. This provision, however, is costly to enforce. If pursued, the PBGC must try to recapture "excessive" payouts from individual participants, some of whom may not be able to repay and all of whom have a right to appeal.[14]

Benefit increases. In principle, benefit enhancements during the pretermination period present a significant moral hazard problem. The PBGC insures 100 percent of benefit increases adopted five years prior to termination. It also insures benefit increases more recent than five years at the rate of 20 percent each year the increase is in effect. Therefore, only 20 percent of increases awarded 12 months prior to termination are guaranteed. Suppose a pension benefit is $120 per year of service, and the firm increases the benefit to $220. If termination occurs in five years, the entire $220 benefit would be guaranteed at termination. If termination occurs in two years, $160 would be guaranteed (the original $120 benefit plus 40 percent of the $100 increase).

Increases in benefits in exchange for lower wages may be rational behavior for failing firms. Consider the one-worker firm used above. If the interest rate is zero, the $120 annual benefit per year of service is worth $60,000 when the worker is age 45 with 20 years of service (retirement occurs at 55; death at 80). A troubled firm can obtain a loan from the worker, guaranteed by the PBGC, by doubling the pension benefit to $240, thus increasing pension value as of age 45 to $120,000. In exchange, as the benefit becomes fully insured over five years, the worker ought to be willing to give up $60,000 in cash wages over his 10 years of remaining tenure.

Further, because his next 10 years of pension accrual (from age 45 to retirement at age 55) amounts to $60,000 instead of $30,000, an

[14] Under certain circumstances, the PBGC can pursue the plan sponsor for these overpayments, but this would not be typical.

additional $30,000 in wage concessions ought to be possible. Thus, if the worker's wage was $30,000 per year plus a $120 pension benefit, he would earn the same compensation if his insured pension benefit was doubled to $240 and his cash wage reduced to $21,000 per year.[15]

Some risk premium would be required at first because the loan is not fully guaranteed for five years. But because this guarantee is phased in at 20 percent per year, the premium could be reduced rapidly. After five years, the loan is fully guaranteed by the PBGC; thus the worker earns the same compensation in the two schemes, and the firm obtains working capital at a risk-free rate.

While this is a potentially important problem, it has been the subject of little study. The only study I know of was done by the General Accounting Office (see below). The study found "numerous" benefit increases in a sample of terminations it studied for the 1983–85 period, but it did not quantify the magnitude of the increases in relation to claims.

Another example is found in the steel industry. In 1978, the United Steelworkers of America renegotiated shutdown benefits from a "rule of 70" to a "rule of 65", thereby reducing the age-plus-service requirement to receive early benefits on a plant shutdown.

Quantitative Effects of Defunding

VanDerhei study. The above discussion demonstrates numerous avenues available to firms to defund their plans prior to termination; and certainly firms have taken advantage of these provisions. VanDerhei's study (see Chapter 6) made a quantitative estimate of the overall effect of defunding prior to terminations. In particular, VanDerhei had a list of 48 claims filed against the PBGC through 1985 for which he also had records on Form 5500 filings in prior years.

It is inappropriate to infer behavioral effects simply by tracking funding ratios in soon-to-be-terminated plans. Funding ratios are influenced by volatility in asset values and interest rates, not just changes in contributions and benefits. Thus, VanDerhei calculated funding ratios in soon-to-be-terminated plans, indexed by overall funding ratios in the defined benefit universe. All these funding ratios in a given year were converted to a common PBGC interest rate prevailing at the time. These calculations were made for the year of termination and for each of five years prior to termination.

The study showed that, on average, funding ratios among claimants

[15] In the old contract, the worker would earn $300,000 in salary in the next 10 years and have $90,000 in pension benefits, for a total of $390,000. In the new contract, he earns $210,000 in cash wage and $180,000 in pension benefits, which also totals $390,000.

TABLE 7–8 Defunding Prior to Termination

Years Prior to Termination	*Standardized Funding Ratio*	*Defunding*	
		Annual	*Cumulative*
5	77%	—	—
4	72	−5	−5
3	68	−4	−9
2	53	−15	−24
1	45	−8	−32
0	27	−18	−50

Standardized funding ratio: Funding ratios in soon-to-terminate plans divided by average funding ratio in pension plan universe during same year, evaluated at the same interest rate. Result is multiplied by 160 percent, the average funding ratio over the period using PBGC close-out rates. Results based on 148 terminated plans from 1980 to 1985.

SOURCE: Jack VanDerhei, "An Empirical Analysis of Risk-Related Insurance Premiums for the Pension Benefit Guaranty Corporation," final report submitted to the PBGC, 1988.

amounted to 17.1 percent of the funding ratios in the pension universe at the time of termination. Five years prior to termination, these plans had funding ratios equal to 48.5 percent of funding ratios for the pension universe. Because the average funding ratio over the period was 160 percent (using the PBGC immediate annuity interest rate), this finding means that the average terminated plan in the sample exhibited a termination funding ratio of 27 percent at the time of termination and 77 percent five years prior to the event. Defunding was evident during the entire five-year period prior to termination (see Table 7–8).

The GAO study. These results are similar to those found in a March 1987 study performed by the U.S. General Accounting Office entitled *Pension Plans: Government Insurance Problem Threatened by Its Growing Deficit*. The study evaluated the 33 largest claims paid by the PBGC from 1983 to 1985. By normalizing liabilities to interest rates prevailing at the date of termination, the study found that funding ratios fell from 56 percent of vested benefits five years prior to termination to 34 percent at termination.

These results are not as revealing as the VanDerhei study because they do not adjust for generally increasing asset values over the period of study, which underestimates reductions in funding for those plans relative to the entire defined benefit plan universe. Nevertheless, the GAO results are consistent with those found in the VanDerhei study.

The GAO study also calculated the ratio of actual to minimum contribution amounts. The results are shown in Figure 7–4 for the five years preceding termination. There is a clear trend toward lower contribution rates as the termination event approaches.

The GAO study concluded that this defunding process was attributable to several factors, including inadequate funding standards,

FIGURE 7–4 Decline in Ratio of Actual to Minimum Contributions

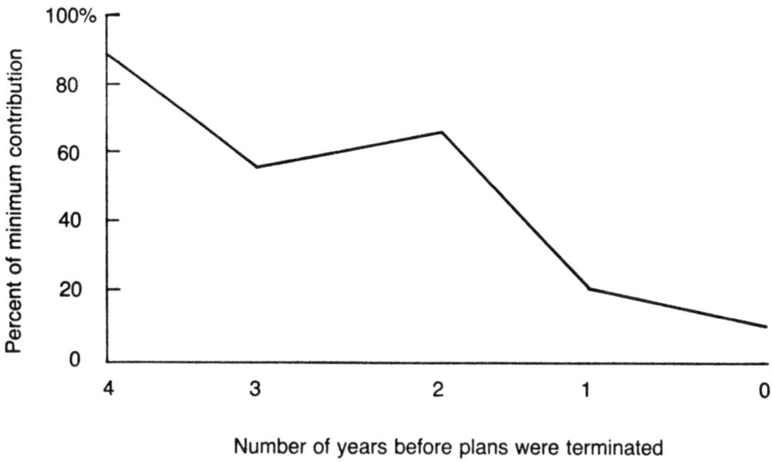

SOURCE: U.S. General Accounting Office, "Pension Plans: Government Insurance Program Threatened by Its Growing Deficit," Report to the Subcommittee on Oversight, Committee on Ways and Means, House of Representatives, March 1987.

increases in benefits prior to termination, waivers, and unpaid contributions. Consistent with data shown in Tables 7–3 and 7–4, the study found that waivers and unpaid contributions alone accounted for 30 percent of the PBGC's claims for these plans. Of this amount, 23 percent was due to waivers, 32 percent to overdue unpaid contributions, and 45 percent to contributions due but unpaid at termination.[16] A summary of the GAO findings is presented in Table 7–9.

Trends in relative funding. The combination of persistent low funding levels for some plans in the universe and defunding prior to termination has important effects on claims paid by the PBGC. Moreover, the problem appears to be growing over time. In column 1 of Table 7–10, funding ratios are listed for insufficient terminations taken over by the PBGC. In column 2, comparable funding ratios are listed for all defined benefit plans, evaluated at the same PBGC interest rates. The funding ratios of PBGC claims indexed to overall market termination funding ratios are shown in column 3.

The results show a clear reduction in relative funding ratios of terminated plans over time. From 1975 to 1980, relative funding ratios averaged 42 percent; from 1981 to 1987, they averaged 28 percent.

[16] While required contributions are due only 8.5 months after the close of the plan year, they become due immediately on a termination. Following the Pension Protection Act of 1987, estimated contributions are required to be paid to the plan quarterly, with the balance, if any, due 8.5 months after the close of the plan year.

TABLE 7–9 Results of the GAO Study

Category		*Amounts*
Period of sample		1983–85
Plans in sample		33
Funding ratio at termination (%)		34
Funding ratio 5 years prior*		56
Percentage of claims attributable to waivers and unpaid contributions		30
Waivers	23%	
Overdue contributions	32	
Due and unpaid at termination†	45	
Total	100	

* Funding ratios five years prior to termination converted to same interest rate used at termination.

† Contributions are due 8.5 months after end of plan year but become due immediately on termination.

SOURCE: GAO, "Pension Plans: Government Insurance Program Threatened by Its Growing Deficit," Report to the Subcommittee on Oversight, Committee on Ways and Means, House of Representatives, March 1987.

These data are consistent with the notion that firms are learning over time how to take better advantage of the insurance system. The goal of funding reform is to reverse this trend.

CONCLUSION

In this chapter, an attempt was made to demonstrate the shortcomings of ERISA in controlling exposure for the Pension Benefit Guaranty Corporation. Despite the introduction of minimum funding rules, target funding ratios have not been affected by ERISA. In fact, the data suggest relatively poorly funded plans have become even more poorly funded during the post-ERISA period.

In addition to the persistence of large exposure levels, firms have discovered how to defund their plans prior to filing a claim with the PBGC. They do this by obtaining or simply requesting waivers, changing actuarial assumptions, increasing benefits, awarding lump-sum payments, or simply not paying required contributions to the plan.

In short, the PBGC insures against a pension underfunding exposure over which it has little control. Because its price does not reflect exposure and risk, firms have incentives to maximize the benefits of the insurance by increasing exposure. Clearly, the problem of controlling exposure needs to be addressed: exposure levels need to be consistent with premium levels permitted by Congress. Efforts toward reform are the subject of the next chapter.

TABLE 7–10 Funding Ratios: PBGC Claimants versus Universe

Year	*PBGC Claimants (1)*	*Defined Benefit Plan Universe* (2)*	*Relative (1)/(2) (3)*
1975	34%	94%	.36
1976	51	104	.49
1977	40	101	.40
1978	37	93	.40
1979	40	88	.45
1980	46	107	.43
1981	42	128	.33
1982	38	131	.29
1983	55	139	.39
1984	42	154	.27
1985	29	146	.20
1986	33†	128	.26
1987	32	138	.23

* Liabilities adjusted to end-of-year PBGC interest rates; reflects all vested liabilities.

† This number excludes the restored LTV terminated plans.

SOURCE: Appendix A to book, Tables A–7 and A–10; Wyatt Company, *1987 Survey of Actuarial Assumptions and Funding* (Washington, D.C.: 1988); and Richard Ippolito and Walter Kolodrubetz, eds., *The Handbook of Pension Statistics, 1985* (Chicago: Commerce Clearing House, 1986).

APPENDIX
Impact of ERISA on Funding Levels

This appendix evaluates the impact of ERISA on funding levels for the pension system and for underfunded plans. The impact of ERISA cannot be measured simply by observing funding levels over time. Funding levels also are affected by exogenous shocks to trust asset values; and firms react to these shocks gradually. A model incorporating behavioral changes and exogenous asset shocks is needed to estimate the underlying funding ratio the firm is trying to maintain.

Overall Funding Ratios

Consider a simple model of pension funding. The funding ratio is $f = A/P$, where A denotes trust assets and P denotes economic pension liabilities. Suppose the firm's pension contribution policy is described by the following equation:

$$\begin{aligned} C_t &= \Delta A_t - rA_{t-1} \\ &= df_{t-1}\Delta P_t + b(f^* - f_{t-1})P_{t-1} \qquad (7\text{–}1) \end{aligned}$$

TABLE 7–11 Impact of ERISA on Funding Levels

Parameter	*Coefficient*	*t-Statistic*
d	.313	2.95
b	.177	2.82
f^* (target funding ratio)	.693	9.28
E (impact of ERISA on f^*)	.014	.13
Observations	31	
Mean of dependent variable	.687	
Standard error of estimate	.042	

Note: The dependent variable is the current funding level; the equation is estimated by nonlinear least squares [see Equation (7–2)].

SOURCE: Richard A. Ippolito, *Pensions, Economics and Public Policy*, Pension Research Council Monograph (Homewood, IL: Dow Jones-Irwin, 1986), chaps. 4 and 5.

The firm's net contribution to the pension plan (C_t) is by definition equal to the net change in assets (ΔA_t) minus trust earnings (rA_{t-1}) where r is the rate of return. This amount equals some portion d, times the existing funding ratio, times the change in pension liabilities (ΔP_t), plus some portion b of the difference between the desired or *target* funding ratio (f^*) and the *actual* funding ratio (f_{t-1}), all times pension liabilities (P_{t-1}). The parameters d and b (presumably numbers between zero and unity) reflect the notion that firms cannot accommodate funding deficiencies instantaneously (due to either financial or IRS constraints).

Manipulating Equation (7–1) I can derive an equation that permits an estimate of the target funding level (f^*) for the pension industry as a whole:

$$f_t = f_{t-1}[1 + r + (d - 1)\Delta P_t/P_{t-1}] + b(f^* - f_{t-1}) \qquad (7\text{–}2)$$

The intuition behind the "stock adjustment" model in Equation (7–2) is that by observing firms increasing contributions when funding levels are low and decreasing them when they are high, firms reveal the target funding level (f^*) they are trying to attain. While actual funding levels are affected by market valuations, the target funding levels can be used as an index of long-term trends in the pension industry.

It is easy to introduce a test for ERISA in this model: simply replace f^* with $f^* + E\cdot\text{ERISA}$ in Equation (7–2), where ERISA is a dummy variable equal to unity for years after 1974, zero otherwise. A coefficient E that is significantly positive supports the hypothesis that ERISA increased average pension funding levels.

Equation (7–2) was estimated by nonlinear least squares for a time series over the 1950–81 period.[17] The results are presented in Table

[17] The time series stop in 1981 because in the following years the underlying series for the Federal Reserve Flow of Funds Accounts was changed, making data after 1982 incomparable to the earlier periods.

7–11. Estimates on the adjustment parameters d and b are within the expected range; they are significantly greater than zero but less than unity. For example, the parameter b implies that firms, on average, close about one fifth of the gap between desired and actual funding ratios in a single year. The target funding ratio (f^*) is estimated to be 69.3 percent (the 95 percent confidence intervals are 54.5 and 84.1).

The results are inconsistent with the hypothesis that the target funding level is affected by ERISA: the coefficient on the ERISA variable is insignificantly different from zero; the t-statistic is almost zero.

Underfunded Union Funding Ratios

In this section a more specific question is asked: If overall funding ratios did not change as a result of ERISA, does the evidence indicate that the most underfunded pension plans in the system were required by ERISA to enhance funding levels, thereby reducing expected levels of transfers? To test this hypothesis, I evaluated contribution behavior after ERISA for pension plans covering unionized workers. Funding ratios in these plans are one-third lower than nonunion plans (Ippolito, 1986) and represent the vast majority of past PBGC claims (see Table 3–5).

To develop this test, the contribution Equation (7–1) is rewritten for a particular firm:

$$C_t = df_{t-1}\Delta P_t + b(f^{**} - f_{t-1})P_{t-1} \qquad (7\text{–}3)$$

where

C_t = contributions to the pension plan during period t
f_{t-1} = actual funding ratio last period
f^{**} = post-ERISA target funding ratio
P_{t-1} = pension liabilities last period

Let the target funding ratio be related linearly to the actual funding ratio, and industry growth IG:

$$f^* = a_0 + a_1 f_{t-1} - a_2\text{IG} \qquad (7\text{–}4)$$

That is, adjusting for the economic well-being of the firm as measured by the industry growth rate, the higher the actual funding ratio, the more likely will the target funding ratio also be high.

The minimum funding rules under ERISA are presumably designed to increase firms' target funding ratios. In particular, because union funding levels are relatively low, the impact of ERISA can be modeled in the following way:

$$f^{**} = f^* + a_3\,\text{Union} + a_4\,\text{Union}\,f_{t-1} \qquad (7\text{–}5)$$

TABLE 7–12 Impact of ERISA on Contribution Rates

Variable	*Coefficient*	*t-Statistic*
Intercept	.47	14.53
f_{t-1}	−.69	17.01
$f_{t-1}\Delta P_t/P_{t-1}$	.92	56.18
Union	−.170	3.36
Union f_{t-1}	.107	1.49
Small (<1,000 participants)	.078	3.89
Industry variables*	X	
R^2	.75	
Obs.	1,144	

Note: The dependent variable is the contribution rate divided by liabilities; the equation is estimated using ordinary least squares [see Equation (7–6)].

* Industry variables included two-digit industry dummy variables and a three-digit industry growth variable (measured by employment levels, 1972–81).

SOURCE: Annual Pension Plan 5500 Form Reports, 1978, 1981.

where

f^* = pre-ERISA target funding ratio
f^{**} = post-ERISA funding ratio

If ERISA was designed to close the union-nonunion funding gap, the coefficient a_3 will be positive (union plans in general will have increased their target funding levels disproportionately) and the coefficient a_4 will be negative (the lower the union plan's funding level, the larger the increase in its target funding ratio mandated by ERISA).

Combining these equations, the following estimable equation is derived

$$C_t/P_{t-1} = ba_0 + df_{t-1}\Delta P_t/P_{t-1} + (a_1 - 1)bf_{t-1} + ba_3\,\text{Union} + ba_4\,\text{Union}\,f_{t-1} - ba_2\text{IG} + \text{error} \qquad (7\text{–}6)$$

If ERISA required union plans to close the funding gap, the coefficient on the union variable should be positive; the coefficient on the union-funding ratio interaction term should be negative. Equation (7–6) was estimated for 1,144 pension plans, using a three-year net contribution rate from 1978–81 and 1978 as the base year for liabilities and funding ratio calculations. The results are reported in Table 7–12. They not only reject the notion that ERISA required underfunded union plans to enhance funding levels, they show that the funding situation in these plans has become even worse.

The sign on the union variable is significantly negative, suggesting union plans reduced their target levels after ERISA. The positive sign on the union funding-level interaction term suggests the target funding ratio has been reduced even more by plans with the lowest funding levels to start with. While the data reject the notion that ERISA exerted a positive effect on overall funding levels, they are consistent with the notion that the most underfunded plans are becoming even more underfunded in the presence of PBGC insurance.

CHAPTER 8

Toward Controlling Exposure

Chapter 6 observed that, despite the introduction of a variable-rate premium structure, the maximum allowable premium set by Congress was sufficiently low ($50) so as to preclude setting prices proportional to exposure. Risk was ignored entirely, and insured benefit levels were not reduced. In some cases, the subsidies inherent in these prices account for over 80 percent or more of estimated market premiums (VanDerhei 1988). Thus, the emphasis on reform has been on rewriting the minimum funding rules to reduce exposure to the corporation in the long run and to work in the direction of controlling the amount of defunding prior to termination.

These efforts have helped policymakers focus on the intended exposure level of the insurance: is insurance available to protect only against volatility in asset prices (target funding ratios should be 100 percent) or is some degree of systematic exposure permissible under the program (target rates can be less than 100 percent)? The drift in legislation appears to be toward its first concept. In this chapter, the funding proposals developed by the PBGC and sent to Congress in 1987 are considered, as are the provisions of legislation ultimately enacted in the form of the Pension Protection Act of 1987. In the next chapter, the resource cost of these reforms compared to alternatives is considered.

PBGC FUNDING PROPOSAL

In response to a deficit that had grown to $4 billion by the end of 1986, the Pension Benefit Guaranty Corporation developed a comprehensive set of funding proposals. The proposals retained current funding rules for plans that were at least 110 percent funded on a termination basis (using interest rates assumed in the plan). For firms below this level, a series of rules were imposed to encourage all firms to attain a 110 percent funding level.

Given that some defunding prior to termination was still possible and given volatility in asset values and interest rates, the 110 percent target funding ratio proposal did not guarantee zero claims to the PBGC. Rather, it generated an expected reduction in exposure by requiring all firms to work in the direction of maintaining generally higher levels of funding.

Faster Amortization Rules

Past service liability. The main element of the proposal was a provision for shorter periods to amortize underfunding attributable to past service liability. It is important to recognize that underfunding for purposes of this provision is calculated on a termination basis. It is mainly intended to affect plans that use flat benefit formulas and unit credit funding methods.[1]

Plans characterized by salary-related formulas, using projected funding methods, would not likely be affected by either the PBGC proposal or the rules enacted in the Pension Protection Act (see below). This is because funding on a projected benefits basis almost certainly would generate overfunding on a termination basis. In contrast, as described in Chapter 7, flat benefit plans would more likely be affected because they routinely create past service liability by periodically increasing the benefit level.

In general, the proposal reduced the amortization period for past service liability from 30 years to some shorter period; the length of the period would be shorter if the existing funding ratio in the plan were lower and the plan's liabilities more mature. The proposal suggested various approaches to setting these limits. One is illustrated by the schedule of amortization periods given in Table 8–1.

The independent variables in the proposal are shown in the row and column labels. The columns reflect various levels of termination funding ratios based on actuarial interest rates.[2] The row elements represent the percent of total contributions required by Section 412 of the Internal Revenue Code not attributable to normal cost contributions. This ratio is higher if the portion of total contributions attribu-

---

[1]This is the funding method used to illustrate funding problems for flat benefit plans in Chapter 7.

[2]An actuarial interest rate is the one assumed by the plan's actuary for purposes of calculating required funding. This rate typically has been lower than market long-term interest rates.

TABLE 8–1 PBGC Proposed Amortization Periods for Past Service Credit

*Percent 30-year Amortization of Total 412 Contribution**	*Termination Funding Ratio*				
	90%	*70%*	*50%*	*30%*	*10%*
10	30	30	30	30	30
30	30	30	30	30	20
50	30	28	14	10	7
70	25	13	9	7	6
90	16	11	8	6	5

*Numbers in table are representative of several similar PBGC proposals; the table assumes a 7.5 percent interest rate.

table to amortization of past service liability and actuarial gains and losses is high.

The higher this ratio and the lower the plan's funding ratio, the faster the required amortization for new past service liability. In Table 8–1, which assumes a 7.5 percent interest rate, the amortization periods range from 5 to 30 years.

Several aspects of the proposal deserve attention. First, the amortization period was not static; the plan's contribution rate would be recalculated based on the plan's status each year. Thus, as the plan's funding condition improved, its required contribution rate would decrease. Second, the proposal did not exempt past underfunding from the rule; therefore its implementation would have generated relatively rapid changes in observed funding ratios among poorly funded plans. Third, the proposal was directed toward plans underfunded in a termination sense, most likely flat benefit plans. It would have substantially reduced the ability of such plans to maintain perpetual underfunding, merely as a result of periodically increasing benefits to reflect wage increases.

Actuarial gains and losses. Because the proposal permitted plans to choose their own interest rate assumption, an obvious loophole was available: firms could escape the intention of the faster amortization rules by changing their interest rate assumptions. Prior to the Pension Protection Act of 1987, the difference between the assumed rate of return and actual investment experience was amortized over 15 years. In the proposal, the difference was amortized over five years. Thus, attempts to evade the funding rules triggered a requirement for firms to redeposit the monies soon thereafter.

Other Rules and Provisions

In addition to faster amortization periods; the proposal was characterized by rules designed to prevent reductions in funding levels under other circumstances. These provisions were not applied in addition to the contribution rates described in Table 8–1. The proposal required each plan to calculate the funding contribution under all three rules plus the old funding requirements and to choose the highest resulting contribution. The other two rules are as follows.

Funding deterioration. If for any reason other than a waiver an underfunded plan's funding ratio fell below the level in the prior year, incremental underfunding attributable to gains and losses and a portion of benefit increases would be amortized over three years.

Cash flow. As a complement to Table 8–1, a special rule would apply when the pension plan's benefit payments exceeded contributions. The special rule required (notwithstanding the amortization schedule in Table 8–1) contributions to be sufficient at least to cover benefit payments, including lump-sum distributions and annuity purchases.

Waivers. The amortization period for waivers was set at 15 years multiplied by the plan's funding ratio, but in no case to exceed 15 years. Thus, a plan with a 60 percent funding ratio that obtained a waiver would be required to amortize its value over nine years.

PROVISIONS OF THE PENSION PROTECTION ACT OF 1987

In December 1987, new funding rules were enacted as part of the Pension Protection Act (PPA). The legislation follows the general nature of the rules contained in the PBGC proposal. The major funding provisions of the new law are shown in Table 8–2. These will be the subject of discussion in this section and the remaining sections of the chapter.

Faster Amortization Schedules

The hallmark of the new law is shorter amortization periods for prospective increases in underfunding. In a nutshell, the law borrows the idea behind the amortization schedule in the PBGC's proposal shown in Table 8–1, without taking explicit account of the plan's maturity; it reflects only the plan's funding ratio. Like the PBGC proposal, the funding ratio is calculated on a termination basis, except the interest rate used in the calculations is not the actuarial interest rate but instead some market rate.

Specifically, if the plan is underfunded, then new past service liability arising after December 31, 1987, must be amortized annually for plan years beginning January 1, 1989, or later according to the following schedule:

$$\text{Percent} = .30 - .25(F - .35) \leq .30, \quad F < 1.00 \qquad (8\text{–}1)$$

TABLE 8–2 Funding Provisions of the Pension Protection Act

Provision	*Old Law*	*New Law*
Amortization periods (number of years)		
Existing past service liability	30	18
New past service liability	30	.30–.25(*F*–35)†
Gains and losses—asset values	15	5
Gains and losses—actuarial assumption	30	10
Waivers	15	5
Shutdown benefits (post-event)	15	7‡
Actuarial assumptions		
General: "reasonable"	In aggregate	Individually
Interest rates	None	Within 10% of 30-year Treasury (4-year weighted average)
Defunding protection		
Waivers each 15 years	Five	Three
Liens for unpaid contributions	None	Arise 60 days after due date
Control group liability for contributions	No	Yes
Benefit increase limit	None	Security required if *F*<60%
Effective date of new law	1988 plan year except 1989 for new past service credit and shutdown provisions	
Steel transition rule	Annual increase in funding ratio not required to increase by more than 1 percent per year for five years.	

Note: For more detail, see Appendix E to book.

*"New" past service credit is past service credit arising after 1988.

†Contribution as percent of underfunding: *F* denotes the plan's funding ratio on a termination basis (using interest rate assumption stated in table). The maximum contribution does not exceed .30.

‡Under some conditions, the rate of amortization could be higher.

where F is the plan's termination funding ratio calculated after new benefits are awarded using a rate within the range of 90 to 110 percent of the 4-year average of the 30-year Treasury bond rate.[3]

The required contribution for past service liability is the greater of

[3]Technically, the legislation requires the plan to use a rate consistent with annuity purchase rates, subject to the restriction that they remain within the corridor described above. In addition, the U.S. Treasury has the authority to use a weighted average of the 4-year average of 30-year rates. At the time of this writing, it was contemplating a 4–3–2–1 weight scheme with the highest weight attached to the most recent year.

TABLE 8–3 First-Year Contributions for New Past Service Liability after 1988

Termination Funding Ratio	*Contribution as a Percent of New Underfunding*
100% or more*	8.79%
80	18.75
60	23.75
40	28.75
20	30.00
0	30.00

*This is the first-year amortization amount assuming an 8 percent actuarial interest rate. In subsequent years, the amortization rate falls in real terms. To be directly comparable with the other numbers in the table, the assumption must be made that the actuarial assumed interest rate is equal to the rate calculated by the U.S. Treasury for purposes of enforcing the funding rule in Equation (8–1). See footnote 4 in text.

the value implied by the schedule in Equation (8–1) or the required contribution under the old law. There are no other cash flow funding deterioration rules as in the PBGC proposal.

The schedule of contribution requirements implied by Equation (8–1) is shown in Table 8–3. If the termination funding level falls below 100 percent, the contribution requirement for benefit improvements increases markedly. If the funding ratio is 80 percent, the first-year contribution is 18.75 percent; if 60 percent, the requirement is 23.75 percent, and so on, up to a maximum of 30 percent.

If the funding ratio is 100 percent or more, the amortization schedule remains the same as under the previous law: new benefits may be amortized over 30 years. These amounts are amortized in equal nominal installments (like a house mortgage) and thus depend on the actuarial interest rate. Using continuous compounding and an 8 percent rate (a typical actuarial rate used in 1986), the first-year contribution over 30 years is 8.79 percent.[4]

Notwithstanding the faster amortization requirements, large[5] benefit increases in the plan are not permitted under the new law if, either before or as a result of the benefit increase, the funding ratio is less than 60 percent, unless security is posted to cover the incremental underfunding caused by the benefit increase (up to the 60 percent level).

To illustrate how the schedule works, consider the one-worker

[4]This rate, however, is not directly comparable to the ones described in Equation (8–1). This is because once the plan is fully funded, it must follow the pre-PPA minimum funding rules. But these rules use an actuarial interest rate, which is typically lower than market rates, and thus the 8.79 percent contribution rate is applied against a higher underfunding number. For simplicity, I depict the 8.79 percent number in Table 8–3 under the assumption that the actuarial assumed rate equals the rate required in Equation (8–1).

[5]Large is defined to include benefit increases amounting to $10 million.

TABLE 8–4 Illustration of Faster Amortization Schedule

	Contributions		*Funding Ratio*	
Year	*Old Law*	*New Law*	*Old Law*	*New Law*
0	—	—	—	—
1	$500	$2,812	80.6%	83.7%
2	500	2,172	81.3	86.6
3	500	1,711	81.9	88.9
4	500	1,372	82.6	90.7
5	500	1,114	83.3	92.2

Note: Liabilities increase from $60,000 to $75,000 at the end of year zero; assets equal $60,000 in year zero (100 percent in Treasury bills); the interest rate and asset earnings are zero; there are no existing service liability or experience gains or losses; plan frozen after benefit increase in year zero.

pension discussed in Chapter 7. A 45-year-old worker with 20 years of service has an annual pension benefit of $120 per year of service beginning at age 55. The interest rate is zero, and all assets are invested in three-month T-bills so that earnings on assets are also zero. If death occurs at age 80 (with certainty), the termination liability equals $60,000 for service incurred to date. Assuming assets also equal $60,000 and there are no amortized required contributions for gains and losses and no past service liability, the plan sponsor would be required to contribute only normal cost to the plan ($3,000 per year).

If the firm increases the benefit to $150, the liability increases to $75,000, and the termination funding ratio is now 80 percent. Thus, according to Equation (8–1), in addition to normal cost the firm is required to make a first-year contribution equal to 18.75 percent of the new $15,000 in liabilities, or

$$\begin{aligned}\text{Contribution} &= [.30 - .25\,(.80 - .35)] \times 15{,}000 \\ &= .1875 \times \$15{,}000 = \$2812 \qquad (8\text{–}2)\end{aligned}$$

Assume for the sake of maintaining a simple calculation that the plan is frozen following the benefit increase: service beyond age 45 is not counted in the pension benefit. Then, in the second year, if asset values do not change, the funding requirement falls to 17.8 percent because the funding level after the year-one contribution is 83.75 percent (assets are $62,812, and liabilities are $75,000).

According to the previous law, the annual minimum contribution using a zero interest rate was only 3.33 percent of $15,000 (the underfunding was amortized over 30 years), or $500. Table 8–4 compares funding levels under the old and new laws for five years after the benefit increases when the interest rate is zero. After five years, the funding ratio under the old law is increased from 80.6 percent to 83.3 percent, compared to 92.2 percent under the new law.

The above example is given for illustration only. For positive interest rates, the pre-1987 30-year amortization schedule is more front loaded than it would be with a zero interest rate. For example, if an 8 percent interest rate is used, the first-year contribution under the new rules would only be roughly twice the first-year contribution under the old rules, rather than over five times as depicted in the table.[6] Thus, though the example shown in Table 8–4 serves to illustrate the qualitative impact of the new amortization periods, it generally overstates their quantitative effect.

Changes in underfunding attributable to reasons other than benefit increases are also amortized over shorter periods in the new law. Gains and losses attributable to plan investment experience or to changes in actuarial assumptions must be amortized over 5 and 10 years, respectively, instead of 15 and 30 years. In addition, waivers are amortized over 5 years, and shutdown benefits are amortized over 7 years instead of 15 years.

Transitional Rules

The new amortization schedules do not apply to past underfunding. Underfunding that existed as of December 31, 1987, is not amortized according to Equation (8–1) but instead over 18 years. This is in comparison to the 30-year schedule for amortization of past service liability used under the old law. Thus, in the case of a zero interest rate, the contribution rate for existing underfunding is increased from 3.33 percent to 5.55 percent. For an 8 percent interest rate, the contribution rate increases from 8.79 percent to 10.49 percent.

In addition, special transitional rules apply to certain large integrated firms in the steel industry. These firms, which comprise a large portion of the PBGC's current risk and exposure, have a special rule: they are not required to make contributions by amounts that would increase their funding ratios by more than 1 percent per year for five years. Ultimately, however, as transitional rules are gradually replaced by the new amortization rules, funding ratios across pension plans ought to be higher than they otherwise would have been under previous law.

---

[6]Using an 8 percent interest rate, the present value of a $2,400 annuity from age 55 to age 80 discounted back to age 45 is approximately $11,655. A benefit increase from $120 per year of service to $150 increases this amount by $2,913. If assets equal $11,655, the termination funding ratio is 80 percent; thus, the new rules require a contribution equal to .1875 × $2,913, or $546. In comparison, amortizing the amount $2,913 like a house mortgage over 30 years generates a payment of $256. This example assumes the actuarial interest rate equals the interest rate used by the U.S. Treasury for calculating Equation (8–1).

SHORTCOMINGS OF NEW MINIMUM FUNDING RULES

The new law instituted stricter funding rules than those originally specified in ERISA and addressed some of the ways to defund prior to filing a claim. The law, however, may not be successful in reducing PBGC claims in all cases or under all economic conditions, and much depends on how successful firms will be in circumventing the intent of the new law. In this section, I consider several reasons why future claim levels might not be affected by the amounts perhaps intended by Congress when it enacted the new funding requirements.

Defunding

The previous chapter indicated that a significant portion of the PBGC's claims arise not so much from low funding levels as from rapid defunding prior to termination. The new funding laws affect only underfunded plans, calculated in a termination sense. Because substantial underfunding among firms with risky exposure has historically tended to arise during the few years prior to termination, it becomes important to learn the efficacy of the new funding laws in preventing defunding during the pretermination period.

Steps toward controlling defunding. Virtually all the ways to defund a pension plan enumerated in the previous chapter are still available at some level under the new law. Most have been curtailed, however, some perhaps in important ways. At the same time, it must be recognized that gaming potential is dynamic: firms may find new ways to defund under the new law.

The steps taken in the Pension Protection Act to reduce the defunding problem are worth considering. First, consider waivers. The number of permissible waivers has been reduced from five to three every 15 years, which reduces the underfunding potential for terminations like Rath Packing and Continental Steel, who each obtained five waivers prior to termination (see Chapter 7). In addition, contributions are now required quarterly instead of 8.5 months after the end of the plan year. This requires firms to make their waiver requests sooner than was previously allowed, thereby reducing the periods of zero contributions pending resolution of a waiver request.

Much depends, however, on how the Internal Revenue Service treats the waiver process. The Pension Protection Act requires the IRS to determine that the waiver request is based on a "temporary hardship," not imminent failure.[7] And further, the IRS is permitted (though not required) to obtain collateral for the plan from the plan sponsor for all waiver requests over $2 million. If the IRS takes a conservative

[7]The temporary hardship requirement refers to the entire control group.

approach to granting waivers, this method of defunding could be substantially reduced. Because tax records are not publicly available, however, empirically measuring the IRS's behavior over time will not be possible, except as claims show up at the PBGC.

Unpaid contributions also have been addressed in some detail in the new law. As stated above, contributions are required quarterly instead of 8.5 months after the end of the plan year; thus, the IRS can learn of missed payments sooner. The likelihood of firms making no contributions for two years prior to termination and being undetected (a not uncommon experience prior to 1987—see Chapter 7) becomes remote.

More important, if firms miss contributions, a lien automatically arises against the plan sponsor (including the entire control group) for the full amount of the missed contribution. If the PBGC can "perfect" the lien against the plan sponsor's assets, the claim becomes secured in bankruptcy and has a higher priority than unsecured creditors' claims.[8] If the lien cannot be perfected, the amount of the missed contributions takes on a tax-status priority in bankruptcy, which is lower than secured status but higher than general unsecured status.

In addition to the above changes, the new law requires collateral to be posted to fund benefit increases amounting to $10 million in plans less than 60 percent funded. Also, amortization periods have been reduced for shutdown benefits, changes in actuarial assumptions, and waivers, thereby reducing the amount of defunding affiliated with these events.

Potential shortcomings of the new provisions. Though the new law is intended to reduce defunding prior to termination, the potential for continued moral hazard continues to exist. For example, consider that under the new amortization rules, contribution requirements typically will tend to increase when firms are in financial difficulty, perhaps because of plant shutdowns or falling funding ratios attributable to lower contribution amounts. This may make it easier for firms to convince the IRS to grant waivers and may push some firms into bankruptcy that otherwise might survive.

In addition, the new funding rules might make it easier to meet the distress tests under SEPPAA, as amended by the Pension Protection Act. PPA requires as a condition of receiving a PBGC transfer, that the bankruptcy court determine that without the PBGC transfer, the plan sponsor will be unable to emerge from a Chapter 11 reorganization proceeding. The combined effect of faster amortization of shutdown benefits, past underfunding, and waivers may make it easier to demon-

---

[8]Because this provision has a size threshold of $1 million in missed contributions, it will not affect the behavior of most PBGC claimants, though it will substantially affect those posing the largest dollar exposure to the PBGC.

strate the burden of high contribution requirements on the future survival of the firm, unless the pension plan is terminated.

Greater contribution requirements may also result in more unpaid required contributions. While the PBGC in principle can perfect liens against unpaid contributions (that is, file a notice in a court to attach assets), other creditors, knowing the potential that the lien will be perfected, may not leave any assets unattached for the PBGC to perfect. The race to attach assets has two negative implications. First, liens for unpaid contributions will more likely take the form of priority claims rather than secured claims (which still is significantly better than general creditor status). Second, the race itself could precipitate more bankruptcies than would otherwise occur.

There is also some downside potential from the IRS becoming overly aggressive in its waiver process. As shown in Chapter 7, waivers among PBGC claimants have accounted for a significant portion of the claims amounts. But the vast majority of waivers have not resulted in claims against the PBGC, suggesting that most "loans" granted through the waiver process are not written off as "bad" in some sense. If the IRS becomes too stringent in its handling of the process, it could contribute to failure of some financially troubled firms, thus leading to more failures and more (though perhaps smaller) claims against the PBGC.

Plant shutdown decisions may also be affected by faster required amortization. Instead of shutting down plants three to five years prior to termination, it may now be optimal for firms to close them, say, one to three years prior to termination, thereby evading much of the impact of faster funding requirements. In effect, the cost of shutting down a plant has been increased by the Pension Protection Act.

None of this discussion suggests the new funding rules will not significantly reduce insurance claims to the PBGC. Rather, it suggests a final evaluation of the legislation must await a determination of the success of potential claimants in gaming the new system.

Falling Interest Rates

All of the stricter funding rules are predicated on the notion of underfunded pension plans at a point in time. For example, return to our one-worker example. A 45-year-old worker with 20 years of service will retire at age 55 and die at age 80; his annual pension benefit will be $120 for each year of service. If the 4-year average 30-year Treasury bond rate is 6 percent, the termination liability for this firm based on service as of age 45 is roughly $17,000. Suppose assets are also $17,000 so that this plan is fully funded.

For the sake of simplicity, I will assume the portfolio is composed entirely of three-month Treasury bills and thus is virtually unaffected by changes in nominal interest rates. This permits us to concentrate on the first-order impact of interest rate changes on liabilities without having to carry along a second-order potential impact on the asset side. In general, as long as the pension plan is diversified across bonds and equity, plan assets should not be unduly sensitive to changes in interest rates.[9] Thus, the qualitative results illustrated using the Treasury bill portfolio is applicable in general.

To illustrate the point, consider a simple example: suppose the interest rate falls from 6 percent to zero. In this case, the potential liability facing the PBGC for this plan increases to $60,000: the funding level becomes 28 percent.

The rules do not require the firm to impose the faster amortization schedule in Equation (8–1) against the $43,000 in underfunding because the firm must calculate benefits using a 4-year average of 30-year Treasury bond interest rates.

Suppose the Treasury implements a simple four-year average interest rate requirement. In this case, the averaging rule requires the use of a 4.5 percent interest rate (6 percent for three years and zero percent for one year). Liabilities by law are calculated as approximately $23,000, implying a funding ratio of 74 percent instead of 28 percent. Thus, the first-year required additional contribution is only .30 − .25(.74 − .35) = .2025, × $6,000 ($23,000 − $17,000), or $1,215, which is less than three percent of the underfunding amount.

The U.S. Treasury could ameliorate this effect by using market interest rates instead of four-year averages. This is unlikely to occur, but the Treasury almost certainly will attach weights to the averaging process. A likely possibility is a 4–3–2–1 weighting scheme, with the highest weight attached to the most recent year. In this case, the plan would be required to use a 3.6 percent rate instead of 4.5 percent, which would increase the first-year contribution from $1,215 to $2,491. A market interest rate, however, would generate a contribution equal to $12,900.[10]

More generally, even if the Treasury used market rates, efforts to

---

[9]The intuition behind the expectation that assets lose value with increasing interest rates is attributable to pension long-term bond holdings. When interest rates increase (say, owing to higher expected inflation), bondholders incur a capital loss. But bond issuers incur a capital gain. Because pension plans also hold corporate equity shares—the primary *issuers* of bonds—plans should earn corresponding capital gains on equity holdings to offset losses on the bond side. Thus, diversification across bonds and equity offsets the first-order impact of nominal interest rate changes. Changes in *real* interest rates will reduce values of all assets in the portfolio; but as a first-order approximation, most of the volatility in nominal long-term interest rates is likely attributable to changing expectations of future inflation, not changes in real rates.

[10]Using the zero market interest rate, the funding ratio is 28 percent and total underfunding is $43,000. Substituting the 28 percent funding ratio into the funding formula, the contribution requirement is 30 percent [see Equation (8–1)]; multiplying this by $43,000 yields a total contribution of $12,900.

improve funding do not prevent large exposure levels from arising when interest rates fall. Thus, when termination funding ratios are high, potential claimants could increase benefits during periods of high interest rates. If this is followed by a period of low interest rates, additional exposure could arise.

Actuarial Asset Values

Similar problems arise if trust assets experience substantial reductions in value, because the law permits actuaries to "smooth" asset values instead of using market valuations. Thus, if asset values fall, plans can pretend they are still high, thereby forestalling the requirements for higher contributions.

More particularly, the Internal Revenue Code permits actuaries to value assets using a consistent averaging formula if the resulting estimate is within 80 percent to 120 percent of market-value assets. Average value can reflect the average of asset prices over a five-year period, including the current year.

Consider an example. Liabilities are $100 million; assets also equal $100 million. Asset values weighted by the security composition of the portfolio have not changed for four years; say this index is 100. In year five, asset values fall by 20 percent to $80 million. When this occurs, exposure to the PBGC increases by $20 million, yet actuarial assets are calculated as the five-year average, or $96 million.

Because this number is within 20 percent of actual market value (80), assets in this example can be set equal to 96 for funding purposes. Even though the funding ratio is 80 percent and exposure to the PBGC is $20 million, plans can mitigate the new minimum funding rules by portraying the plan as if it had a 96 percent funding ratio and $4 million in exposure.

These problems could have been largely circumvented had the law required the use of market-value assets and market interest rates in the funding rules. By not doing so, the law imposes a potential wedge between actual exposure facing the insurance company and exposure calculated by actuaries for purposes of satisfying the funding requirements.

IMPLICATIONS OF THE NEW FULL FUNDING LIMIT

Thus far, discussion of the Pension Protection Act has been limited to the new rules it imposes on underfunded plans. While this was supposed to be the focus of the new law, the overall impact of the legislation may be more constraining to well-funded plans. This is because as part of the Omnibus Budget Reconciliation Act of 1987

(OBRA), Congress imposed a new *full funding limit* on well-funded plans, thereby reducing their ability to contribute to the pension plan on a tax-deductible basis.

Impact on Pension Plan Funding

Under the previous law, firms were permitted to contribute the following amounts to the pension plan: the sum of the normal cost contribution, which essentially is an amount that funds the current-year increase in service accruals (see Chapter 7), plus an amount to amortize existing levels of underfunding attributable to past service liability and experience gains and losses. Plans were permitted to be fully funded in an ongoing sense (recognizing salary projection); once this level was attained, only normal cost contributions were permitted. Because the actuary was reasonably free to choose assumptions, the plan could still become moderately overfunded in an ongoing sense, despite the so-called full funding limit. For example, Table 7–1 showed that in 1986, roughly 20 percent of participants were in plans over 125 percent funded in an ongoing sense.

The Pension Protection Act changed the full funding limit in the following way: it prevents *all* contributions to the pension plan (including normal cost) if the plan has assets in excess of 150 percent of *termination* liabilities. For purposes of the test, the actuary must use an interest rate within the range of 90 to 110 percent of the 4-year average of 30-year Treasury bond rates.

Table 8–5 shows the distribution of termination funding ratios for 1986 using 90 percent of a simple average of this rate over the 1982–86 period (the Secretary of the Treasury has the authority to change the weights on these rates through regulation). The data show that fully 57.9 percent of all plans, representing 55.8 percent of all participants, will be precluded from making contributions to their plans (plans with fewer than 100 participants are not included in the table).

Interestingly, the data show that though the law was originally intended to affect only a small number of relatively underfunded plans, it actually will impact most plans. Only 27.8 percent of the plans have termination funding ratios within the 100–150 percent corridor where much of the old law prevails (some faster amortization schedules still apply to these firms). A portion of these firms, however, will potentially "bump" against one or the other of the corridor constraints.

The impact on the funding limit is large for several reasons: (1) 150 percent of termination liabilities is small in relation to ongoing liabilities at current interest rates (see below); (2) the new constraints do not even permit contributions for normal cost; and (3) the actuary has no opportunity to effectively expand the limit by adjusting the plan

TABLE 8–5 Funding Ratios Using Four-Year Treasury Rate, 1986

Funding Ratio	*Plans*	*Participants*
Less than 25%	0.4%	0.2%
5–49	1.6	1.8
50–74	4.1	3.7
75–99	8.2	9.6
100–124	12.1	11.9
125–149	15.7	17.0
150 or more	57.9	55.8
Average: 144		

Note: Liabilities are discounted at 90 percent of the simple average of constant-maturity 30-year Treasury bond rates from 1983 to 1986. This rate turned out to be 9.5 percent.

Table reflects plans with 100 or more participants only.

SOURCE: 1984 Form 5500 Annual Pension Plan Reports, projected to 1986.

assumptions.[11] As such, the new law ensures defunding of all plans in excess of the 150 percent limit.

That is, suppose contributions are set so that combined with investment returns, benefits can be financed without liquidating pension plan trust assets. Then, if the new rule sets contributions at zero, benefit payments will erode the asset base until the funding ratio falls below 150 percent of termination liabilities.

The impact of the new limit will be broader and more significant if the interest rates drift higher than current levels. This can be seen in Table 8–6. This table represents the average pension plan in 1986 (based on Form 5500 Annual Report data). Column 2 shows that on an ongoing basis, the typical plan was 87.8 percent funded in 1986. Ongoing liabilities are calculated at a 2 percent interest rate. The ability to retain this funding level depends on the calculation of termination liabilities which in turn primarily depend on the long-term nominal rate of interest.

Ongoing liabilities are much less dependent on changing interest rates because the inflation component that determines interest rates also affects salary projections and inflation adjustments to retirees.[12] For the calculations in Table 8–6, I assume ongoing liabilities are based

[11]By converting from an ongoing concept to a termination one, actuaries are denied the opportunity to choose worker turnover and wage growth assumptions. Further, the law specifies the interest rate that can be used.

[12]Even though payments during retirement are typically not explicitly related to inflation, as a practical matter firms, at least partially, adjust benefits for inflation, thus further insulating true economic liabilities from the inflationary component of nominal interest rates. The actuary can effectively fund for postretirement adjustments by increasing the assumed rate of wage growth for active workers.

TABLE 8–6 Relation of Termination to Ongoing Liabilities

Interest Rate	Termination Funding Ratio† (1)	Ongoing Funding Ratio*: Old Law (actual) (2)	Ongoing Funding Ratio*: New Law‡ (maximum)§ (3)
5.0%	106.8%	87.8%	123.2%
7.5	126.2	87.8	104.3
10.0	149.3	87.8	87.8
12.5	176.5	87.8	74.5
15.0	209.3	87.8	62.8
20.0	299.4	87.8	43.8

*Ongoing liabilities are approximated by discounting liabilities at a 2 percent interest rate.

†Calculated prior to deterioration of assets to meet the new 150 percent constraint.

‡Calculated after asset levels have deteriorated until the new 150 percent full funding limit has been attained.

§Funding ratios in excess of 100 percent might also be constrained by the old full funding limit which is still operable.

SOURCE: Simulations based on 1984 Form 5500 Annual Pension Plan Reports, projected to 1986.

on a constant 2 percent interest rate, regardless of the level of the nominal interest rate.

The table recalculates termination funding ratios and full funding limits as a percent of ongoing pension liabilities for interest rates from 5 to 20 percent. Evaluated at a 7.5 percent interest rate, the termination funding ratio for the typical plan is 126.2 percent; thus, at this interest rate, the full funding limit is similar in the new and old laws because both continue to permit some additional funding.

At a 10 percent interest rate, however, the average termination funding ratio is almost at the 150 percent limit (it equals 149.3 percent), and thus the typical pension plan is about to be constrained from making further tax-deductible contributions. As column 3 shows, this means the funding ratio for real or ongoing benefits is constrained to 87.8 percent, instead of the 100 percent allowed under the old law.[13] This essentially reflects the impact of the law in 1986: in 1986, 90 percent of the 4-year average of 30-year Treasury bond rates was 9.5 percent.

If the interest rate increases beyond 10 percent, plans are faced with even lower ceilings on their permissible funding ratios on an ongoing basis. For example, when the interest rate is 20 percent, the

[13]This ratio is calculated as follows: The permissible termination funding ratio of 150 percent is proportional to the ratio 100/67, where 100 denotes assets and 67 denotes termination liabilities. Because the ongoing ratio is .878 and assets are 100, ongoing liabilities are 113.8. The full funding limit permits assets to be no higher than 100 (67 in termination liabilities times 150 percent). Thus, only 87.8 percent of ongoing liabilities may be funded (100 divided by 113.8).

termination funding ratio for the typical plan in 1986 would have been 299.4 percent. Because the plan sponsor would not contribute to the fund on a tax-deductible basis until assets fell below 150 percent of termination liabilities, its ongoing funding ratio would decrease.

If the interest rate remained at 20 percent, the ongoing funding ratio would effectively fall to 43.8 percent before further contributions would be permitted. At this interest rate level, firms are permitted to fund less than half of the ongoing liabilities they have incurred, in comparison to 100 percent under current law.[14]

Potential Impact on PBGC

The potential effects stemming from higher interest rates are not restricted to plans having no exposure to the insurance company. This can be demonstrated by a simple, stylized simulation. Suppose the current interest rate is 10 percent. Based on this rate, the distribution of termination funding ratios from the 1984 Form 5500 data projected to 1986 is given in columns 1 and 2 of Table 8–7. Consistent with Table 8–6, the average termination and ongoing funding ratios are 149 percent and 88 percent, respectively.

For the sake of simplicity, ignore the four-year averaging of rates and assume the full funding limit under the new law is calculated at the existing long-run rate. Let this rate increase suddenly from 10 to 20 percent owing to higher inflation expectations.

The distributions of funding ratios at the higher interest rates are given in columns 3 and 4 of Table 8–7. These numbers portray funding ratios the instant following the increase in the interest rate. They do not account for reductions in the asset base caused by the imposition of the new full funding limit. The termination funding ratio now averages 299 percent; the ongoing funding ratio is still 88 percent because it is essentially unaffected by higher inflation (recall that I calculate ongoing liabilities using a constant 2 percent interest rate). At the 20 percent interest rate, fully 94 percent of all plans (weighted by participants) are affected by the 150 percent termination funding limit and thus are precluded from making tax-deductible contributions to the pension plan.

Assume real rates of return in the portfolio are zero, and benefits are paid out at the rate of 8 percent of ongoing liabilities per year. Because contributions are not permitted for all plans above the 150 percent limit, assets will deteriorate accordingly until each plan's funding ratio falls below the 150 percent limit, after which I assume

---

[14]Referring to the previous footnote, when the termination funding ratio is 299 percent, termination liabilities are not 67 but rather 33. One hundred and fifty percent times 33 equals 50, which is only 43.8 percent of ongoing liabilities (equal to 113.8).

TABLE 8–7 Potential Reduction in Funding Levels under New Full Funding Limit (dollars in billions)

	Interest Rate (in sequence)					
	i = 10		*i* = 20		*i* = 10	
Funding Ratio	*Termination* (1)	*Ongoing** (2)	*Termination†* (3)	*Ongoing* (4)	*Termination‡* (5)	*Ongoing‡* (6)
Less than 25%	0.3%	0.6%	0.0%	0.6%	0.3%	0.6%
25–49	1.8	6.5	0.3	6.5	1.8	22.0
50–74	3.6	24.5	0.4	24.5	4.9	52.5
75–99	9.0	33.0	1.7	33.0	32.5	19.0
100–124	11.0	22.5	1.1	22.5	23.0	2.8
125–149	15.5	9.0	2.5	9.0	18.5	0.5
150 or more	58.8	3.9	94.0	3.9	19.0	2.6
Average	149%	88%	299%	88%	107%	62%
Underfunding	$19.5	$122.4	$1.4	$122.4	$37.3	$254.2

Note: Distributions are on a participant basis.

Illustration is based on estimated 1986 data projected from the 1984 Form 5500 Annual Pension Plan Reports. The simulation assumes that (1) the interest rate increases from 10 to 20 percent; (2) the new interest rate is used immediately rather than smoothed by a four-year average; (3) the 20 percent rate remains in effect for five years; and (4) assets are drawn down at the rate of 8 percent of ongoing liabilities (representing benefit payments).

*Ongoing liabilities are calculated using a 2 percent interest rate.

†Calculated prior to deterioration of asset levels owing to the new full funding limit.

‡Calculated subsequent to asset deterioration owing to the new limit; and before additional contributions are made to reattain the new 150 percent full funding limit at the new, lower interest rate.

plans maintain this limit. I also assume all plans below the 150 percent limit maintain their ongoing funding ratios at the same level.[15]

Assume the 20 percent interest rate prevails for five years. At the end of this period, suppose inflationary expectations fall to their previous level, so that interest rates return to 10 percent. Because relatively well-funded plans were precluded from making contributions when interest rates were high, the funding ratios in the new equilibrium will have deteriorated over the five-year simulation period. The new funding distributions reflecting lower asset levels and the reemergence of the 10 percent interest rate are given in the last two columns in Table 8–7.

Ongoing funding ratios are 62 percent compared to 88 percent on average at the start of the simulation period, with $254 billion in unfunded liabilities compared to $122 billion at the start of the

[15]In reality, plans with funding levels below 100 percent ought to increase their funding levels over time owing to the stricter funding requirements in the law for such plans.

simulation. Termination funding ratios are 107 percent compared to 149 percent, with $37 billion in exposure compared to $19 billion. The latter numbers imply that the potential exposure to the pension insurance company roughly doubles.

In short, the imposition of the new funding limit can work at cross purposes to the intent of the legislation. While the law takes steps to improve funding for some plans, it raises the possibility that the insurance corporation's exposure could increase. Moreover, the legislation permits less than 100 percent funding on a tax-deductible basis for most plausible interest rate levels; and therefore, another bias in favor of defined contribution plans is created because those plans are still permitted to fully fund on a tax-deductible basis (more on this in Chapter 9).

The problems raised by the new full funding limit could be solved if Congress would redefine the full funding limit in terms of ongoing liabilities. Instead of permitting 100 percent of these liabilities to be funded, it could set the permissible level lower, say, at 90 percent (the exact number to be set to generate the same tax revenue as the 150 percent termination limit at interest rates prevailing at the time the law was enacted). This would generate the same target tax revenue but insulate ongoing funding ratios from changes in nominal interest rates.

OTHER REFORM PROPOSALS

The provisions of the Pension Protection Act were the result of a long discussion addressing how best to reduce the growing financial problem at the Pension Benefit Guaranty Corporation. The nature and magnitude of this problem was discussed at length in Chapters 3 through 5. Proposals submitted by the PBGC in 1987 as well as the provisions of the new law were evaluated in chapters 6 through 8. Not yet discussed are proposals raised during the debate process but not reflected in official proposals or legislation. It is appropriate to present these ideas now as a prelude to the next chapter, which discusses efficiency aspects of various reform ideas, and to Chapter 10, which deals exclusively with ideas for a rational economic insurance policy.

The areas not reflected in the new legislation that were actively considered and debated (inside and outside government) involve benefit reductions, provisions for liens, and changes in the bankruptcy law. The reform ideas I discuss below are listed in Table 8–8.

Benefit Reductions

Maximum benefit. Discussion of benefit reductions followed the standards set out in the Multiemployer Pension Protection Amendments Act of 1980 (MPPAA). As discussed in Chapter 5, MPPAA

TABLE 8–8 Ideas for Reform Not Legislated

Category	*Description*
Benefit reductions*	
Maximum guaranty	Reduce maximum to be consistent with multiemployer program
5-year cliff benefits	Freeze benefit accruals (except service) for five years prior to termination (replaces five-year phase-in)
Shutdown benefits	Eliminate from guarantees, or create separate trust protected by supplemental coverage
Age of first receipt	Normal benefits available at age 62; full actuarial reductions for earlier receipt
Liens†	Attach assets of plan sponsor to cover underfunding amounts
Bankruptcy‡	
Priority	Give pensions absolute priority in bankruptcy proceedings
	Eliminate 30 percent net worth limitation on tax-priority claims
Eliminate Chapter 11 termination	Restrict termination to Chapter 7 of the bankruptcy code
Chapter 11 with PBGC approval	Permits termination in Chapter 11 only if PBGC approves

*The Pension Protection Act restricted increases in benefit generosity if the plan's funding ratio was less than 60 percent funded (on a termination basis) and the benefit increases exceeded $10 million.

†The Pension Protection Act permits liens for due and unpaid contributions (not counting waivers) when these amounts reach $1 million.

‡The Pension Protection Act permits Chapter 11 terminations on finding of the court that reorganization otherwise will be unsuccessful.

guarantees maximum benefit levels roughly half as generous as the single-employer program. It was shown that the existing maximum benefit formula in the single-employer plan may have had a substantial impact on limiting the accumulation of the PBGC's deficit through 1987 (see Table 5–3). Application of MPPAA-like reductions in this maximum would have important effects on the amounts of claims for future years.

Five-year cliff guaranty. MPPAA also imposes five-year cliff guarantees compared to a five-year (20 percent per year) phase-in of new benefits in the single-employer program. As mentioned in Chapter 7, no effort has been made to quantify the impact of the phase-in on PBGC claims. But, based on their study, the General Accounting Office (see Chapter 7) concluded that the problem was substantial and recommended application of the five-year cliff rule.

Shutdown benefits. Shutdown benefits are also virtually nonexistent in multiemployer plans. In many multiemployer plans, workers may be mobile among firms, and thus shutdown of one plant or firm may not affect employment or pension accruals. In addition, the shutdown of one plant in the group would translate into higher liabilities to all other firms.[16]

In single-employer plans, shutdown benefits are common among industries that pose the most risk and exposure to the PBGC; notably, the steel and automobile industries. On plan termination, benefits payable to participants affected by plant shutdowns prior to the termination event are guaranteed and thus payable by the PBGC (up to the maximum guarantee limit). Because these benefits are not prefunded and represent unusually generous benefits to unusually young participants, they have been the subject of much debate.

Various ideas have been considered to control the shutdown problem, including requiring the benefits to be prefunded; separate funds to be used to accommodate these benefits with a different set of guarantees; and special surcharges to be applied to plans with these benefits to help offset their expected cost on the insurance system (see Chapter 6).

Standardized normal retirement age. Another idea discussed in Chapter 5 integrates the shutdown problem with the notion of benefit reductions for early retirement. The idea is to redefine the PBGC guaranty so that all full benefits would be payable at the age at which social security payments were available, say, age 62 or 65. If age 62 were chosen, then regardless of the plan provisions, insured full benefits would commence at age 62. Insureds could receive benefits earlier (say, as early as age 55), subject to full actuarial reduction. (The implications of this change were illustrated in Figure 5–1.) Essentially, this benefit change eliminates the problem of shutdown benefits, which are problematic only because they award full benefits much earlier than age 62. The change also reduces benefits in plans that have relatively generous early normal retirement ages.

Lien against Underfunding

Another reform idea involved the creation of liens against real property held by plan sponsors. This approach is essentially a substitute for funding rules. If some firms do not fund their plans sufficiently, the resulting exposure can be eliminated by attaching assets of the firm, thereby making the PBGC a secured lender to the firm.

---

[16]Under MPPAA, the insurable event occurs when the plan is unable to pay current benefits at the guaranteed level. When this occurs, the PBGC is required to provide the plan with sufficient funds to pay benefits at the guaranteed level. The provision of funds is in the form of a loan subject to repayment to the PBGC. If one firm fails then the remaining participating plan sponsors absorb the underfunding previously allocated to the failed firm.

Perhaps the most dramatic lien proposal was made by the House Ways and Means Committee (HR 3345, 100th Congress). This bill proposed that if a pension plan's funding level fell below 70 percent, the PBGC could attach the plan sponsor's assets by the *entire* amount of the underfunding.

When the Pension Protection Act was enacted, these broad powers were not included. Instead, the PBGC was awarded the opportunity to attach liens (which must be perfected to be enforceable) in amounts equal to due and unpaid contributions (not counting waivers) when these amounts reached $1 million. This provision tends to restrict the lien potential to the last year or two prior to a termination.

Bankruptcy Law

Change pension priorities. It has long been known that workers' pensions could largely be protected by a simple change in the bankruptcy laws. That is, if pensions were put at the front of the queue of all creditors on bankruptcy (including secured creditors), the risk of bankruptcy would essentially be transferred from workers to creditors. Creditors, in turn, would risk-rate the pension liability by requiring higher interest rates for credit when the risk of default is larger and the amount of exposure posed by the pension fund is greater.

A variant of this proposal eliminates the priority claim now constrained to 30 percent of the plan sponsor's net worth. That is, ERISA permits the PBGC in bankruptcy proceedings to enter a priority claim (tax-status claim) for underfunded, guaranteed benefits up to 30 percent of net worth. The problem is that net worth is often not large in a bankruptcy proceeding. The alternative is to eliminate the net worth cap entirely, which would increase the PBGC's priority above general creditor status (though it would still be lower than secured creditor status).

Eliminate Chapter 11 as distress criteria. Another proposal would eliminate filing for Chapter 11 of the Bankruptcy Code (reorganization), leaving only Chapter 7 (dissolution) as criteria for transfers from the PBGC. This change alone may not have much impact on behavior because it keeps intact two other distress criteria that do not require any bankruptcy filing (see Chapter 5). Assuming all criteria except firm insolvency are eliminated, however, the essential idea is to substantially reduce the incentive for some firms to declare Chapter 11 bankruptcy for the sole reason of collecting government subsidies (much of this from the PBGC).

Chapter 11 with PBGC discretion. One advantage of precluding a termination until a Chapter 7 filing is that fewer claims would be presented to the PBGC. However, because the PBGC would not be part of the creditor group in earlier negotiations with the firm (perhaps in a

Chapter 11 filing), further deterioration in pension plan funding prior to the filing of Chapter 7 would likely occur.

One way to give the PBGC more leverage is to permit Chapter 11 termination if the PBGC agreed to it. Essentially, this would give the PBGC more leverage in the Chapter 11 proceedings because without the PBGC transfer, all creditors would receive less and the firm would be more likely to file for Chapter 7 of the bankruptcy code.[17]

The Pension Protection Act did not include any changes in the Bankruptcy Code. However, the law did modify the distress criteria under a Chapter 11 filing to require the bankruptcy judge to determine that unless a pension termination takes place, as a part of the Chapter 11 proceeding, the firm will not be able to successfully reorganize. The determination does not require PBGC approval.

CONCLUSION

The Pension Protection Act (PPA) of 1987 was an important change in pension law. Motivated by a growing deficit at the PBGC, legislators sorted through literally dozens of ideas for reform. The hallmark of the legislation was a substantive change in the minimum funding rules for underfunded pension plans and changes intended to reduce the pretermination defunding problem. Ironically, the Omnibus Budget Reconciliation Act of 1987 (the umbrella legislation for PPA) imposed equally dramatic changes in funding rules, limiting maximum contributions for the majority of better-funded pension plans.

The net effect of the Pension Protection Act on PBGC solvency will not be calculable for many years. Transitional rules soften the legislative impact in the short run. It is also unclear whether firms will be successful in outwitting the intent of the new law, so that claims will not be affected as much as Congress intended. More certain is that improvements to the solvency of the insurance fund have come at some cost. These costs as well as a broader discussion of other efficiency (cost) issues surrounding pension insurance will be presented in the following chapter.

---

[17]A discussion of bankruptcies is found in White (1988).

PART THREE

Toward Economically Rational Pension Insurance

CHAPTER 9

Efficiency Aspects of Pension Insurance Rules

Thus far, the discussion has generally been focused on the financial condition of the federal insurance company. Reform ideas have been judged on how successful they are in reducing claims to the PBGC in the long run. Rules constraining insurance losses on the PBGC, however, are not imposed at zero cost. To the extent that rules distort the way firms do business, there is a real resource cost to the insurance system. This chapter will discuss efficiency concepts and consider reform ideas in this context. In the next chapter, these ideas are put to work in the form of the new pension insurance system.

ILLUSTRATION OF EFFICIENCY CONCEPTS

An example will help illustrate the idea of efficiency. Suppose there are two states in a country: a cold-weather state and a warm-weather state. The inhabitants produce and consume only two things, apples and oranges. In the cold state, workers can produce either a dozen apples or a half-dozen oranges (or any linear combination). In the warm state, workers can produce a dozen oranges or a half-dozen apples (or any linear combination).

Workers prefer a diet composed of 50 percent apples and 50 percent oranges. If the states do not trade with each other, this variety is attained if workers in each state devote twice as much time to producing the product they have the least advantage in producing; and they end up with four apples and four oranges to consume in each state.[1]

---

[1]Consider the cold state. It takes twice as many hours to produce an orange (O) compared to an apple (A). A total of H hours are available for production; they are therefore allocated according to the formula:

A better solution is for each state to produce only the product in which it has an advantage in production. Thus, overall production in the country is maximized if the cold state produces only apples and the warm state only oranges: total production equals 12 oranges and 12 apples. To retain a balanced diet, the two states can trade six apples for six oranges. Through specialization and trade, production is increased by one third.

Now suppose this country has a problem: individuals perpetuate crime then cross state lines to evade state prosecution (the states have no extradition agreement). To stop the crime problem, the government closes the only road that connects the states, so criminals cannot leave either state. The good news is that there is now less crime. The bad news is that because the road is closed, the states can no longer trade.

Now the workers in each state have a choice: to incur a *consumption inefficiency* or a *production inefficiency* (or some of both). That is, suppose the cold- and warm-weather states decide to continue producing what they produce best, all apples or all oranges. In this case, total production is unaffected by the road-closing policy, but workers in each state must eat only apples or only oranges. Because they prefer to eat some of each, they are all worse off under the road-closing policy. We can call this a *consumption inefficiency*. Consumption is inefficient because everyone would be better off if they could consume some apples and some oranges instead all one or the other.

Alternatively, suppose that to attain variety, each state devotes two thirds of its resources to production of the product in which it has the least advantage and one third to the product in which it has the most advantage. As demonstrated above, using this allocation of resources, both states produce four apples and four oranges. Workers are better off in the sense that they have attained variety in their diet. But now there is less total production. Before the road-closing policy, production totaled 24 apples and oranges; now there are only 16 apples and oranges available. We can call this a *production inefficiency:* production is one-third lower because of the road-closing policy.

$$H = h_A A + h_O O$$

where

h_A = number of hours required to produce one apple
h_O = number of hours required to produce one orange
A = number of apples produced
O = number of oranges produced

If $A = O$ (apple production equals orange production), then $h_O O = (2/3)H$ (because, by definition, $h_O = 2h_A$). If all resources devoted to apples yield one dozen apples, then it must be true that one-third this time yields four apples; and because $A = O$, they also have four oranges. A similar calculation shows the same net result for the warm state.

Clearly the policy of closing the road imposes a loss on workers in both states. This may not have been the most efficient policy to deal with crime. It may have been cheaper to let crime continue if its level was not high compared to the gains from trade; or it may have been more efficient for states to set up an extradition agreement or to devote more resources to preventing crime.

In the area of pensions, similar efficiency issues arise. Congress set up a mandatory insurance program without an appropriate pricing system. As a result, a certain level of unproductive activity is encouraged to maximize transfers available from the insurance company. This itself creates a distortion because it provides a mechanism for some financially troubled firms to force financially sound firms to help pay for pension promises in the former firms.

Efforts to fix this problem, however, are not without cost implications. Creation of nonprice solutions to help stop moral hazard in the insurance system may help reduce the problem facing the insurance company. But it may also adversely affect other pension plan sponsors and participants, leading them to engage in even more costly policies. Unless caution is used, additional layers of distortion and burden can be imposed, with a detrimental effect on the entire defined benefit plan system. These effects can be evinced in the form of either a higher cost of offering defined benefit plans (production inefficiency) or a bias toward defined contribution plans relative to defined benefit plans (consumption inefficiency).

PENSION INSURANCE AND EFFICIENCY

Potential Problems with Market Prices

There is no "perfect" price system for insurance coverage. In general, the more that prices reflect exposure and risk, the lower the amount of cross-subsidy characterizing the system. This tends to generate the appropriate amount of insurance coverage and moral hazard across all insureds. If measures of risk are imperfect, however, some distortions will remain.

For example, drivers under age 25 are usually rated high risks for automobile insurance. This means some young drivers who would be considered low risks in a full-information world pay large subsidies to others in the insurance pool. If there were one-risk category, these same good (but young) drivers would pay a smaller subsidy—but more other drivers would also pay subsidies. In general, the narrower the risk categories, the fewer the insureds who pay "wrong" prices; but those who are misclassified tend to pay "very wrong" prices.

Because the market will tend to establish more risk classes as long as the marginal reductions in premiums to good risks outweigh the cost of creating new categories, the solution is efficient (the creation of more classes would not reduce prices to good risks beyond some point).[2] Nevertheless, the potential for risk-based price systems to badly misclassify some risks is often used as an argument for imposing a maximum premium.

Problems with Mandatory Coverage with Market Prices

Insurance contracts invariably distort economic activities because of either moral hazards or rules designed to control these hazards. The goal is to minimize this interference and, at the same time, protect the integrity of the insurance system. One fundamental source of inefficiency in the existing pension insurance program stems from its mandatory nature: workers and firms are covered by the insurance whether or not they want to be. This problem is exacerbated by constraints on the PBGC against charging market premiums or reducing insured benefits.

As shown in Chapter 6, under the current system many firms and workers pay subsidies to poorly funded plans in high-risk firms and thus may not wish to be included in the insurance program. Mandatory coverage with inappropriate prices encourages moral hazard amongst bad risks and induces good risks to leave the system. But even if the system were characterized by free market prices and could be administered at zero cost, many firms and workers might not want to be covered by pension insurance. Thus, mandatory participation will lead to inefficiencies.

Benefits of uninsured underfunding: An example. In this section, I will illustrate a case where mandatory pension insurance coverage imposes economic inefficiencies. Consider a firm with a unionized labor force.[3] The union has some control over the financial viability of the firm: it can raise wages above competitive levels, which ultimately will lead to firm failure. Even though union members ultimately lose their jobs, they may benefit from this strategy as a group because they collect supracompetitive wages during the time it takes the firm to fail. Stockholders knowing this potential are reluctant to invest in the firm.

To solve this problem, suppose a bargain is struck giving the union a stake in the long-term viability of the firm: a large portion of

---

[2]Just because a free market system is efficient does not imply that it must generate a higher social welfare than a system that artificially regulates fewer risk categories. Because of nonlinearities, the "harm" imposed on fewer badly misclassified good risks might be greater than the lesser harm imposed on a greater number of insureds who are only mildly misclassified.

[3]The issues raised in this section are treated in detail in Ippolito, 1986.

compensation is paid in the form of a pension, but the pension is not funded. In the event of firm failure, the union members lose the entire value of their deferred wages in the form of valueless pensions. Thus, the union now has an incentive to help the firm remain competitive over the long run.

To illustrate, suppose the interest rate and wage growth are zero. Workers start work in the firm at age 25. The pension pays $150 per month from age 55 until death, which I assume occurs at age 80 (that is, the monthly benefit is $5 per year of service). The present value of the pension is $45,000 at age 55; total compensation is $6,500 per year during work years. Of this, workers receive $5,000 in cash wages, and the remaining $1,500 is deferred and returned in the form of a pension during retirement ($1,500 per year times 30 years of work is $45,000, exactly the value of the pension). In this example, the pension is worth 23 percent of total compensation (total compensation is $6,500 per year times 30 years, or $195,000).

If the funding level in the pension is zero and the firm fails, a 55-year-old worker loses $45,000 in pension benefits; a 35-year-old worker loses $15,000 ($1,500 forgone wages for 10 years); a 70-year-old retiree loses $18,000 ($150 per month for 10 remaining years of retirement). Given these potential losses, the union has an incentive to work with the firm to ensure its long-term viability.

Consequences of mandatory insurance. Now suppose pension insurance is mandated. All workers have their benefits insured, and thus the incentive scheme set up by the firm is eliminated. Workers now have an incentive to raise wages: their pensions are insured, and thus no pension loss occurs on firm failure. This will create more firm failures than anticipated by the insurance company, based on historical experience prior to the creation of pension insurance. Either firms must find other, less efficient ways to control unions, or firms susceptible to a union "hold up" (notably, firms with a high intensity of specialized durable capital) will find ways to operate without unions (perhaps by transferring production to foreign countries or to other regions in the country).

Finally, firms and unions caught by the enactment of pension insurance will have incentives to transfer the extra cost created by the insurance to the PBGC. For example, firms may agree to pay union members shutdown benefits and higher monthly benefits in lieu of higher wages. Thus, instead of paying $150 per month in benefits, they might agree to increase benefits to $200 payable perhaps at age 50 if a plant shutdown occurs.

In short, while free market prices would substantially reduce distortions in the current single-price system, they do not ensure an absence of distortions. The mandatory nature of the system itself imposes resource costs on some firms. Given that Congress mandates pension insurance coverage, the problem is determining the next-best solution.

Optimal Insurance under Mandatory Coverage: Market Prices and Benefit Reductions

One solution that reduces the problem posed by mandatory insurance coverage is to combine a market rate premium structure with several benefit options. Free market prices (that is, prices reflecting risk and exposure) reduce cross-subsidies among different risk groups and thus reduce distortions inherent in flat price formulas. Market prices alone, however, do not eliminate market distortions. Many insureds will be required to purchase more insurance than they otherwise would if they had a free choice. This suggests that the market could be made more efficient by permitting insurance against a smaller portion of pension benefits.

For example, a low-option policy could be set at some minimal level, presumably to address congressional concerns that pension participants would have inadequate income if their pension plan were terminated. This level could be set at the plan's benefit level or at the average of all pension payments in the universe (in relation to wage and service), whichever is lower. Payments would be made starting at age 62. In this way, firms and workers who wanted less insurance could choose the low-option alternative.

In terms of the union example above, suppose guaranteed benefits were $100 per month starting at age 62. In comparison to the $150 benefit level payable in the plan starting at age 55, a 55-year-old worker would lose roughly 50 percent of this pension upon firm failure if the insured benefit were only $100 payable at age 62. The guaranteed benefit for a 50-year-old worker receiving $200 per month under a plant shutdown provision would be reduced from $72,000 ($200 per month for 30 years) to $21,600 ($100 per month for 18 years). This would reduce the moral hazard problem of firms increasing the amount of the expected transfer from the insurance company and would maintain some incentives for unions to preserve the financial viability of the firm.

In short, a pension insurance system characterized by free market premiums and an assortment of insurance protection levels would minimize the distortions inherent in mandatory insurance coverage.

NONPRICE/BENEFIT REFORMS

Unfortunately, Congress has not set a pricing scheme meaningfully related to market rates (see Chapter 6). Thus, we are facing two serious congressional constraints: insurance coverage is mandatory, and premiums are essentially the same for all insureds. Given these constraints, a second-best solution is to reduce guaranteed benefit levels. This option minimizes the PBGC's need to distort all firms' behavior to prevent gaming by a small minority of firms against the insurance company. In short, the lower the guarantee level, the smaller the need to directly affect exposure, and the smaller the incentives for corporations to try to game the system.

Had the low-level guarantee suggested in the above paragraphs (benefits no higher than average industry benefits payable no earlier than age 62) been in effect in 1986, it is doubtful that LTV Corporation, for example, would have been in a position to make anything like a $2 billion claim against the PBGC insurance system. As discussed in Chapter 7, "Underfunding Exposure: The Evidence," over 50 percent of the claim was attributable to shutdown and early normal retirement ages. An additional reduction would have occurred if age-62 benefits in steel industry pension plans exceeded average age-62 benefits in all insured pensions.

If all pension plans were assessed a market insurance premium, then each plan could determine whether it was willing to pay for higher benefits than these. When there are large cross-subsidies in the pricing structure, however, there is an argument for reducing these transfers to what can be considered a reasonable minimum. Otherwise, those receiving subsidies have incentives to take a larger portion of the wage package in the form of insured pension benefits. This increases the taxes on those who do not benefit from the system (encouraging them to leave) and reduces the incentive for workers to help firms remain competitive.

In short, from an efficiency perspective, the appeal of benefit reductions is that they minimize the adverse impact of the regulated price scheme. The idea is to set benefit levels to make a closer match between revenues and expected claims for all firms.

Outlawing Underfunding

In the absence of meaningful changes in pricing and benefits reform, the only avenue left to control claims is to limit firms' exposure levels facing the PBGC. This can be done by enacting stricter minimum funding rules, by making it easier to attach assets in firms with underfunded pension plans, or by changing the bankruptcy laws to increase pension priorities above other creditors.

The first two solutions have the potential to interfere with optimal production and financing policies of many firms. This potential arises because the solution effectively outlaws substantial underfunding when underfunding may serve important economic functions. In fact, we know underfunding must be valuable to firms because there is a large forgone tax advantage of not fully funding a tax-free accumulation vehicle, and also because large amounts of underfunding characterized defined benefit plans long before the creation of pension insurance.[4]

In 1986, fully one out of four plans with at least 100 participants was underfunded in a termination sense (see Table 6–1) and hence will be impacted by the new minimum funding rules. It is unlikely that 25 percent of all plans pose significant risks to the PBGC. A more likely explanation for underfunding is that overall firm productivity is higher for some firms when they operate with underfunded pension plans. Otherwise, all firms would fully fund in an ongoing sense (and thus overfund in a termination sense), thereby taking full advantage of tax-free accumulation in the pension trust. By constraining the option to underfund, some gaming potential against the PBGC is removed, but some unmeasurable productivity effect will also be imposed on other firms that operate underfunded pension plans but pose little risk to the PBGC.

The potential for interference would be reduced if funding requirements were combined with estimates of default risk. The impact of the funding rules would more likely be restricted to firms posing significant exposure to the insurance company.

This principle was partially recognized in the Pension Protection Act. This legislation did not attach assets of all firms with pension underfunding. Instead, it permitted liens to arise only when minimum contributions in excess of $1 million were not paid to the plan. As noted in Chapter 8, because the liens arise late in the process, few assets may exist at this point that are not already subject to some other lien.[5] But the upside of the provision is that the lien solution tends to affect only firms with an imminent claim on the PBGC, thus reducing the overall burden of the rule.

More generally, the main ingredient of the new legislation is to require all underfunded plans, regardless of the risk they impose, to substantially increase their funding levels. The intent is to eliminate much of the exposure faced by the PBGC. The effect may be to reduce the attractiveness of defined benefit plans for some firms.

The underfunding provisions of the Pension Protection Act, however, were less intrusive than they could have been. For example,

---

[4]Ibid.

[5]It is not clear if the solution is more efficient if the PBGC successfully perfects its liens. A common solution to firms in financial difficulty is to use what assets are still free of lien to obtain bank loans to finance operations during reorganization. If the firm misses its pension contribution (a common occurrence prior to termination—see Chapter 7) and if the PBGC acts fast enough to attach the remaining assets, then the likelihood of a successful reorganization is reduced. That is, the likelihood is increased that the firm will utlimately enter Chapter 7 of the Bankruptcy Code, rather than structure a successful reorganization under Chapter 11. The recovery rate for the PBGC (and all other creditors) almost surely is lower in a Chapter 7 proceeding than in Chapter 11.

one easy way to eliminate most underfunding in the defined benefit system is to require all pension plans (including flat benefit plans) to project benefits to retirement ages using some wage/benefit growth assumption reasonably related to the interest rate assumption. This funding rule would be more effective in limiting the exposure facing the PBGC than the rules imposed by the Pension Protection Act because (1) it does not postpone strict funding requirements until the firm is in financial difficulty and (2) it mandates funding in the ongoing sense, thereby providing a sizable cushion for exposure in a termination sense. While this rule would have reduced exposure to the PBGC, however, it would have greatly aggravated the distortions imposed by mandatory full funding requirements because it eliminates all underfunding (not just underfunding in a termination sense).

Bankruptcy Changes

Potential changes in bankruptcy rules are likely to be more efficient solutions than more stringent funding rules to reduce exposure. This is because bankruptcy changes work indirectly to either reduce benefits or impose market-determined insurance rates. Two potential changes include restricting the insurance event to Chapter 7 of the Bankruptcy Code and changing the pension priority in the event of either Chapter 11 or Chapter 7 of the code.

Restructuring the insurance event to Chapter 7 (dissolution) instead of Chapter 11 (reorganization) of the U.S. Bankruptcy Code eliminates the potential for ongoing firms to essentially trap the government into subsidizing their pension benefits. If some ongoing firms in an industry are successful in obtaining the subsidy, it becomes more important for other firms in the industry to follow suit; otherwise, some firms will have a competitive advantage over those who do obtain the subsidy. Restriction of the insurance only to Chapter 7 bankruptcies is an indirect way to reduce the level of benefits offered in the system: only firms in dissolution are eligible for the PBGC transfer.

In the absence of price and/or benefits flexibility, arguably the most efficient change in the law would be a change in priority claims of pensions in bankruptcy. In particular, suppose that in bankruptcy, pensions had to be paid before all other claimants (including secured creditors). The effect of this rule is that creditors would set interest rates reflecting the risk of pension default and exposure.

Just as above, however, the solution is not best because it makes insurance coverage mandatory, which might not be optimal in all cases. This solution would work better if the priority claim were limited to a minimum benefit, say, no higher than the average benefit in all pension plans, payable no earlier than age 62.

If Congress is unwilling to set market rates directly, however, it is unlikely to change bankruptcy laws to increase the pension priority for the same reason: indirectly, a high pension-priority bankruptcy rule merely represents a "back door" free market rate system.

Arguments for Mandatory Participation

If the insurance price structure reflects large cross-subsidies, there is an obvious need to require mandatory participation; otherwise, all the good risks would opt not to participate. Even if premiums are set to fully reflect risk and exposure (my assumption in this section), at least three arguments are used to justify it. These are selection bias, information problems (including agency costs), and catastrophic risk. None of these arguments, however, appear to be compelling.

Selection bias. All voluntary insurance is subject to adverse selection. Despite insurance companies' ability to collect important information, insureds usually know more about their own risk than the insurance company. Thus, when 65-year-olds apply for annuities until death, they are not a random sample from the population. They likely overrepresent a group that has a longer life expectancy. This is why defined benefit coverage is required of all workers within large groups (like blue collar or white collar) in the firm and why optional lump sums are rarely permitted.

Adverse selection is not a trivial problem in pension insurance. In this case, however, the insurance company has large amounts of available data describing a potential insured, including its financial history, the performance of its industry, and the characteristics of the plan and firm. Moreover, the insurance company can monitor audited reports of the insureds' funding levels and portfolio holdings. Just as in any kind of insurance, prices would not be perfectly set, but there are good reasons to believe that reasonably accurate prices could be attained. If so, the selection problem would appear less than paramount.

Information problems. A second argument is that workers may want to have their pensions insured if they possessed all the facts and had the time and ability to process the information. A related issue pertains to the incentives of the stockholders versus the workers (the so-called agency problem). Even if workers desire coverage, the firm's management decides whether coverage will be obtained.

One solution to this problem, if it exists, is to require all firms' actuaries to provide workers with an explanation of the insurance option, together with estimated premium payments required by the PBGC. On a one-time basis, all firms could be given the opportunity to opt out of the insurance. If workers are unionized, insurance coverage could be the subject of collective bargaining; otherwise, the decision would require, say, a two-thirds vote by workers in the firm (where the election would be held by, say, an actuarial or accounting firm).

Catastrophic claims. Perhaps the best argument for mandatory participation in a free market for pension insurance is the potential for catastrophic claims. Suppose 100 firms are covered by a pension insurance contract. All have the same small risk of making a claim (say, 1 in 100 each year), and each claim costs $100. Ignoring the cost of operating the insurance company, the economic premium is one dollar per plan per year.

Suppose no claims occur in years one and two, and then five occur each year during years three and four. Consider the insurance company's position in year three. It has five claims totaling $500 but only $300 in accumulated premiums; at the end of year four, it has $1,000 in accumulated claims and only $400 in accumulated premiums. If it tries to raise premiums, insureds have an incentive to leave the system to insure elsewhere. Thus, the insurance company goes bankrupt, and the claimants receive only 40 percent of expected protection. This result occurs even though over a 10-year period, claims may average $100 per year, as expected.

One way to circumvent this problem is for the insurer and the insureds to commit to a long-term contract. Effectively, a premium surcharge may be levied during the early years, say, a $2 premium instead of $1. During year three in the above example, $600 in accumulated premiums would be available to pay $500 in claims. In year four, $300 in accumulated premiums would be available to pay part of the additional $500 in claims in that year. The insurance company would borrow $200 against forthcoming premiums based on its guaranteed contracts.

If in years 5 through 10 zero claims were received (consistent with the original expectation that $1,000 in claims would occur every 10 years on average), a rebate of excess premiums during these years could be given to the insureds. This kind of industry group concept will be implemented in the pension insurance system described in Chapter 10.

The catastrophic claims problem is a good argument for the insurance carrier to mandate long-term contracts but not for the government to mandate participation of all pension plans in the agreement.

DISTORTION FOR OVERFUNDED PLANS

Thus far, the discussion has been limited to the potential for distortions imposed by insurance rules on the behavior of firms with underfunded plans. The Omnibus Budget Reconciliation Act (OBRA), however, imposes a distortion on the choice of types of pension plans for firms wishing to have well-funded plans. While OBRA required underfunded plans to become better funded, it also generally required well-funded plans to become less well funded.

As discussed in Chapter 8, prior to OBRA, firms were permitted to fund up to 100 percent of ongoing liabilities. OBRA changed this limit to 150 percent times termination liabilities. It is easy to show that for some defined benefit plans, particularly those disproportionately populated by workers (as compared to retirees), the new full funding limit is tantamount to legislating persistent underfunding in an ongoing sense. This encourages these firms to use defined contribution plans instead because the latter plans still provide for full utilization of the tax-exempt trust funds. An example will illustrate the point that OBRA essentially attaches a special excise tax against defined benefit plans.

Consider a firm's ability to fund a defined benefit plan for a worker entering the firm at age 40. For simplicity, suppose there is only one worker in the firm. This example mimics plans sponsored by new, growing firms with predominantly young workers.

Suppose the chances of this worker quitting, being laid off, or dying prior to age 65 (retirement age) are zero. At age 65, the worker will receive a lump sum pension equal to 10 percent times years of service times wage at retirement. The worker effectively pays for this pension by contributing $1 per year (in the form of forgone wages) in real terms. That is, in the absence of the pension, the worker's salary would be $11 per year. Assume the inflation rate, the interest rate, and wage growth are all 10 percent per year. Thus, in real terms, the present value of the worker's pension at age 65 is $25.

Trust Fund Balance: Pre-1988 Rules

Consider the pre-1988 funding rule: the firm is permitted to project wages by 10 percent, then discount by the 10 percent interest rate. Its ongoing liability after one year is thus $1 (10 percent times current wage $10, times one year of service, projected at 10 percent per year, discounted by 10 percent per year)

$$\begin{aligned} PVO(1,0) &= .10 \times 1 \text{ year} \times \$10e^{(.10-.10)25} \\ &= \$1 \end{aligned} \qquad (9\text{–}1)$$

where $PVO(1,0)$ is the present value of the ongoing pension after one year of service evaluated in year-zero dollars.

In fact, under this rule, the firm can put all subsequent worker contributions into the trust fund to accumulate at a tax-free 10 percent interest rate. For example, consider year 15 of the accumulation: the wage then is $44.81 ($10 accumulated at 10 percent wage growth for 10 years), service is 15 years, and there are 10 years to retirement. Thus, the ongoing benefit liability in year-15 dollars is:

$$\begin{aligned} PVO(15,15) &= .10 \times 15 \text{ years} \times \$44.81e^{(.10-.10)10} \\ &= \$67.22 \end{aligned} \qquad (9\text{–}2)$$

In year-zero dollars, this amount is discounted 15 years at the 10 percent interest rate:

FIGURE 9–1 Trust Funding: Old and New Funding Rules

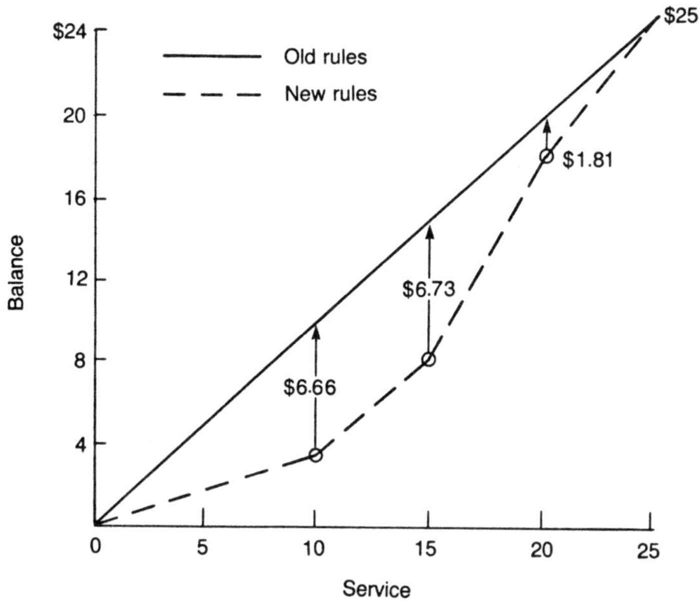

$$PVO(15,0) = \$67.22e^{-.10(15)} = \$15 \quad (9\text{–}3)$$

The firm's normal cost calculation is the difference between benefits at age 65 and current benefits, prorated over years left until retirement (see Chapter 7). Because the present value of benefits at age 65 will be $25 in real terms the difference between this and benefits accrued at year 15 ($15) spread over 10 years is $1: the firm's normal contribution in year 15 is $1 (valued in year-zero dollars).

Figure 9–1 depicts the growth of the trust fund in year-zero dollars; it is a linear schedule starting at zero and reaching $25 in 25 years (it increases at the rate of $1 per year). These trust fund amounts at various ages are also reflected in the first row of Table 9–1.

Trust Balance: Post-1988 Rules

Now consider the post-1988 funding rules: the firm is restricted to maintain a trust fund with assets no more than 150 percent of the present value of terminated benefits (*PVT*). In year one, 150 percent of terminated benefits is 12.3 cents:

$$PVT(1,0) \times 150\% = .10 \times 1 \text{ year} \times \$10e^{-.10(25)} \times 150\% = .123 \quad (9\text{–}4)$$

TABLE 9–1 Tax Cost of New Funding Rules: Illustration

	Years of Service				
Category	*0*	*10*	*15*	*20*	*25*
Trust balance ($real)					
1. Old rules	$0.00	$10.00	$15.00	$20.00	$25.00
2. New rules	$0.00	3.34	8.27	18.19	25.00
3. Difference	0.00	6.66	6.73	1.81	0.00
4. Average difference during interval	—	3.33	6.69	4.27	.90
Taxable interest					
5. Average per year during interval	—	.33	.67	.42	.09
Tax during interval					
6. (33%) per year	—	.11	.22	.14	.03
7. Total	—	1.10	1.10	.70	.15
8. Cumulative tax	—	2.10	2.20	2.90	3.05

Note: See text for assumptions.

Termination liabilities are similar to the ongoing liabilities in Equation (9–1) except the 10 percent salary projection factor is missing in the termination calculation. This is why, even allowing for multiplication by 150 percent, the termination funding limit is only 12.3 percent of the ongoing liability limit in year one.

From the perspective of using the trust fund, the firm can contribute only 12.3 percent of the worker's implicit one-dollar contribution to the pension (in the form of forgone wages). Implicitly, the rest must be saved outside the trust. If the firm pays a tax rate of 33 percent, 87.7 percent of the implicit contribution accumulates at the 6.67 percent after-tax interest rate (10 percent, minus the 33 percent tax, times 10 percent).

In year 15, the trust fund is restricted to hold $8.27 in real terms:

$$PVT\ (15{,}0) \times 150\% = .10 \times 15 \text{ years} \times \$10e^{-.10(10)} \times 150\% = \$8.27 \qquad (9\text{–}5)$$

Under the old funding rules, the firm could hold $15 in real terms in year 15 in the trust fund; thus, at the 15-year service level, the firm is saving $6.73 outside the pension fund at the after-tax interest rate ($15 in real contributions, minus $8.27 in the trust fund).

The maximum amount of assets in the trust fund under the new rules is shown by the nonlinear schedule in Figure 9–1 and the second row of Table 9–1. The difference between the two requirements is the amount of pension accumulations that must be saved outside the pension fund (row three of the table, also depicted in the figure).

By year 20, the new rules permit almost the entire ongoing liability to be reflected in trust assets. In the new scheme, $18.19 may be held in trust (in year-zero dollars), compared to $20 under the old rule; the gap in the two full funding rules narrows because contributions to the trust fund increase rapidly at older ages under the new rule. Between years 15 and 20, the average contribution to the trust fund is almost $2, double the amount in the old funding scheme.[6]

Tax Assessment

It is easy to obtain an estimate of the tax impact of the new rules. Over each segment of the schedule in Figure 9–1, the average difference between the two trust accounts is calculated (row four in Table 9–1). Taxable interest is 10 percent times these differences (row five of the table). The tax assessed on these interest amounts is assumed to be 33 percent times these amounts each year. Annual tax assessments on interest earned outside the trust are shown in row 6 of Table 9–1.

Row seven lists the total tax assessment during each interval. For example, during the first 10 years, 11 cents in taxes each year amounts to $1.10 over 10 years. The last row accumulates these amounts. These numbers show that over 25 years, an additional tax is paid on savings outside the pension under the new rules amounting to approximately $3 in real terms, which is approximately 12 percent of the value of the pension, $25.

If, instead, the firm offers a defined contribution plan, it would be entitled to deposit the full amount of the implicit pension contributions (forgone wages) into the pension trust fund, all of which would accumulate at the pre-tax rate of interest. Thus, the new rules create a tax bias in favor of defined contribution versus defined benefit plans. Moreover, if long-term interest rates increase beyond 10 percent, the bias will become even larger.

Defined benefit plans historically have numerous inherent advantages: they permit firms to over- or underfund, to deter labor mobility, and to discourage retirement beyond normal retirement age.[7] In addition, they provide a vehicle that permits spreading of investment risks among worker cohorts and between workers and stockholders. The new funding rules further interfere with the first advantage. The remaining advantages are intact, except they now cost more to effect.

---

[6]The example understates the impact of the new rule because I assume the firm can always make contributions to the fund to keep itself at the 150 percent limit. In fact, once below the limit, the pre-1988 funding rules apply (normal cost plus amortization of underfunding), and thus permitted contributions may be even less than those implied in the table.

[7]Defined benefit plans typically discourage retirement after normal retirement merely by not making actuarial adjustments to benefits after this age.

Given the new costs, new firms may be more likely to find other (perhaps less effective) means to control their work forces and share investment risks with workers in ways that will have more advantageous tax implications compared to defined benefit plans.

Balanced Work Force

The use of a one-worker plan mimics the impact of the new full funding limit on new, growing firms with predominantly young workers; but it somewhat overstates the impact of the new rule in a more mature firm. This is because for older workers, 150 percent of termination liabilities typically exceeds ongoing liabilities. Because the rules are applied in the aggregate, the "surplus" amounts for older workers can be applied to the "deficit" amounts for younger workers. The net permissible trust balance is thus higher than depicted above for older firms with a mix of younger and older workers. The tax effect, however, is still significant.

To illustrate, consider a firm where each worker starts at age zero and retires at age 25. Workers never quit and are never fired. The firm is neither growing nor contracting, and thus employment is constant. For simplicity, assume there are 25 workers in the firm: one worker joins each year, and one retires each year.

The firm pays a lump-sum pension to each retiree in the amount of 10 percent per year of service, times wage. The current wage is $10 per year.

Liabilities for the plan are obtained by adding the liability for each of 25 workers in the firm, each with a service level varying from zero to 25 years. Assuming the interest rate and the expected wage growth rate are each 10 percent, the calculation of ongoing benefits is depicted by

$$PVO = \int_0^{25} .10 \times a \text{ years} \times \$10\, da \qquad (9\text{–}6)$$

which sums benefits for workers with $a = 0$ to 25 service years. The solution to the above expression is $312. That is, ongoing liabilities at any given time for this firm are $312 in real terms.

The termination value of benefits is exactly the same as in Equation (9–6), except liabilities are not projected by 10 percent salary growth. Salary growth is not permitted in a termination liability calculation. To partly offset the omission of salary growth, the new full funding limit permits termination liability to be multiplied by 150 percent. That is, the new full funding limit is expressed as follows:

$$\text{Limit} = 150\% \times \int_0^{25} .10 \times a \text{ years} \times \$10 \times e^{-.10(25-a)} da \qquad (9\text{–}7)$$

The solution to this equation is $237. In the more general model, the new 150 percent full funding limit permits 75 percent (237/312) of ongoing liabilities to be funded; the remaining 25 percent must be saved in a tax-exposed trust. This means the interest earnings on this $75 is subject to the corporate tax. If this tax rate is 33 percent and interest earnings are $7.50 (10 percent interest rate times $75), the effective tax levied against the pension savings amounts to $2.50 per year (33 percent tax times $7.50 in interest earnings). If we think of this tax being paid effectively by each year's retiree when he obtains the annual lump-sum payout ($25 in real terms), then each year's retiree receives a benefit roughly 10 percent less than the benefit under the old funding limit. Since all contributions to a defined contribution plan (of equal generosity) would accumulate in the tax-exempt trust fund, the firm can evade the excise tax by switching to a defined contribution plan.

CONCLUSION

In this chapter, an attempt was made to show the potential costs of offering pension insurance without concern for fundamental insurance principles and economic efficiency. In an ideal world, pension insurance coverage would be voluntary, the levels of insurance would be variable, and prices would be set to reflect exposure, risks, and the cost of writing insurance. By mandating insurance coverage, the government imposes costs on some firms that may operate more productively in the absence of insurance. This distortion would be minimized if firms had choices of various insurance options and if premiums were freely determined to reflect risk and exposure.

By mandating insurance coverage and effectively outlawing market pricing, the potential for inefficient outcomes increases. The system builds in a mechanism for well-funded plans with financially sound sponsors to subsidize underfunded plans with financially unsound sponsors. Because the latter firms do not pay a premium related to their risk and exposure, incentives are created for them to game the subsidizing plans, which in turn encourages those firms to evade the tax by not participating in the defined benefit system.

The distortions would be markedly reduced if the levels of mandated insurance were reduced to a basic level of protection. This would dramatically reduce the magnitude of the transfers and thus limit the long-term impact of the program. By declining to limit the program and by combining this constraint with mandatory participation and an essentially flat pricing scheme, a formula is written that virtually guarantees substantial long-term distortions in the defined benefit system. A mechanism is created for billions of dollars to be transferred from one to another set of firms sponsoring defined benefit plans.

In view of the constraints it has placed on the insurance system, Congress is left with two alternative policies: either let the system proceed unchecked, thereby facing the risk of endangering the continuation of financially sound defined benefit plans, or mandate reduced exposure by forcing underfunded firms to become more fully funded. The latter approach was adopted in the Pension Protection Act of 1987. This policy may itself create other distortions because it requires some firms that otherwise would optimally finance internally to either engage in more external financing at higher interest rates or switch to less efficient ways to include workers in the firms' financing.[8]

Ironically, the new legislation may not be successful in attaining its first goal (reducing the incentives for well-funded pension plans to switch to defined contribution forms). The 1987 Omnibus Budget Reconciliation Act forced well-funded plans to offset the higher contribution (and thus higher tax deductions) used by poorly funded plans by imposing stricter funding limits on well-funded plans. At a 10 percent interest rate for a pension plan characterized by zero steady-state growth and 25-year careers by participants (with no retirees), the new full funding limit is the equivalent of assessing a 10 percent tax on the contributions to a defined benefit plan versus a defined contribution plan. For new, growing firms populated predominantly by young workers, the effective tax rate is closer to 12 percent.

The possibility that stricter funding standards may not reduce claims expectations proportionately must also be considered. Even though funding standards are stricter, potential claimants may still be successful in defunding their plans prior to termination. Efforts aimed at limiting this ability—superfast funding requirements of waivers and shutdown benefits—may ensure satisfaction of the distress criteria required to qualify for the PBGC transfer. Moreover, the integrity of the new funding constraints can be substantially affected if interest rates increase substantially and then decrease (see Chapter 8).

In addition to these problems, the PBGC insurance program has been plagued with uncertainty in benefit guarantees. Because the insurance protects nominal benefits, the guaranteed real levels vary with the interest rates and with workers' ages. It is not uncommon for a termination to cause some workers to lose 90 percent of their real expected pensions. The average loss of real pension benefits on termination can vary from 30 percent to 60 percent, depending on the level of the nominal interest rate (see Chapter 2).

In the face of these issues, it is inviting to think about an entirely new pension insurance program, one that recognizes congressional constraints for mandatory participation and a maximum premium level but pays attention to the efficiency and long-term integrity of the insurance system and defined benefit plans. This will be the subject of the last chapter of the book.

---

[8]One alternate might be for the firm to deliberately reduce wages early in the career and to pay higher wages later. This might be a less efficient solution because it forces workers to have "too little" consumption at younger ages and "too much" at older ages.

CHAPTER 10

Proposal for an Economic Insurance System

Chapters 6 through 8 discussed reforms attained for the federal pension insurance system and ideas proposed for future reform. Chapter 9 discussed some of these ideas in the context of economic efficiency. In this chapter, many of the ideas discussed or implied in these and other parts of the book are brought together to describe an economically rational pension insurance program.

This is a good place to reconsider the ideas of Dan McGill mentioned in Chapter 1. Prior to the enactment of ERISA, he developed a set of principles to guide the development of a national pension system. His policy would have been operated by the federal government but would have differed from ERISA legislation in the following ways. The insurable event would be firm failure, not "distress" or reorganization; guaranteed benefits would exclude (*a*) benefit increases within five years of termination and (*b*) all shutdown benefits; and funding rules would be changed to (*a*) require standardized assumptions and (*b*) reduce amortization periods on past service credit from 30 to 20 years.

If these provisions had been included in ERISA, the Pension Benefit Guaranty Corporation would have accumulated significantly lower claims over its history. And except for the past service amortization period, which was partly addressed (for underfunded plans only) in the Pension Protection Act of 1987, all of his ideas would still have had a significant impact on the solvency of the program if they had been enacted in 1987.

In my view, if Congress will not permit market pricing and will continue to require mandatory participation, the single most important reform that could be instituted in the existing program is to restrict the amount of the basic insured benefit and age of first receipt. I would guarantee a maximum benefit equal to the plan benefit or the average of all pension benefits (as a percent of wage and service), whichever is lower, payable no earlier than age 62. This concept mimics principles of the unemployment compensation insurance program, which restricts benefits to something proportional to average wages and sets a limit on the period of collection. This would substantially reduce the distortions created by the current system and various attempts to fix it.

Rather than weave reform ideas around the existing program, however, my intention in this chapter is to build an entirely new program, one that incorporates McGill's notions and others discussed above. The system I describe could be operated either by the PBGC or by private insurance companies. I will describe the system, however, as if it will be operated by the private sector, subject to government regulation. My preference for the private-sector solution is grounded on the presumption that it will be more efficient owing to the competition of ideas and varieties of policies that otherwise would less likely be developed in a system operated by a single, nonprofit insurance company.

By its nature, the discussion in this chapter is suggestive and leaves many questions unanswered. It also leaves many options unexplored: it assumes one set of congressional constraints and develops one hypothetical carrier's policy to satisfy those constraints. Discussion of a full pension system with all of its attendant regulatory and private-sector options would itself fill a rather lengthy book.

UNDERLYING CHARACTERISTICS OF PROPOSAL

Congressional Constraints

In developing this proposal, I assume the solution has boundaries owing to various congressional constraints. Setting out such constraints is a somewhat arbitrary exercise. The ones I chose to assume simply represent my interpretation of limits likely to be imposed by Congress on any type of reformed pension insurance system. The specifics would probably vary depending on who draws up the list. But the themes in most lists, I suspect, would reflect (1) some paternalistic element—workers must be protected against loss of basic pension benefits at older ages and (2) some transfer element—insurance prices must be constrained to reflect some cross-subsidies from low- to high-risk firms.

For the sake of describing an operational system, I assume these constraints take the following specific forms (summarized in Table 10–1): (1) the insurance program is mandatory; (2) the insurance must at least cover a basic benefit equal to the lower of the plan benefit or the average of all pension benefits (as a percent of wage and service),

TABLE 10–1 Assumed Congressional Constraints

Category	*Provision*
Coverage	Mandatory
Maximum premium	$200 per participant per year ($1985)
Type of policy	Renewable term
Maximum coinsurance	40 percent for active workers at termination; 20 percent for retirees
Minimum benefit guarantee	Lower of plan benefit or average of all pension annuities (adjusted for age and service), payable at age 62

payable in an unreduced form no earlier than age 62; (3) pension insurance policies, like most life insurance policies, must be term renewable; (4) the coinsurance charge against workers can be no greater than 40 percent for vested active workers and 20 percent for retirees older than age 62 (except as affected by the minimum benefits limit (see item 2 above)); and (5) the premium is limited to $200 per participant per year (in 1985 dollars) for minimum insured benefits (see item 2).

The role of the *regulatory agency* is to enforce these constraints.

Role for the Industry Group

The proposal outlined here is designed to operate in a competitive insurance market. Subject to the congressional constraints enumerated above, each insurer would be free to design its own policies and to set rates based on its own assessment of risks and exposure. The PBGC would provide its historical data on all insureds and claims to help insurers set prices.

I assume an *industry group* will provide various functions. It will operate an assigned risk pool for so-called uninsureds (pension plans that cannot find insurance for basic benefits for less than $200 per participant per year). The pool rules will be designed by the regulator. In addition, the industry group will provide reinsurance to protect against individual insurance company bankruptcies and will enforce a surcharge-rebate scheme to handle catastrophic claims events.

It is expected that each insurance company will protect itself from exposure to claims disproportionate to all insurance companies. They will do this by diversifying coverage across a wide variety of firms and industries. It is also presumed that all insurance companies will reinsure portions of their major clients with other carriers to protect themselves against insolvency from taking one usually large claim. Because the industry group essentially acts as a guarantor in the case of a carrier insolvency, presumably it will require these precautions in any event.

A problem arises, however, if the entire industry experiences "catastrophic" events. This means claims over time may not exhibit a small variation but instead may evince a "bunching" in some time periods. For example, in serious recessions, funding ratios may fall and the rate of firm failure may increase; or, an entire industry may fail over a short time period. In these cases, the insurance companies as a group may not have accumulated sufficient premiums to cover claims, and insureds will have incentives to find insurance through new insurance companies unencumbered by unusual past losses.

To maintain a stable system, the insurance group will impose surcharges on all insureds to fund an industry reserve, which would be available to insurance companies according to some predetermined formula when overall insurance industry claims experience increases by some specified amount beyond expectations. The surcharge can be increased or lowered (or rebates given), depending on experience and the size of the surplus pool.

Insureds wishing to exit the defined benefit system will be responsible for paying their share of any surcharge in effect at the time of the departure and for some period of time (perhaps five years) after departure (perhaps guaranteed by a bond on exit). In addition, all insurance carriers, including new entrants writing pension insurance, will be required to charge the same proportional surcharge to their clients. These rules prevent free-riding by insureds who try to flee the system (that is, switch to either defined contribution plans or to a new-entrant carrier) during or after some catastrophic loss period, once it is apparent that they are not the ones to use the insurance during the period.[1]

It is presumed that Congress mandates the equivalent of a *term-renewable policy*, which is common in life insurance policies. This kind of policy prevents insurance carriers from increasing the premium when it becomes apparent that a client is "sick" or "dying." That is, it prevents insurance carriers from reassessing probabilities of default for particular insureds after the initial determination. Changing risks, however, may be taken into account in decisions to permit firms to attain lower funding levels or to obtain protection for higher real benefits. In addition, risk assessments may be altered if the client voluntarily changes its risk classification, say, by changing its line of business through merger or acquisition (this is akin to increasing life insurance premiums if a client starts smoking midstream in the contract).

New pension plans would be assigned a premium based on their

---

[1]In principle, each firm could write separate long-term contracts with their clients. This solution is more costly because clients must protect themselves from the insurer raising prices to increase profits or offset poor underwriting judgment.

financial and other risk characteristics at the time of entry. The insurance company, however, is permitted to increase prices across the board to reflect its overall claims experience.

Assigned Risk Pool

The insurance policy proposal presented here revolves around the establishment of a maximum premium, for basic benefits insurance equal to $200 per participant per year, indexed to wages; the VanDerhei study suggested that if free market prices were applied to the existing insurance contract in 1985, roughly 7 percent of the participant population would have paid a price in excess of $200 (see Chapter 6). Pension plans paying a premium less than the maximum face no special funding rules and no constraints on benefit payments (except those related to a coinsurance feature of the policy and those not reflected in liability calculations, such as shutdown benefits). Firms wishing to buy insurance at a cost greater than $200 per participant per year are free to do so.

Otherwise, plans constrained by the maximum premium are put into the *assigned risk pool*. Plans in the pool face special funding rules and constraints on benefit levels.

These constraints are discussed in greater detail below. The insureds in the assigned risk pool are allocated to all participating insurance companies, presumably in proportion to the amount of voluntary pension insurance they write. This method ensures that subsidies will be financed equitably by all those outside the pool.

ILLUSTRATIVE POLICY BY A PRIVATE INSURER

In this section, I will discuss a hypothetical insurance policy offered by a competing insurance carrier. The policy will satisfy the constraints imposed by my hypothetical Congress (see Table 10–1) and will reflect various principles described in previous chapters. The elements of the insurance policy are listed in Table 10–2 and will be discussed in turn.

The policy I describe does not insure a terminated benefit. As discussed in Chapter 2, the problem with a termination-type guarantee is that the coinsurance factor varies greatly with participants' ages and the interest rate. Workers do not know which portion of their real promised pension is protected. In addition, it is difficult for the carrier to satisfy the coinsurance limits imposed by my hypothetical Congress with this type of guarantee. The coinsurance limits may be satisfied at, say, an 8 percent interest rate but be violated if the rate increases to 10 percent.

In the policy described here, *guaranteed pensions* for active participants *are indexed to the lesser of prices or Treasury bill rates*

TABLE 10–2 Features of an Illustrative Economic Insurance Policy

Category	*Characteristic*
1. Pension promise	Indexed* from date of plan termination until death for active participants. For retirees, indexation is retroactive to age of retirement.
2. Portion of real pension insured	50 percent (equivalent to a roughly 30 percent coinsurance factor compared to ongoing benefits)
3. Insurance firm portfolio	100 percent Treasury bills.
4. Premium formula	$q\,[(1-c)L^{*} - A(1-g)] + yM$ plus expense and subsidy amounts q = Probability of termination L^{*} = Liabilities reflecting indexed insured benefits g = Percent permissible pre-claim defunding c = Coinsurance portion of L^{*} M = Exposure attributable to portfolio risk y = Cost of holding hedging instruments.
5. Risk assessment	A risk premium is assessed on the basis of the risk characteristics of the portfolio. These risk measures may include the beta value and long-bond share characterizing the portfolio. Assuming this exposure can be hedged, the price is captured by the term yM above.
6. Liability calculation	Must use fixed assumptions: All benefits (including flat benefits) must be calculated in a termination sense, using a discount rate not to exceed the lower of 1 percent or the average of the real T-bill rates over the most recent 20 years. Assume all retirements occur at highest-cost ages (usually ages first eligible).† Turnover and mortality assumptions reflect industry averages.‡
7. Increases in real benefits	Not covered on past service (maintenance of real benefits is anticipated in premium calculation—see category 6)
8. Shutdown benefits	Not permitted; but plan may provide for annuities to be indexed to prices from the date of plant shutdown until the normal retirement age§
9. Lump-sum options	Not permitted, except for de minimus amounts
10. Defunding	Permitted with permission of insurance firm. Otherwise, covered up to g percent erosion of plan's funding ratio (indexed to all plans' funding ratios). Beyond this, the plan's benefits are frozen in real terms, benefit payments are reduced to insured levels, and portfolio is converted to 100 percent Treasury bills.

TABLE 10–2 *(concluded)*

Category	*Characteristic*
11. Insurable event	Chapter 7 of the U.S. Bankruptcy Code; abandonment of the plan outside the insurable event is protected by a pledge of security in the amount of 20 percent of insurable benefits.
12. Plan administrator	The insurance company.

*Indexed to lower of the inflation rate or the T-bill return.

†Rule is relaxed if established plans can demonstrate a statistical distribution that justifies a different assumption.

‡Can be stylized to plan only if actuarial assumptions are based on statistical evidence for the plan.

§If these shutdown benefits are permitted, the plan may not incorporate anticipated layoffs in its turnover assumption.

from the date of termination until death, reduced by a fixed coinsurance factor. For retirees, indexation is retroactive to the age of retirement, reduced by a fixed coinsurance factor: the retiree receives either the insurance benefit or his current benefit, whichever is lower.[2]

The guarantee formula does not presume benefits are also explicitly indexed in the pension plan. Pension benefit formulas, however, are relevant to enforce a reasonable coinsurance policy, particularly their explicit and implicit indexing provisions. For purposes of my example, I assume the plans my carrier insures pay benefits that are implicitly or explicitly tied to wages at, or around, retirement age, and some ad hoc policy will accommodate inflation after retirement. If, for example, the pension plan never paid postretirement inflation adjustments, a different guarantee would have to be written to prevent negative coinsurance from characterizing the insurance contract described below.

The coinsurance factor chosen must be sufficiently large to discourage moral hazard *and* to offset full indexing of the insured benefits after retirement, not usually available in the private sector. For example, Allen, Clark, and Sumner (1986a) showed that while private pension benefits were routinely increased during retirement on an ad hoc basis, benefits during retirement eroded in real terms by a few percentage points per year during the 1970s. For example, if the erosion rate is 3

[2]The added condition on retirees reduces the possibility that insured benefits exceed current benefits: negative coinsurance factors could create moral hazard problems. The insured benefit might exceed current benefits in the policy my hypothetical insurance carrier offers if a pension plan had not made postretirement cost-of-living adjustments for several years and if inflation were significant. The condition does not eliminate the potential for negative coinsurance for some retirees, as will be demonstrated in an example below.

percent per year, then roughly one third of real benefits will be eroded over 15 years.

The policy I describe has roughly a 30 percent coinsurance factor for active workers; that is, the insured benefit has a value roughly 70 percent as high as benefits that would be collected if the plan did not terminate. It turns out that this is roughly equivalent to applying a 50 percent coinsurance factor to a completely indexed pension. The PBGC coinsurance factor generally has ranged between 25 percent and 35 percent, depending on the prevailing interest rate. That is, termination liabilities have amounted to roughly two thirds to three fourths of ongoing liabilities.[3]

Real insured benefit. The insurance policy written by my hypothetical carrier is summarized as follows. In the event of a pension termination, all workers' accruals to date are insured *in real terms* and reduced by one half. Existing retirees will have their real benefits recalculated as of the date of their retirement, reduced by 50 percent. The retiree will receive this benefit or his current benefit, whichever is lower, indexed until death.

To protect the insurance carrier from indexing more than its portfolio can deliver, indexing is done at the inflation rate or the Treasury bill rate, whichever is lower. Because T-bill rates generally exceed the inflation rate over the long run (see Table 18 in Appendix A), this policy produces an expected cushion to the carrier, which in a competitive market, will be reflected neither in the price of the insurance nor in a rebate scheme set by the carrier.

To see how the insurance works, consider a 55-year-old worker at termination. In this example, I suppose that his annuity according to the benefit formula in the pension plan is .5 percent, times wages of $10,000, times 15 years of service, or $750 per year. The plan provides for a single retirement age (60), and death always occurs at age 80. The real three-month Treasury bill rate is zero (the T-bill rate equals the inflation rate).

This worker's insured benefit equals his $750 annuity reduced by one half, or $375; this amount is indexed from termination date (age 55) to death (age 80). Because the real T-bill rate is zero in this example, this yields a pension value in real terms at retirement age equal to $7,500 ($375 in real terms collected from age 60 to age 80). Because his first year annuity is indexed from the date of termination, and since the real interest rate is zero by assumption, the real value of the insured benefit at age 55 is also $7,500.

This amount (generally financed partly by assets in a terminated plan and partly by the insurance firm) will be invested entirely in

---

[3]These numbers can be derived by dividing funding ratios in Table 3–8 by those shown in Table 3–7.

TABLE 10–3 Coinsurance in an Illustrative Indexed Insurance Policy

Age (1)	*Ongoing Liabilities (2)*	*Termination Liabilities (3)*	*Coinsurance† (4)*	*50 Percent Real Liabilities (5)*	*Coinsurance‡ (6)*
45	$ 3,441	$ 750	78.1%	$ 2,500	27.3%
50	6,883	2,250	67.3	5,000	27.3
55	10,324	5,025	51.3	7,500	27.3
60 (retire)	13,766	10,000	27.3	10,000	27.3
65	9,161	7,145	22.0	7,500	18.1
70	5,522	4,610	16.5	5,000	9.4
75	2,483	2,258	9.0	2,500	−.6
Total—active	$34,414	$18,025	47.6%	$25,000	27.3%
Total—retired	$17,166	$14,013	18.3%	$15,000	12.6%

Assumptions: Start age is 40; retirement occurs at age 60; and death occurs at age 80. Interest rate, inflation rate, and wage growth rate are 8 percent. Ongoing plans make ad hoc adjustments to retirees equal to one half the inflation rate.

†Numbers in this column equal column 2 minus column 3 all divided by column 2.

‡Numbers in this column equal column 2 minus column 5 all divided by column 2.

Treasury bills. By investing all assets in T-bills and restricting inflation adjustments to the lesser of the T-bill rate or the inflation rate, the insurance firm will avoid the risk posed by mismatching its assets and liabilities (see Chapter 2).

This example is developed further in Table 10–3. It is assumed that the interest rate, the inflation rate, and expected wage growth all equal 8 percent per annum. It is assumed that this pension plan is typical in the sense that if it continues, it is expected to make ad hoc adjustments to retiree benefits equal on average to one half the inflation rate. In this case, the present value of the ongoing benefit for a 55-year-old worker is $10,324. That is, the worker's $750 annuity is expected to be indexed to wages until retirement and then is subject to 4 percent erosion each year thereafter (ad hoc benefit increases are 4 percent, but the interest rate and inflation rate are 8 percent). The present value of a 20-year annuity discounted at 4 percent to age 60 is $10,324. Because wage growth equals the interest rate, the net discount rate to age 55 is zero (see Chapter 2); thus, the present value of the ongoing benefit at age 55 is also $10,324.

Coinsurance for workers. On termination, the current PBGC insurance system freezes nominal benefits until death. Thus, all benefits are discounted at 8 percent. The value of a $750 annuity starting at age 60, discounted at 8 percent and discounted back to age 55 at 8 percent, is $5,025. The PBGC coinsurance factor for this worker is 51.3 percent.

The indexed policy written by my hypothetical carrier (subject to a 50 percent coinsurance factor) has a value of $7,500 (see above) and thus imposes a coinsurance factor equal to 27.3 percent. In fact, recomputing pension values for all active participants, the coinsurance factor is a fixed 27.3 percent (column 6 in Table 10–3), well within the 40 percent boundary set by my hypothetical Congress. The average PBGC coinsurance for active workers in this example would be 47.6 percent (see column 4 in Table 10–3).

Coinsurance for retirees. Coinsurance factors fall significantly for retirees under either the PBGC or the real insurance scheme. In the case of PBGC insurance, the "extra" 4 percent discounting applies to fewer years for retirees; thus, a 70-year-old retiree has a coinsurance factor equal to 16.5 percent.

In the real insurance scheme, the 70-year-old retiree's benefit is recalculated in real terms at his retirement age. If this retiree had 20 years of service when he retired at age 60 (the same service I suppose all retirees had), and assuming that real wages have not changed since retirement, his age-60 benefit in real terms would be $1,000.[4] Reducing this by 50 percent, leaves a $500 annuity indexed to prices. The present value of this annuity to the age-70 retiree is equal to $5,000 ($500 in real terms collected for 10 more years of service), which is more than 90 percent of the value of his ongoing amount. The ongoing annuity is worth $670 in real terms (it had eroded 4 percent per year for 10 years) but will erode over his remaining 10 years at the rate of 4 percent compared to the indexed pension. In present-value terms, a $500 indexed annuity for 10 years is worth $5,000 in real terms. A $670 partially indexed annuity is worth $5,522.

It is noted parenthetically that the age-75 retiree receives more insured benefits in my indexed scheme than he would have if the plan had not terminated. This occurs even though his first posttermination-year annuity is less than current benefits.[5]

Other policies. The indexed insurance policy illustrated in Table 10–3 could be altered in numerous ways. For example, the coinsurance factor could be increased, or retirees' annuities could be frozen in nominal terms akin to current PBGC policy. My choice is somewhat arbitrary and serves to illustrate the basic coinsurance features of an indexed insurance policy. Further, by indexing all benefits, including

[4]That is, the plan pays .5 percent per year times a $10,000 wage (real terms), times 20 years of service.

[5]The insured annuity in this case is $500. His current benefit in real terms is $548 ($1,000 at retirement at age 60, eroded by 4 percent inflation each year from age 60 to age 75). But because the $500 insured annuity is indexed and his current annuity is only 50 percent indexed, the present value of the insured benefit exceeds the value of his current benefit.

retirees' benefits, the optimal portfolio strategy is simple (100 percent T-bills). If retirees' benefits are frozen in nominal terms, the 20 percent coinsurance limit set by my hypothetical Congress for retirees (see Table 10–1) could be violated under some interest rates, and the portfolio must be composed of T-bills to match active liabilities and of long-term bonds to match retiree liabilities.

In addition to numerous potential variants to the above policy, my hypothetical insurance carrier also will offer a *basic benefits plan*, consistent with the minimum insurance required by Congress. The plan pays a full benefit at age 62 equal to the weighted average of all plans' full benefits available at age 62 (as a percent of wages and service); payments prior to age 62 use a formula approved by the insurance carrier that reflects full actuarial adjustments.

All of the same rules enumerated above apply to the basic plan. In particular, the basic plan is indexed and subject to 50 percent coinsurance. When liabilities—and thus exposure—are calculated, they will conform to the generally lower liabilities calculated under the basic plan.

The basic plan option is available only to insureds whose plan benefits are more generous than the basic plan (generosity is measured in terms of the age of eligibility and size of benefits at a given age and service). Otherwise, the insured benefit may be more valuable than the ongoing benefit.

DEFAULT RISK

Setting the appropriate premium requires estimation of several parameters: namely, the probability of default, underfunding exposure (including pre-claim defunding), insureds' portfolio risk, and the cost of writing and administering the insurance. I will ignore the expense factor. I also assume the cumulative PBGC deficit will be financed prior to the start of the new system by either a lump-sum tax on existing insureds or a transfer from the U.S. Treasury.

As in any insurance, there is no perfect model to predict the occurrence of claims, but sufficient data is available to establish classes of risks in the population. In the case of pensions, presumably pension plan, plan sponsor, and industry characteristics (notably financial indexes) will be used to assess risk.

The discussion of the PBGC experience in Chapter 3 indicates that default risks are disproportionately related to industry type and union plans. In a previous study of firm failures offering defined benefit plans over the 1978–83 period, for example, I found that the probability of failure for a firm comprised of 50 percent union workers was approximately double the average; and that plans experiencing a 15 percent

TABLE 10–4 Factors Affecting Default Risk

Factor	*Impact on Risk*
Current assets/current liabilities	−.102*
Equity/total firm value	−.208*
Plan sponsor size (assets)	−.009
Net income/assets	−.236*
Unionization of plan	−.028
Steel industry†	.270*
Five-year probability of termination in (stratified) sample 6.5%.	

Note: Numbers show incremental impact of factor on the probability of an insufficient pension plan termination at the PBGC from 1980 to 1984.

*Asterisk denotes coefficient statistically significant at the 95 percent level of confidence.

†Plans sponsored by firms in the industry characterized by a two-digit Standard Industrial Classification Code equal to 33 (primary metals group).

SOURCE: Jack VanDerhei, "An Empirical Analysis of Risk-Related Insurance Premiums for the Pension Benefit Guaranty Corporation," Final report submitted to the PBGC, 1988.

decline in employment over the 1972–81 period were also approximately 50 percent more likely to fail than average.[6]

Pension defaults were statistically analyzed in the VanDerhei study (see Chapter 6); the factors identified are shown in Table 10–4. VanDerhei analyzed the probability of a PBGC claim during the 1980–84 period from a sample of 1,518 defined benefit plans (with at least 100 participants) filing Forms 5500 in 1980. In his sample (stratified to oversample terminations), 6.5 percent of the plans made a claim against the PBGC during a five-year period. Coefficients denoted by an asterisk are significant at the 95 percent confidence level; otherwise, they are not statistically different from zero.

His findings show that plan sponsors with better financial characteristics (higher ratios of assets to liabilities, higher equity ownership shares, higher net income to assets) have lower probabilities of termination. The interpretation of the financial-variable coefficients is illustrated by the first entry: a decrease in the plan sponsor's ratio of current assets to current liabilities from, say, 1.0 to .75 increases the probability of terminating with a claim by 2.5 percent (equals −.25 times the coefficient −.102).

His results also show that, accounting for financial measures, pension plans in the primary metals industry exhibit a five-year termination probability 27 percent higher than plans outside the steel industry. Accounting for various financial characteristics of the plan sponsor, no additional information is provided by union status of the plan; the coefficient on unions is small and not statistically different from zero.

[6]See Ippolito, 1986.

EXPOSURE AT EXISTING ASSET VALUES

Control of exposure is a critical element in setting any insurance price and deserves particular attention in the case of pensions. The essential idea is that because premiums are collected on the basis of observed exposure, controls must be administered to prevent this exposure from expanding prior to the filing of a claim. Otherwise, premiums systematically will fall short of claims experience. Premiums must be assessed on the basis of expected exposure in the event of a claim. The discussion in this section will concentrate on control of funding levels relative to the average of funding levels among all insureds, assuming overall asset values do not change over time. In the next section, the discussion accounts for volatility of asset values.

Liability Calculation

To ensure a match between insured liabilities and those subject to the premium assessment, all benefits in the premium formula are expressed on a termination basis, discounted at a rate not to exceed the lower of 1 percent or the average real three-month Treasury bill rates over the most recent 20 years. These interest rates are consistent with guaranteed benefits in the indexed insurance policy.

The rule requiring liabilities to be calculated on a real basis prevents plans (particularly flat benefit plans) from imposing unfunded past service credits on the insurance system by increasing nominal benefits. The rule does not preclude the use of flat benefit formulas, but rather it requires firms to express these benefits in real terms for purposes of assessing exposure.

Similarly, to retain the integrity of the calculation over time, increases in *real* pension plan generosity are not insured except insofar as the increase applies only to future service. Real benefit increases due solely to increases in real wages in the firm are insured, if they have been incorporated in liability projections for purposes of paying premiums. In addition, I adopt McGill's proposal (see above) by excluding from the guarantee any real benefit increases granted during the five years preceding a claim.[7]

To calculate exposure for premium purposes, other actuarial assumptions are imposed by the carrier. In particular, assumed retirement ages must conform to the earliest eligible ages. Turnover and mortality assumptions also must conform to those set out by the insurance company. If statistical evidence to justify different assump-

[7]The rules could be changed if, at the time the insurance contract was signed, it was anticipated that real benefits would be increased within a specified range. In this case, premiums could be set to reflect this anticipated additional exposure. A five-year cliff rule, however, still would be appropriate in these contracts.

tions can be provided by the insured's actuary, alternative assumptions will be permitted by my hypothetical carrier.

Control of Defunding

Once the plan's liabilities and thus its underfunding ratio are calculated, several steps must be taken to ensure that the ratio is reasonably related to the underfunding ratio at the time of a claim. Toward this end, two plan benefit provisions are prohibited: shutdown benefits and lump-sum payments. The more general problem of defunding must also be addressed.

Shutdown benefits. Shutdown benefits are not included in the normal calculations of funding and thus can impose significant underfunding on the insurance firm prior to and at the time of termination. Following McGill, these benefits are not covered by my hypothetical insurance carrier's policy. The plan, however, can make a special promise to workers affected by a shutdown: it can promise to pay benefits at retirement age indexed at the lower of the inflation rate or the T-bill rate from the shutdown date to the age of normal retirement.

The provision locks in real benefits for special early retirees but does not increase exposure for the carrier. This is because indexation of benefits is assumed for all workers except those who quit the firm prior to retirement age.[8] In this event, the pension plan cannot factor shutdown possibilities into its turnover assumptions.

Lump-sum payments. Lump-sum payments present obvious opportunities for plans to circumvent the coinsurance feature of the insurance (see Chapter 7). Therefore, these payments should not be permitted in the plan, except insofar as they apply to de minimus amounts as defined by the insurance company.

General rule for defunding. Once the plan's exposure has been calculated at the start of the insurance period, generally no problem will arise if the plan's funding level is increased relative to the overall average of pension plans (in this case, they would receive a reduction in their exposure assessment). The problem arises when the plan sponsor wishes to reduce its funding ratio relative to the average.

The general rule constraining defunding is stated as follows: *If in relation to all plans' funding ratios,*[9] *the insured's funding ratio reaches a level 20 percent below the level at the time the contract is written, without receiving an exemption from the insurance firm, all*

---

[8]In the proposal, no indexing protection prior to normal retirement age is required for participants who quit the firm prior to the earliest permissible retirement age.

[9]The measure of overall funding ratios needs to be specified in the contract. The carrier might, for example, purchase this information from a large actuarial firm that would provide annual data based on a sample of its clients, assuming they were representative of the pension universe.

service accruals are frozen. After this point, accruals are permitted only insofar as future contributions maintain the defunding gap at no more than 20 percent.

The freeze in accruals must be accompanied by other actions. First, upon a freeze, the portfolio is converted entirely to Treasury bills to protect the insurance company against market volatility.[10] Second, the freeze triggers the payment of *insured benefits only* from the trust fund. The insured is free to continue paying full benefits promised by the plan but only by augmenting insured payments from the trust fund with monies contributed from the firm. These actions ensure that the underfunded portion of guaranteed benefits will be frozen at $1-F^*(1-.2)$, where F^* is the funding level observed when the firm started the policy (indexed to overall pension funding levels).

Third, and finally, the insurance policy written by the carrier will specify that following a plan freeze, (*a*) no insurance will be written for any new defined benefit plan that covers any of the same workers in the frozen plan, and (*b*) the insured is precluded from obtaining insurance from another carrier to cover any new plan designed to circumvent the coinsurance feature of the insurance. A defined contribution plan may be created (or an old one enhanced) if it provides (1) no past service credit, (2) equal contribution percents to all workers' accounts, and (3) no integration rules with the frozen plan.

That the policy permits some defunding prior to termination (equal to 20 percent) is a concession to the nature of the insurable event: firm failure. A firm encountering financial failure will likely have difficulty paying its required contributions. It is akin to a life and health insurance company, which expects to pay significant health benefits prior to the payoff of a life insurance policy. However, these benefits usually will be constrained by the carrier to reduce the moral hazard problem, just as defunding is constrained to 20 percent of the contracted amount (indexed to overall funding levels among insureds).

It is tempting to exempt "well-funded" pension plans from the defunding rule. If an insured has a funding ratio for insured benefits of, say, 140 percent, why not permit the plan to reduce the ratio to 100 percent without triggering a freeze? If the portfolio were 100 percent T-bills, this might be possible. Given the carrier's exposure to asset-value volatility, however, a 100 percent funding ratio presents substantial potential exposure to the carrier, compared to a ratio of 140 percent. This issue is discussed in more detail below.

The defunding rule does not preclude plans from contracting with

---

[10] As a practical matter, this conversion does not have to be made literally if other equally effective portfolio changes can be made at lower costs. For example, some combination of options and futures market transactions executed at the time of the benefit accrual freeze might protect the insurance carrier during the period in which the insured's funding deficiency is corrected.

the insurance firm to increase exposure. The plan may ask the insurance company to permit the plan to increase its exposure to some higher level. If the insurance company does not perceive a moral hazard problem—for example, the firm's financial condition and future prospects appear sound—higher exposure may be permitted, just as insureds may obtain higher life insurance coverage, subject to acceptance by the insurance company (usually in conjunction with a medical exam or other medical information). In some cases, the insurance company may permit the additional exposure with restrictions; for example, it might permit more underfunding exposure in exchange for a temporary lien on real property to last, say, three years.

Exposure Calculation

The discussion thus far suggests that underfunding (per plan per participant) for purposes of determining a premium is calculated as follows:

$$U^* = L^*(1-c) - A(1-g) \qquad (10\text{–}1)$$

where

A = Current trust assets at market value
L^* = Termination liabilities evaluated by using a 1 percent (or lower) interest rate, and other assumptions subject to insurance company restrictions
c = Coinsurance factor, equal to .5
g = Maximum permitted defunding (percent of assets), equal to .2

The funding ratio for the purpose of paying premiums is denoted by F^*:

$$F^* = A\,(1-g)/L^*\,(1-c) \qquad (10\text{–}2)$$

Funding levels for premium calculations under this insurance policy are approximated in Table 10–5 for the population of pension plans in 1986. Because the numbers are derived from Form 5500 data, I could not exactly recalculate retiree liabilities to conform to the indexed policy.[11] To approximate, I recalculated active participant liabilities at a 1 percent discount rate, reduced by a 50 percent coinsurance factor. I included 100 percent of termination liabilities for current retirees,

[11] In my carrier's insurance policy, benefits for retirees are recalculated in real terms as of their retirement date, reduced by half, and then indexed to death. Because the age distribution and retirement ages are not given in the Form 5500 data, these recalculations could not be made.

TABLE 10–5 Distribution of Exposure Levels

Funding Ratios (%) $A(1-g)/L^*(1-c)$	*Plans†*	*Participants*
100 or more	71.5%	69.9%
75–99	15.4	15.0
50–74	9.0	10.8
Less than 50	4.1	4.3
Average: 110		

L^* denotes vested liabilities, discounted at 1 percent; A denotes trust assets; g is percent of permissible defunding (set equal to .2); and c is the coinsurance factor (set equal to .5).

†Excludes plans with fewer than 100 participants.

SOURCE: 1984 Form 5500 Annual Pension Plan Reports.

discounted at 7.25 percent. This treatment of retirees is a proxy for calculation of their liabilities in real terms and reducing these by 50 percent.

The numbers in the table demonstrate that at the announced levels of permitted defunding ($g=.2$) and coinsurance ($c=.5$), 70 percent of all plans would pose no exposure for purposes of calculating the premium for the policy discussed above (beyond that affiliated with asset volatility—see below); 15.4 percent of plans would have up to 25 percent of their insurable benefits unfunded; and 13.1 percent of plans would have more than 25 percent of insurable benefits unfunded.

Administration of Insurance

Given the moral hazard potential in the insurance, the monitoring and reporting costs inherent in maintaining control of the insurance can be large. My hypothetical carrier will minimize these costs by requiring insureds to make the insurance company the administrator of the fund. Competition among carriers and/or constraints in the contract will ensure that the administrative cost will not be excessive.[12] The carrier will maintain all liability data, pay benefits, file annual reports to the government, etc. The carrier will also electronically or manually monitor all transactions with the custodial bank and retain authority to impose all constraints required to effect a plan freeze under conditions set forth in the contract (see above).

In this way, the insurance company has all the data required to operate the plan. It can calculate liabilities in the plans by using

[12]A new contract can be signed, say, annually. If a carrier tries to increase administrative cost assessments, the insured is free to shop for a new insurer. If a longer-term contract is beneficial to both parties, some limit in the range of administrative costs can be specified. The range can be indexed to some industry measure of various cost components.

insurance company assumptions and can continuously monitor the market value and portfolio composition of trust assets. It therefore is able to monitor funding levels: if the defunding rule is broken, the insurance firm can ensure that the accrual freeze procedure is enforced.

By having the insurance company administer the fund, monitoring costs of the insurance are substantially reduced, and, in the event of a claim, no time is lost or cost imposed owing to requirements to audit plan records to set benefit levels. The plan sponsor loses no flexibility in the plan. It can still set funding levels (subject to defunding rules), choose its portfolio, and set benefit levels. Because the insurance firm administers the plan, however, it is aware of the plan's financial characteristics and condition and can implement insurance rules without impediments created by imperfect and untimely information passing from the plan sponsor to the insurance firm.[13]

ADJUSTMENTS FOR PORTFOLIO RISK

The insurance company faces risks even if all insureds retain sufficiently high funding ratios, so in a typical time period, guaranteed exposure levels are zero. The problem arises because of volatility in asset values. The easiest way to think about this is to suppose all insureds have target funding ratios of 100 percent of guaranteed benefits; and there is no problem of defunding prior to termination (g=0). To make the numbers easy, suppose assets equal 100.

Factors Affecting Risk

Table 10–6 illustrates a highly stylized example. Each of four pension plans holds 100 percent funding ratios against insured benefits, and each has chosen to invest 100 percent in a single class of securities: one in the Standard & Poor's 500 stock index, one in a small stock index, one in long-term bonds, and one in Treasury bills. We will follow these portfolios for only one period, so it is convenient and inconsequential to ignore interest and dividend accruals. It is assumed that insured benefits are indexed and that expected rates of return on investments are constant.

It is assumed that the small stock index has a *beta value* of two relative to the S&P. This means that if the S&P 500 index falls by 10

[13]The possibility must also be entertained that firms in growing financial trouble may have incentives to misrepresent reportable information to the insurance firm. Because Congress probably would not permit workers to accept insurance losses beyond those specified in the coinsurance clause and a court claim may not be paid in full in bankruptcy proceedings, the onus is on the insurance carrier to maintain direct monitoring of pension funds.

TABLE 10–6 Illustration of Portfolio Risk

Portfolio	*Initial Value*	*S&P Stock Index Falls 50 Percent*	*Inflation Doubles*
1. 100% S&P index (Beta=1)	100	50	100*
2. 100% small stocks (Beta=2)	100	0	100
3. 100% long bonds (infinite horizon)	100	100	50
4. 100% T-bills	100	100	100

*For the sake of the example, it is assumed that inflation effects on stock prices net out to zero.

percent, the small stock index falls by 20 percent. If, after our initial snapshot (when premiums are assessed in these plans), the S&P index falls by 50 percent, the insurance company has exposure equal to 50 in the S&P stock portfolio and to 100 percent in the small stock portfolio. I assume that interest rates are stable during this period, so that exposure in the bond and T-bill portfolios remains at 100.

Now suppose stock values are stable, but the inflation rate doubles. And, for simplicity, assume the long bonds have infinite lives and real interest rates are zero. This makes it easy to calculate that long-bond values will be reduced by 50 percent.[14] The insurance company faces exposure equal to 50. Once again, the T-bill portfolio remains at 100: higher inflation rates merely translate to higher interest rates in each succeeding T-bill turnover, and hence no capital losses are sustained. Thus, in portfolios comprised of stocks and bonds, exposure to the insurance carrier can increase owing to volatility of the underlying value of these securities.

It is tempting to think that the exposure calculations are symmetric; that in riskier portfolios, exposure can fall as well as increase. But this is only partially correct. First, increases in asset values do not always benefit the insurance company. This is illustrated in Table 10–6. If either of the portfolios doubles from 100 to 200, the exposure of the insurance firm would still be zero. That is, if a termination occurs when insurance plans have surpluses, the insurance company does not receive a portion of the excess.

Second, the probability of firm failure (and thus a claim) is not independent of market conditions. If stock market values double, fewer firms are likely to fail; if stock values decrease by 50 percent, more firms are likely to fail.

[14]The price of an infinitely lived bond is $1/i$, where i is the interest rate. Thus, if the interest rate doubles, bond values fall by 50 percent.

Third, when portfolios have lots of volatility, the probability of insolvency of the insurance firm increases. If stock values decrease by 50 percent and remain there for several periods, the cumulative claims by more highly exposed plans can threaten the insurance company's solvency. Thus, insuring more volatile portfolios requires higher returns to insurance company investors and larger reserve requirements, which translate to higher premium requirements.[15]

These arguments suggest that the rate structure must reflect portfolio risk. When the pension plan portfolio comprises only T-bills, this risk is essentially zero: the beta value is zero, and exposure to inflation risk is virtually zero. As the insured holds higher beta portfolios or portfolios with higher shares of long-term bonds, the risk of higher exposure increases, which in turn should be reflected in premium rates.

Calculations of Additional Exposure

Calculation of portfolio exposure requires analysis of portfolio volatility over time. For example, the average level of beta and long-bond share held by pension plans during the years 1977 through 1983 were .5 and 54 percent, respectively.[16] Column 1 in Table 10–7 shows the volatility in ongoing funding ratios for the average of all plans over the 1960–87 period. The largest reduction in funding ratios (34 percentage points) occurred from 1972 to 1974, when funding ratios fell on average from 86 percent to 52 percent. The three-year cumulative reduction in funding ratios occurred during the same period (29 percentage points from 1972 through 1975).

Consider the portfolio exposure presented by the funding ratio volatility in the table. Suppose the portfolio for the typical pension over the entire period exhibited a beta equal to .5 and bond share equal to 54 percent. Suppose further that the insurance policy was written against ongoing liabilities subject to a 25 percent coinsurance factor; also assume that the defunding factor (g) is zero. This means funding ratios for insured benefits (column 2) are 133 percent higher than the ongoing ratios (owing to the 25 percent coinsurance factor). The funding ratios for insured benefits are shown in column 2 of Table 10–7.

The average insured funding level is 100 percent. But this does not mean no exposure is experienced over the period. In 11 of the 28 years shown, exposure was positive primarily because of market asset

[15]The insurance firm's insolvency probability can be reduced through a surcharge-rebate system with the insurance group (see above), but the cost of operating this system must be assigned to portfolios that pose more portfolio risk.

[16]The beta value describes the entire pension portfolio, including bonds, not just stock. See Ippolito and Turner, 1987.

TABLE 10–7 Portfolio Exposure, 1960–1987

	Funding Ratios		
Year	*Ongoing* *(1)*	*With 25 Percent Coinsurance* *(2)*	*Exposure* *(3)*
1960	72%	96%	4%
1961	77	102	0
1962	70	93	7
1963	76	101	0
1964	80	106	0
1965	80	106	0
1966	74	98	2
1967	77	102	0
1968	82	109	0
1969	71	94	6
1970	75	100	0
1971	81	108	0
1972	86	114	0
1973	67	89	11
1974	52	69	31
1975	63	84	16
1976	74	98	2
1977	72	96	4
1978	65	86	14
1979	69	92	8
1980	84	111	0
1981	77	102	0
1982	85	113	0
1983	92	122	0
1984	95	126	0
1985	88	117	0
1986	90	119	0
1987	102	136	0
Average	75%	100%	3.5%

Note: Funding ratios calculated at beginning of plan year, usually January 1.

SOURCE: 1953–1984, Richard Ippolito and Walter Kolodrubetz, *The Handbook of Pension Statistics, 1985* (Chicago: Commerce Clearing House, 1986). After 1984, Wyatt Company, *1986 Survey of Actuarial Assumptions and Funding* (Washington, D.C.: 1987).

volatility, particularly over the 1973–79 period (see column 3 of Table 10–7 and Figure 10–1). On average, exposure was 3.5 percent of insured liabilities. Thus, in this example, systematic exposure (E) is zero and market exposure (say, M) is $.035L^*$, where L^* denotes insured liabilities.

The above example assumes zero systematic exposure on average. Portfolio volatility exposure would be lower for plans that have higher funding ratios. In the above example, if the coinsurance factor had been 50 percent, the average funding ratio for insured benefits would be 150 percent. There would have been no portfolio exposure to the insurance

FIGURE 10–1 Changing Funding Ratios, 1960–1987

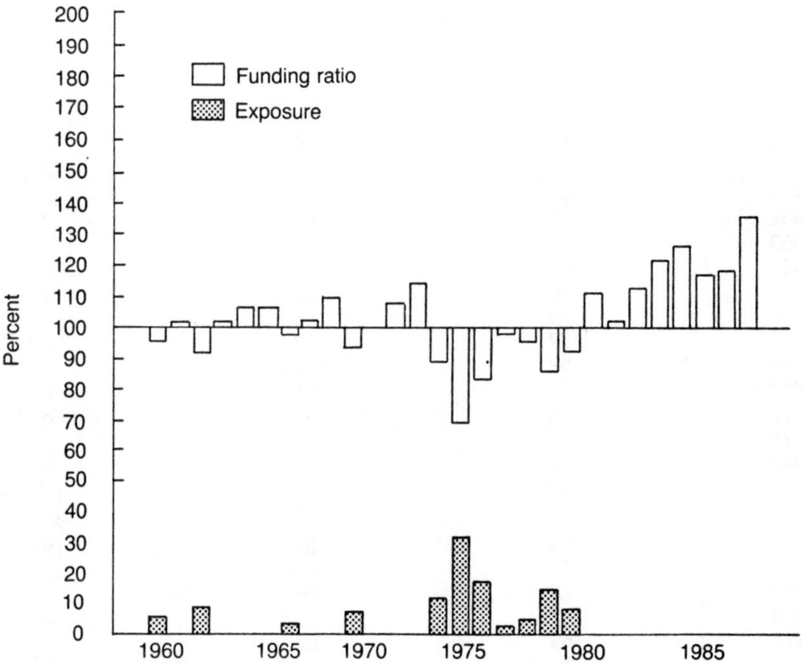

carrier over the entire 28-year period shown in the table because a sufficient cushion would have existed to protect against asset volatility in all years. For example, in 1974, when the ongoing funding ratio was at its lowest level, the funding ratio for insured benefits with a 50 percent coinsurance feature would have been 104 percent.

In general, a series of exposure tables would be created to calculate historical values of market exposure (M). The level of exposure would be a function of portfolio risk characteristics and average funding levels in the insured's pension plan portfolio.[17]

In essence, the insurance carrier is offering a kind of portfolio insurance, except the insurance applies only to plans if they terminate. The carrier will protect its position by continually buying options to sell equity securities in the futures market.[18] The cost of insurance will reflect the price of these options denoted, say, by y.[19]

[17] For a more detailed treatment of this issue, see Marcus, 1983.

[18] This is distinct from some versions of "portfolio insurance" designed to transact in the futures market at some future date, conditional on values of predetermined market variables.

[19] Because the carrier will not be entirely able to hedge its risks, some limit to portfolio exposure will likely be part of the contract.

Rate formula. Assuming all portfolio risks can be hedged, we can now write the premium formula that characterizes an insurance policy:

$$P = qU^* + yM(U^*,R) \tag{10–3}$$

where

P = Per participant premium
q = Probability of default
U^* = Systematic per participant exposure defined in Equation (10–1)
M = Exposure presented by asset value volatility, conditional on U^* and portfolio risk characteristics (R)[20]
y = Cost of holding hedging instruments, per dollar of market exposure

THE INSURABLE EVENT

A prominent feature of the premium charge is the probability for filing a claim, denoted by q. As discussed in previous chapters, the definition of the insurable event has changed somewhat over time. Prior to the enactment of the Single Employer Pension Plan Amendments Act (SEPPAA) in 1986, a claim could be filed by any plan sponsor willing to trade plan underfunding for 30 percent of net worth. SEPPAA constrained the event to be related to one of four distress criteria, including Chapter 7 or Chapter 11 of the Bankruptcy Code, or demonstration that the firm will fail unless the pension is terminated, or that the sole reason for funding deterioration is the contraction of an industry (see Chapter 5). The Pension Protection Act of 1987 changed the Chapter 11 criterion to also require that in the absence of plan termination, reorganization would not be possible under Chapter 11.

While these changes have worked to constrain the insurable event, they still retain significant potential for moral hazard. Paying off claims outside of firm failure is akin to paying life insurance benefits to individuals who are in poor health but not necessarily fatally ill.

The application of sound insurance principles suggests the policy be paid off only on the condition of dissolution of the firm. If the firm continues in whole or part as the ongoing entity, the incentive remains for the insured to distort its behavior to obtain a transfer from the insurance firm.

[20]In the example demonstrated in Table 10–7, if U^* is zero, exposure from market volatility averaged 3.5 percent times liabilities; but if U^* was *negative* 50 percent (target funding ratio equals 150 percent), exposure from market volatility was zero over the time period considered. If the portfolio were invested entirely in Treasury bills, exposure from market volatility also would be zero.

A lesson from the PBGC's experience is that in the absence of strict requirements for firm failure, insureds will try to find ways to obtain payments from the insurance company to acquire transfers for subsidizing their operations, thereby giving them an advantage over their competitors. This advantage, in turn, invites other firms to engage in the same procedure. For these reasons, the insurable event in my hypothetical insurance carrier's contract will be approved by the courts of a filing under Chapter 7 of the U.S. Bankruptcy Code (or similar filings under state laws).[21]

The insurance company will be fully protected by this rule, but situations could arise in which workers would not be paid their pensions. I presume Congress will require workers to receive their guaranteed benefits regardless of disputes between the insurance company and the plan sponsor.

Consider the following example. A plan sponsor has assets in trust equal to insured benefits; after it encounters financial difficulty, the funding ratio falls to 80 percent. The insurance firm reacts by freezing accruals. This, in turn, triggers various protections for the insurance company (discussed above) that freeze the funded portion of guaranteed benefits at 80 percent. (These actions include conversion of the portfolio to Treasury bills and restriction of benefit payments to the guaranteed benefit level from the trust fund.)

Now suppose the firm makes no further contributions to the trust fund, so that ultimately funds available to pay the frozen benefits are insufficient by 20 percent. If the firm enters Chapter 7 of the Bankruptcy Code (dissolution), the insurance company will pay off the claim. But suppose the firm enters Chapter 11 (reorganization), and the pension obligations are dissolved by the bankruptcy court. The pension insurance is not paid off because the insurable event is not satisfied. But because of insufficiency in the terminated pension plan trust fund, workers will receive only 80 percent of their insured benefits.

Congress could solve this problem by requiring firms emerging from Chapter 11 of the Bankruptcy Code to bring their pension obligations with them. In the absence of a change in the law, the insurance carrier can address this problem in at least two ways.

The first option is to decrease insurance benefits by the amount of the underfunding (in this case, 20 percent) at the time of termination in Chapter 11. Workers thus suffer some reduction of benefits beyond their coinsurance portion, which is feasible if the overall coinsurance does not violate the limits which I assume will be set by Congress (see Table 10–1).

Second, the insurance policy could be written with collateral

[21]To prevent the potential for abuse, the language might specifically prohibit the firm from continuing as an ongoing entity, even after a Chapter 7 bankruptcy.

posted in an amount sufficient to pay for 20 percent defunding (plus some allowance to protect against asset volatility). In the event of default outside the insurable event, the insurance company would be fully protected, and workers would receive their full guaranteed benefits for all service credited prior to a pension freeze. The lien would become null and void on a successful filing under Chapter 7 of the Bankruptcy Code (or comparable filings under state law).[22]

THE ASSIGNED RISK POOL

In the insurance scheme described above, all insureds are assessed premiums determined in the free market, unless a price quotation below $200 per participant per year cannot be found for basic benefits coverage. In this event, these plans are put into an assigned risk pool, which is subsidized by those outside the pool. This subsidy, however, is reduced by application of special rules that apply to all plans entering the pool. These rules affect benefit levels and funding rules. The rules governing those in the pool are determined by the regulatory agency.

Special Benefit Limitations

When a plan enters the assigned risk pool in my hypothetical pension system, various rules are triggered to prevent the subsidization of exorbitant pension payments. In the proposal considered here, those paying the subsidy will not be required to subsidize benefits exceeding the average of those available in their own plans and will subsidize only payments made for retirement-age years.

More particularly, plans in the pool are constrained from making full benefits to any participant younger than age 62. Participants may receive benefits prior to this age, but only in amounts reflecting a full actuarial reduction. Moreover, the amount of full benefits to all participants in the plan is subject to a maximum payment equal to the average benefit payment (as a percentage of wage and service) paid by all insureds in the system (adjusted to an age-62 equivalent). Further, postretirement inflation adjustments made while plans are in the pool are limited by the average of all such adjustments in the entire sample of insureds.

Special Funding Rules

As long as insureds remain outside the pool, they may maintain low funding levels indefinitely. They are only precluded from defunding

---

[22] Ibid.

their plan according to rules set out by their insurance carrier. Once in the pool, however, special funding rules are triggered to amortize guaranteed liabilities calculated at the pool-constrained benefit levels.

Suppose a plan enters the pool with liabilities of $100 and assets of $50. Benefit restrictions while in the pool reduce liabilities to $80: the firm is required to amortize the remaining $30 deficiency over a reasonable period of time, say, 12 years. Moreover, normal cost contributions must be at least equal to those calculated to meet additional guaranteed accruals. Calculations must conform to assumptions as determined by the pool regulator; insured liabilities cannot be discounted by a rate in excess of 1 percent.

In addition, once a plan is in the pool, defunding (relative to overall funding levels) is not permitted. If a plan in the pool fails to make a required contribution or permits its funding ratio (indexed to overall funding ratios) to fall below the level it had at the time it entered the pool, all plan accruals are frozen, trust assets must be converted to 100 percent Treasury bills, and benefits are reduced to 50 percent of the pool-constrained benefits (indexed to prices). The freeze persists until the funding deficiencies are remedied by the plan sponsor.

Portfolio Exposure

To prevent plans in the pool from providing unreasonable volatility risks to those subsidizing the pool, plans entering the pool are required to alter their portfolios. The pool rules might require, for example, all portfolios to comprise at least one third Treasury bills; the beta value to be less than the median level for all insured plans; and the share and duration of its bond portfolios to be less than the median for all insured plans.

Termination While in the Pool

If a plan terminates in the pool, basic pool benefits will be indexed and reduced by a 50 percent coinsurance factor.

Participation in the Pool

To be eligible for the pool, firms must show they are unable to find a *basic benefits policy* (akin to the one in the pool) for less than $200. To enforce this, the pool price will not be set below $200 for any pool member. As long as the premium outside the pool is greater than $200, the plan remains in the pool.

Plans can voluntarily exit the pool if they are willing to pay the free market premium. Thus, if the market premium for a plan is $300 per participant, the plan may elect to pay the premium instead of con-

TABLE 10–8 Special Rules for the Assigned Risk Pool

1. Participation	Entitled to participate if insured cannot find insurance for a basic benefits policy for less than $200 per person per year May voluntarily remain outside the pool by paying premiums in excess of $200
2. Price	$200 per participant per year
3. Benefits	Full benefits payable no earlier than age 62. Benefits are the lower of plan benefits or average benefits payable in all pension plans (adjusted to age-62 retirement age)
4. Funding	Minimum funding rules are altered to require contributions based on wage projection (even in flat benefit formulas); the net discount rate cannot exceed 1 percent. Existing underfunding is amortized over 12 years.
5. Termination benefit	If an insurable event occurs to a pool-insured plan, the insurance benefit is equal to the basic pool benefit, reduced by 50 percent, and indexed to the lower of prices or T-bills.

tinuing in the pool. In this event, the plan is subject to whatever rules are set by their insurance carrier. (Rules for the assigned risk pool are summarized in Table 10–8.)

CONCLUSION

In this chapter, an attempt was made to build a pension insurance system that incorporated economic principles and reflected the experience of the Pension Benefit Guaranty Corporation. The proposal is not unique; other equally efficient or better proposals could be developed. It accepts the constraints that the insurance at some level is mandatory and that some maximum premium must characterize the system.

The proposal minimizes the impact on pension plans in firms that pose little risk by (1) permitting pension plans to choose among various insurance policies and (2) minimizing the subsidy to plans that provide lots of exposure and risk. The latter objective is attained by creating an assigned risk pool, akin to casualty insurance, to be populated by plans that cannot find insurance against basic benefits for an annual premium less than $200 per participant in 1985 dollars and are unwilling to pay more. Pool members are subject to a basic benefits package; pension payments cannot exceed average industry benefit payments starting at age 62. They are also subject to special portfolio and funding rules while in the pool.

The insurance policy of the hypothetical carrier described herein pays a benefit set in real terms, reduced by some coinsurance factor. This means regardless of the nominal interest rate, workers of all ages receive a real indexed insured benefit, reduced by a factor of 50 percent. Compared to ongoing benefits in 1986 (which are less than completely indexed), this policy incorporates a roughly 30 percent coinsurance factor for active participants and 15 percent for retirees.

The indexing feature of the insured benefit limits the coinsurance factor. This policy is important in my hypothetical carrier's policy because to protect itself and workers from wholesale defunding by plan sponsors, a pension plan is frozen if its funding level (indexed to average funding ratios in all plans) falls by more than 20 percent. On a freeze, benefits are automatically reduced to the insured level, and the portfolio is converted to 100 percent Treasury bills. Insurance protection is denied to any defined benefit plan created after a freeze. While this procedure freezes future accruals, all workers are assured of absorbing only approximately 30 percent of their expected benefits on termination. My hypothetical assigned risk pool pays the same type of insured benefit if termination occurs while in the pool. The coinsurance factor for these workers and retirees is applied to the basic benefit levels permitted by the pool.

How is the transition made from the existing pension insurance program to a system like the one described above? One way is to make an immediate conversion as of some retrospective date. This would deny huge transfers to perhaps hundreds of plans that have queued at the proverbial PBGC transfer window. Rather than close the window completely and immediately, Congress could give all existing plans the right to qualify for the insurance under the old rules. To qualify, however, the plan must be terminated at the time the new legislation is enacted.

All future service (plus inflation indexing of past service) must be financed by a new plan. The new plan would be covered by the new pension insurance rules. Existing funding rules would continue to apply to the terminated plans.

This transfer rule would have little impact on firms at the front of the PBGC queue. Those further back (that is, those who otherwise would receive transfers in future years) would receive smaller real transfers because inflation will erode the value of benefits frozen at their nominal levels at the transfer date. To reduce moral hazard, a five-year cliff guarantee rule would be imposed to prevent firms from trying to increase benefits in the old plan prior to the conversion date. Alternatively, a retrospective date for the freeze could be chosen.

Suppose expected annual claims against the PBGC are $600 million per year (see Chapter 6). If claims will increase at the rate of 8 percent per year owing to wage increases, and if the long-term interest rate is 10 percent, then claims are discounted at a net 2 percent. Thus, the present value of claims of the existing system in 1987 is $30 billion in real terms. If claims' levels are frozen in nominal terms, the claims are discounted at the full 10 percent (wage growth is zero). The present value of claims is then reduced to $6 billion. Thus, the freeze reduces the cost of the existing system by 80 percent but promises sufficient transfers to those in the front of the queue, to reduce intense political opposition to the new scheme.

The $6 billion transfer would be financed by a one-time lump-sum exit tax on all participants on the day of the transfer. In exchange for approximately $240 per head (there are roughly 25 million participants in single-employer defined benefit plans), firms gain the opportunity to operate defined benefit plans with fewer government constraints and lower subsidy payments.

PART FOUR

Appendixes

APPENDIX A

Statistical Tables

Number	Description	Page
	Labor force statistics	
A–1	Trends in Employment and Wages	208
A–2	Employment in Small and Large Establishments	209
	Defined benefit plans	
A–3	Growth of Participants in Insured Defined Benefit Plans	209
A–4	Pension Plan Terminations and Formations	210
A–5	Distribution of Plans, by Industry	211
A–6	Distribution of Plans, by Size	212
A–7	Distribution of Termination Funding Ratios, 1978–1986	212
A–8	Distribution of Ongoing Funding Ratios, 1978–1986	213
A–9	Reversions in Excess of $1 Million, 1980–1987	213
	Insurance claims	
A–10	Claims Experience: Single-Employer Program	214
A–11	Distribution of Net Claims by Size, 1986	214
A–12	PBGC Financial Summary: Single-Employer Fund, 1974–1987	215
A–13	Largest 100 Claims Excluding LTV, 1974–1987	215
	Benefit payments	
A–14	Participants in Pay Status	219
A–15	Maximum Monthly Benefits, by Year	220
	Investment returns	
A–16	Stock Price Indexes, 1950–1986	221
A–17	Long-Term Bond Rates	222
A–18	Treasury Bill Rates (3 months)	223

TABLE A–1 Trends in Employment and Wages

	Employment*		Nominal Wage†		CPI		
Year	Number	Percent Change	Hourly	Percent Change	Index	Percent Change	Real Wage Change
1950	58.9	2.2%	$1.33	3.7%	72.1	1.0%	2.7%
1951	59.9	1.6	1.45	7.5	77.8	7.9	−.4
1952	60.2	.5	1.52	5.1	79.5	2.2	2.9
1953	61.1	1.4	1.61	5.6	80.1	.8	4.8
1954	60.1	−1.6	1.65	3.3	80.5	.5	2.8
1955	62.1	3.3	1.71	3.5	80.2	−.4	3.9
1956	63.7	2.5	1.80	4.9	81.4	1.5	3.4
1957	64.1	.6	1.89	5.0	84.3	3.6	1.4
1958	63.0	−1.7	1.95	4.2	86.6	2.7	1.5
1959	64.6	2.5	2.02	3.5	87.3	.8	2.7
1960	65.7	1.7	2.09	3.4	88.7	1.6	1.8
1961	65.7	0.0	2.14	3.0	89.6	1.0	2.0
1962	66.7	1.5	2.22	3.4	90.6	1.1	2.3
1963	67.7	1.4	2.28	2.8	91.7	1.2	1.6
1964	69.3	2.3	2.36	2.8	92.9	1.3	1.5
1965	71.1	2.5	2.46	3.6	94.5	1.7	1.9
1966	72.8	2.3	2.56	4.3	97.2	2.9	1.4
1967	74.3	2.1	2.68	5.0	100.0	2.9	2.1
1968	75.9	2.1	2.85	6.1	104.2	4.2	1.9
1969	77.9	2.6	3.04	6.7	109.8	5.4	1.3
1970	78.6	.9	3.23	6.6	116.3	5.9	0.7
1971	79.3	.8	3.45	7.2	121.3	4.3	2.9
1972	82.1	3.5	3.70	6.2	125.3	3.3	2.9
1973	85.0	3.5	3.94	6.2	133.1	6.2	0.0
1974	86.7	2.0	4.24	8.0	147.7	11.0	−3.0
1975	85.8	−1.0	4.53	8.4	161.2	9.1	−.7
1976	88.7	3.5	4.86	7.2	170.5	5.8	1.4
1977	92.0	3.7	5.25	7.6	181.5	6.5	1.1
1978	96.0	4.3	5.69	8.2	195.4	7.7	.5
1979	98.8	2.9	6.16	7.9	217.4	11.3	−3.4
1980	99.3	.5	6.66	9.0	246.8	13.5	−4.5
1981	100.4	1.1	7.25	9.1	272.4	10.4	−1.3
1982	99.5	−.8	7.68	6.9	289.1	6.1	.8
1983	100.8	1.3	8.02	4.6	298.4	3.2	1.4
1984	105.0	4.1	8.32	3.2	311.1	4.3	−1.1
1985	107.1	2.0	8.57	3.1	322.2	3.6	−.5
1986	109.5	2.2	8.76	2.4	328.4	1.9	.5
1987	112.4	2.6	8.98	2.5	340.4	3.6	−1.1
Annualized		1.7%		5.1%		4.1%	1.07%

*Civilian work force, in millions.

†Private, nonagricultural.

SOURCE: *Economic Report of the President,* 1988.

TABLE A–2 Employment in Small and Large Establishments (absolute numbers in millions)

		Workers per Establishment			
		Number		*Percent*	
Year	*Total*	*1–99*	*1,000+*	*1–99*	*1,000+*
1974	63.4	33.3	10.1	52.5%	15.9%
1975	60.4	32.6	9.3	53.9	15.3
1976	62.5	33.9	9.2	54.2	14.7
1977	64.9	35.4	9.4	54.5	14.4
1978	70.2	38.3	10.1	54.5	14.3
1979	74.5	40.3	10.9	54.0	14.6
1980	74.8	40.6	10.7	54.2	14.3
1981	74.7	40.7	10.6	54.4	14.1
1982	74.2	41.0	10.4	55.2	14.0
1983	72.8	40.9	10.0	56.2	13.7
1984	77.9	43.6	10.4	55.9	13.3
1985	81.1	45.3	10.4	55.8	12.8

SOURCE: U.S. Census, *County Business Patterns, Annual Summary*, 1986.

TABLE A–3 Growth in Participants in Insured Defined Benefits Plans (absolute numbers in millions)

	Participants per Plan							
	1–99		*100–999*		*>999*		*Total*	
Year	*Number*	*Percent Change*	*Number*	*Percent Change*	*Number*	*Percent Change*	*Number*	*Percent Change*
1974	1.25	—	4.28	—	17.3	—	22.9	—
1975	1.38	9.9%	4.68	9.1%	18.8	8.6%	24.9	8.7%
1976	1.42	3.0	4.86	3.8	19.4	3.2	25.6	3.1
1977	1.43	.8	4.90	.8	18.7	−3.6	25.0	−2.4
1978	1.41	−1.6	4.98	1.5	18.8	0.5	25.2	.5
1979	1.46	3.5	5.25	5.4	19.8	5.3	26.5	5.4
1980	1.59	8.8	5.49	4.5	21.0	6.0	28.1	5.7
1981	1.63	2.0	5.64	2.8	21.8	3.8	29.1	3.7
1982	1.69	3.9	5.77	2.2	22.2	1.8	29.6	1.8
1983	1.72	1.8	5.76	−.2	22.5	1.3	30.0	1.1
1984	1.69	−1.8	5.69	−1.1	22.8	1.3	30.2	.8
1985	1.60	−5.2	5.68	−.4	23.3	2.1	30.6	1.3
1986	1.58	−1.2	5.58	−1.8	23.8	2.1	31.0	1.3

Note: Percent calculations may not correspond precisely to absolute numbers owing to rounding of absolute number.

SOURCE: PBGC Premium Payers database.

TABLE A–4 Pension Plan Terminations and Formations (participant numbers in thousands)

	Defined Benefit			Defined Contribution			DB : DC (Columns)		
	Formations		Terminations	Formations		Terminations			
Year	Plans (1)	People (2)	Plans (3)	Plans (4)	People (5)	Plans (6)	1 : 4 (7)	2 : 5 (8)	3 : 6 (9)
1975	15,549	627	4,588	17,038	166	3,598	.9	3.7	1.3
1976	4,889	279	9,024	21,030	813	6,889	.2	.3	1.3
1977	6,953	1,639	5,337	28,463	3,315	10,478	.2	.5	.5
1978	9,728	1,125	4,625	55,956	2,754	10,661	.2	.4	.4
1979	15,755	972	3,267	41,122	1,050	7,574	.4	.9	.4
1980	18,849	1,784	4,297	50,493	1,997	8,982	.4	.9	.5
1981	23,789	2,185	4,536	57,748	1,302	8,906	.4	1.6	.5
1982	28,189	1,324	5,043	57,162	1,428	10,108	.5	.9	.5
1983	22,130	1,946	7,230	42,089	1,927	11,417	.5	1.0	.6
1984	12,807	1,335	9,153	28,279	4,345	11,019	.5	.3	.8
1985	17,267	806	12,215	30,355	3,265	13,819	.6	.2	.9
1986	22,076	5,036	10,724	45,061	3,168	14,612	.5	1.6	.7
1987	12,778	4,597	6,584	29,935	8,498	9,318	.4	.5	.7

SOURCE: Internal Revenue Service qualifications data.

TABLE A–5 Distribution of Plans, by Industry

Industry	*Vesteds*	*Funding Ratio*	*Liabilities per Vested*
Manufacturing	59.4%		
Food and kindred products	3.5%	138.7%	$27,810
Textile mill products	1.3	137.7	9,165
Apparel and other textiles	.6	133.5	9,300
Lumber and wood products	.7	152.0	13,086
Paper and allied products	2.6	118.9	26,268
Printing and publishing	1.7	149.2	24,296
Chemical and allied products	5.6	147.7	42,121
Petroleum refining	2.6	145.1	60,969
Rubber and plastics	1.4	135.9	32,417
Leather products	.5	125.2	10,345
Stone, clay, glass, and concrete	1.5	123.1	31,337
Ferrous metals (steel)	3.9	111.1	59,925
Nonferrous metals	.6	130.1	47,468
Fabricated metal products	3.7	130.7	27,517
Machinery (not electrical)	5.2	134.2	34,890
Electrical and electronic machinery	7.7	142.9	30,546
Motor vehicles (auto)	10.7	127.9	48,296
Other transportation equipment	2.9	141.7	36,084
Instruments, photo, medical, etc.	2.7	145.4	29,969
Agriculture, forestry, fishing	.2	145.6	24,729
Mining	.7	170.7	31,125
Construction	.4	159.0	25,513
Transportation, communications, utilities	13.4	148.3	51,612
Wholesale trade	.9	162.3	18,850
Retail trade	5.8	152.5	11,060
Finance, insurance, real estate	7.8	178.0	35,528
Services	5.8	172.7	15,902
Tax-exempt organizations	1.3	163.7	31,498
Other	4.3	N/A	N/A
Total (weighted)	100.0%	148.9%	$35,183

SOURCE: 1984 Form 5500 Annual Pension Plan Reports, projected to 1986.

TABLE A–6 Distribution of Plans, by Size (percent)

Size†	*Plans*	*Participants*	*Assets*	*Liabilities**	*Funding Ratio*
Less than 250	33.7%	3.0%	1.7%	1.7%	131%
250–499	24.2	4.7	2.6	2.6	129
500–999	17.4	6.4	4.0	3.8	130
1,000–2,499	14.1	10.8	7.8	7.2	134
2,500–4,999	5.1	8.8	7.7	7.3	132
5,000–9,999	2.8	10.0	9.5	8.8	133
10,000–24,999	1.7	13.8	14.6	14.5	124
25,000 or more	1.0	42.5	52.1	54.1	119
Total	100.0%	100.0%	100.0%	100.0%	124%

*Liabilities converted to 7.25 percent interest rate.

†Participants per plan.

SOURCE: Form 5500 Annual Pension Plan Reports, 1984, projected to 1986.

TABLE A–7 Distribution of Termination Funding Ratios, 1978–1986 (dollars in billions)

	Percent Participants								
Funding Ratio	*1978*	*1979*	*1980*	*1981*	*1982*	*1983*	*1984*	*1985*	*1986 (est.)*
0–24%	.8%	.8%	2.4%	.3%	.3%	.3%	.3%	.3%	.3%
25–49	8.8	9.7	3.8	2.6	2.5	2.0	1.6	1.8	2.6
50–74	14.2	16.0	11.5	8.3	8.0	7.6	2.8	3.7	8.3
75–99	24.6	26.5	17.1	10.4	9.3	6.7	9.0	9.5	10.8
100–124	25.5	25.8	22.9	14.1	14.2	13.4	10.1	11.7	16.3
125–149	14.9	11.7	22.1	20.1	19.5	18.2	12.2	16.5	18.5
150+	11.1	9.2	22.0	44.1	46.1	51.7	63.8	56.4	43.2
Average	92.9%	88.5%	107.2%	128.8%	130.9%	139.2%	153.9%	145.6%	128.5%
Underfunding ($1986)*	$116.7	$126.0	$73.0	$42.1	$39.5	$35.8	$25.9	$31.8	$49.2
Interest rate†	7.25%	7.50	8.75	10.25	10.75	9.25	10.00	9.75	7.75

*Exposure is adjusted to 1986 dollars and size of pension universe. Funding ratios are calculated for each year using a constant 2 percent discount rate. Assets in year *t* are then set equal to assets in 1986 times the real funding ratio in year *t* divided by the same ratio in 1986. Liabilities in year *t* are set equal to those in 1986 but adjusted to the PBGC immediate annuity rates shown in the table.

†Average PBGC immediate annuity rate during year.

SOURCE: Form 5500 Annual Pension Plan Reports.

TABLE A–8 Distribution of Ongoing Funding Ratios, 1978–1986 (dollars in billions)

	Percent Participants								
Funding Ratio	*1978*	*1979*	*1980*	*1981*	*1982*	*1983*	*1984*	*1985*	*1986 (est.)*
0–24%	2.8%	3.3%	2.4%	2.0%	2.0%	.9%	.8%	.9%	.9%
25–49	16.5	22.2	15.3	13.1	13.2	10.4	10.0	10.1	10.1
50–74	36.4	39.5	34.9	27.5	27.6	18.6	16.9	17.1	16.8
75–99	30.2	25.6	31.1	32.1	33.2	29.3	27.3	28.1	27.3
100–124	9.1	6.1	10.6	16.4	16.4	24.4	25.6	25.1	25.6
125–149	2.6	2.0	3.0	5.2	5.1	9.8	11.2	11.0	11.2
150+	2.4	1.3	2.7	3.8	3.6	6.5	8.0	7.6	8.0
Average	65.3%	60.3%	67.3%	74.4%	74.1%	84.3%	87.5%	86.5%	87.2%
Underfunding ($1986)*	$343.0	$387.5	$325.8	$268.5	$272.4	$203.5	$187.6	$191.3	$189.3

*Underfunding is adjusted to 1986 dollars and size of pension universe, as described in notes to Table A–7, except liabilities in all years are fixed at 1986 levels.

SOURCE: Form 5500 Annual Pension Plan Reports.

TABLE A–9 Reversions in Excess of $1 Million, 1980–1987 (dollars in millions)

Year	*Number of Plans*	*Assets*	*Benefits*	*Reversion*	*Participants*
1980	9	$ 58	$ 40	$ 18	22,242
1981	35	341	183	159	30,512
1982	82	1,136	733	404	123,587
1983	166	3,431	1,823	1,608	168,549
1984	331	7,426	3,862	3,564	382,188
1985	580	15,060	8,393	6,666	693,553
1986	263	8,918	4,630	4,287	262,255
1987	169	3,706	2,279	1,426	159,822
Total	1,635	$40,079	$21,945	$18,134	1,842,708

SOURCE: PBGC, *Annual Report,* 1987.

TABLE A–10 Claims Experience: Single-Employer Program (dollars in millions)

Fiscal Year	*Number of Plans*	*Guaranteed Benefit Liability*	*Plan Assets*	*Funding Ratio*	*Employer Liability*	*Claims Total*	*Claims per Plan*
1975	98	$ 56	$ 19	34%	$ 4	$ 32	$0.3
1976	172	88	45	51	25	18	0.1
1977	129	51	21	40	8	23	0.2
1978	102	125	46	37	7	72	0.7
1979	78	81	32	40	4	45	0.6
1980	100	166	77	46	5	84	0.8
1981	135	178	75	42	27	76	0.6
1982	128	461	174	38	7	280	2.2
1983	140	408	224	55	10	174	1.2
1984	90	47	20	42	1	27	0.3
1985	88	262	75	29	4	183	2.1
1986	86	1,140	375	33	193	573	6.7
1987	30	153	48	32	1	104	3.5
Pending 1987	29	663	346	52	6	312	N/A
Total	1,405	$3,880	$1,576	41%	$300	$2,003	N/A
(Steel Plans)	(183)	(2,110)	(727)	(34%)	(217)	(1,165)	(6.4)

Note: Date for 1986 does not include claims made by LTV Corporation for pension plans later restored by the PBGC.

SOURCE: PBGC, *Annual Report,* 1987.

TABLE A–11 Distribution of Net Claims by Size, 1986 (dollars in millions)

	Guaranteed Benefit Liability		*Net Claim (event basis)**	
Size	*Plans*	*Liability*	*Events*	*Claims*
Greater than $100	9	$4,708	5	$2,788
$50–100	8	518	6	351
$25–50	20	662	7	254
$10–25	23	369	10	134
$5–10	37	255	11	76
$2–5	73	234	41	131
$1–2	109	159	45	61
Less than $1	1,066	190	968	105
Total	1,345	$7,095	1,093	$3,900

* A single insurable event such as bankruptcy of plan sponsor may involve termination of several insufficient pension plans.

SOURCE: PBGC, *Annual Report,* 1986.

TABLE A–12 PBGC Financial Summary: Single-Employer Fund, 1975–1987 (dollars in millions)

Year	*Total Assets*	*Reserve for Guaranteed Benefits*	*Accumulated Results of Operations (loss)*	*Premium Income*
1987	$2,163.3	$3,629.3	($1,548.6)*	$267.6
1986	1,740.3	5,491.8	(3,826.4)	201.4
1985	1,154.6	2,447.0	(1,325.3)	81.7
1984	1,063.3	1,496.6	(462.0)	80.5
1983	1,084.9	1,570.0	(523.3)	81.5
1982	772.8	1,076.0	(332.8)	79.6
1981	467.4	673.0	(188.8)	75.0
1980	429.5	506.0	(94.6)	71.2
1979	332.3	460.0	(146.4)	69.7
1978	244.6	365.0	(137.8)	47.4
1977	175.8	260.0	(95.3)	25.1
1976	127.3	159.0	(41.0)	29.7
1975	56.6	58.3	(15.7)	18.5

*The reduction from 1986 to 1987 includes the restoration of three terminated plans to LTV Corporation. See Appendix D.

SOURCE: PBGC, *Annual Reports.*

TABLE A–13 Largest 100 Claims Excluding LTV*, 1974–1987 (dollars in millions)

Plan Name	*Date of Termination*§	*Plan Assets*	*Reserve for Guaranteed Benefits*	*Plan Underfunding*	*Funding Ratio*
WPSC†—Ohio Valley	11/08/85	$83.5	$339.0	$255.6	24.6%
Republic Steel	09/30/86	6.0	225.2	219.2	2.7
Kaiser Steel Hourly	07/28/87	27.9	228.9	201.0	12.2
Allis-Chalmers Hourly	07/26/85	2.3	176.1	173.8	1.3
WPSC†—Mon Valley	11/08/85	51.5	212.9	161.4	24.2
WPSC† Retirement Income	11/08/85	33.6	127.1	93.5	26.4
Rath Packing Co.	09/13/82	5.6	60.9	55.4	9.1
Wisconsin Steel Nonunion	05/16/80	32.3	87.6	55.3	36.9
White Motor Co. Cleveland Union	11/30/81	11.4	57.1	45.7	19.9
Alan Wood Steel Co. Hourly	11/01/77	7.0	41.8	34.8	16.8
Continental Steel	02/14/86	22.1	56.3	34.2	39.3
Mesta Machine Hourly	06/16/83	19.7	53.8	34.1	36.7
White Farm Hourly	09/14/82	5.2	37.9	32.7	13.6

TABLE A–13 *(continued)*

Plan Name	*Date of Termination*[§]	*Plan Assets*	*Reserve for Guaranteed Benefits*	*Plan Underfunding*	*Funding Ratio*
Kaiser Steel Salaried	02/28/87	0.0	31.5	31.5	0.0
Century Brass Products, Inc.	12/02/85	6.8	36.6	29.7	18.7
LTV—Reserve Mining Hourly‡	05/24/87	44.0	72.7	28.7	60.5
McLouth Steel Hourly	11/30/82	37.7	64.8	27.1	58.2
Allis-Chalmers —Salaried	12/17/87	177.0	202.3	25.3	87.5
Braniff Airways	08/23/82	10.9	36.0	25.1	30.2
Mansfield Tire & Rubber Co.	06/30/79	3.7	27.6	24.0	13.3
Phoenix Steel Claymont Union	08/22/83	3.8	26.6	22.8	14.4
Braniff Airways Teamsters Plan	08/23/82	7.6	29.6	21.9	25.8
Facet Enterprises Hourly	11/13/80	17.9	39.6	21.7	45.2
Penn Dixie Cement Hourly	05/10/81	4.1	23.5	19.4	17.4
White Motor Corp. Salaried	11/30/81	10.2	28.9	18.6	35.5
Auto Specialties Mfg. Unit	12/20/86	5.1	23.0	17.9	22.2
Phoenix Steel— Phoenixville	08/22/83	7.3	25.2	17.9	29.0
White Farm —Salaried	09/04/82	6.2	23.4	17.2	26.3
McLouth Steel —Salaried	11/30/82	15.1	30.0	15.0	50.2
City Stores, Inc.	10/27/80	0.1	15.0	14.9	0.6
Heppenstall Co. Hourly	05/31/79	0.2	14.1	13.9	1.1
Mackintosh— Hemphill	01/31/87	5.0	18.6	13.6	27.0
Chase Brass and Copper Co.	06/28/76	3.2	16.5	13.3	19.3
Washburn Wire	10/31/76	1.2	14.4	13.2	8.1
Braniff Airways, Management	08/23/82	18.8	31.4	12.6	59.9
Continental Steel Corp. Plan B	02/14/86	11.3	23.7	12.4	47.8
Dubuque Packing Co.	11/01/82	40.8	52.4	11.6	77.8
RBS Industries	10/10/86	8.6	19.9	11.3	43.0
Ingersoll Products Corp.	12/31/85	1.2	11.8	10.6	10.2
Diamond REO Trucks, UAW	05/31/75	1.4	11.4	9.9	12.6

TABLE A–13 (*continued*)

Plan Name	*Date of Termination*[§]	*Plan Assets*	*Reserve for Guaranteed Benefits*	*Plan Underfunding*	*Funding Ratio*
Alliance Machine Hourly	05/31/87	2.9	12.4	9.5	23.6
Lundberg, Industries	09/24/87	5.1	13.8	8.7	36.8
Rath Packing Co.	09/13/82	6.0	14.5	8.5	41.3
National Sugar Refining Co.	06/20/82	6.1	14.6	8.5	41.9
AM International	10/15/82	16.6	25.0	8.4	66.4
WPSC†—Monessen	11/08/85	6.8	15.2	8.4	45.0
LTV—Continental EMSCO‡	04/30/88	1.5	9.9	8.4	14.9
Donner Hanna Coke Hourly	12/01/87	3.4	10.8	7.5	31.1
LTV—Reserve Mining—Salaried‡	03/25/87	35.0	42.4	7.4	82.5
Driver Harris Hourly	11/12/85	1.9	9.3	7.3	21.0
Lebanon Steel Bargaining	07/31/83	2.3	9.1	6.8	25.8
White Motor Co. Hourly	11/30/81	−0.1	6.5	6.5	−0.8
Washburn Wire	10/01/79	0.0	6.4	6.4	0.0
White Farm —Hopkins	09/14/82	1.0	7.3	6.3	13.4
Jones & Lamson Machinery	10/09/87	3.9	10.2	6.3	38.2
Volco Steelworkers	10/22/85	0.3	6.1	5.8	5.7
Central Foundry Co. Molders	05/18/81	0.0	5.8	5.8	0.2
Alan Wood Steel Salaried	11/01/77	2.5	8.2	5.7	30.8
Johnson Steel and Wire Co.	09/13/82	1.8	7.5	5.7	24.1
Energy Cooperative	12/04/81	3.7	9.3	5.6	39.5
Allis-Chalmers —Harvey	12/17/87	9.6	15.1	5.5	63.4
Auto Specialty Management	12/20/86	2.2	7.6	5.5	28.3
Chicago West Pullman	05/16/80	11.3	16.6	5.4	67.8
Acme—Hamilton Local 95	05/15/78	0.3	5.5	5.1	5.8
Jeanette Corp. Union	05/31/83	2.6	7.8	5.1	33.9
Mid-Vale Heppenstall	04/30/76	0.5	5.6	5.1	9.2
Wieboldt Stores	07/11/87	5.0	9.9	5.0	49.9
Marhoefer Packing Co.	05/19/78	2.8	7.7	5.0	35.8

TABLE A–13 *(continued)*

Plan Name	*Date of Termination*[§]	*Plan Assets*	*Reserve for Guaranteed Benefits*	*Plan Underfunding*	*Funding Ratio*
Kaiser Steel Fabricating	07/28/87	2.2	6.9	4.7	31.9
AlloyTek, Inc., Hourly	10/31/79	0.5	5.1	4.6	9.7
New Jersey Brewery	12/31/77	9.0	13.3	4.3	67.4
Kaiser Steel, Napa	08/03/87	2.2	6.4	4.2	34.6
Continental Steel Corp. Joliet	02/14/86	2.3	6.4	4.1	35.7
Maryland Glass Corp. Hourly	02/25/81	3.2	7.3	4.1	44.3
Ironton Coke Corp.—Hourly	05/06/82	1.1	5.1	4.0	22.3
Gateway Transportation	06/15/82	0.1	4.1	4.0	2.9
The Union Metal Manufacturing	05/15/85	5.7	9.6	3.9	59.1
McKeesport Steel Casting	04/13/84	0.2	4.1	3.9	5.2
United Steel & Wire Hourly	08/09/85	1.8	5.7	3.9	31.9
Alliance Machine Salaried	05/31/87	2.6	6.4	3.8	39.9
Hotel and Restaurant Employees	09/30/77	0.0	3.7	3.7	0.0
Mullins Mfg.	04/30/75	0.9	4.5	3.6	20.2
Adirondack Foundries Hourly	12/31/87	1.9	5.4	3.6	34.4
New Jersey Zinc	01/01/83	1.2	4.8	3.6	25.5
Retail Clerks Union 1357	10/27/80	0.0	3.5	3.5	0.2
Airlift International	03/25/82	6.4	9.9	3.5	64.4
Van Huffel Tube	11/30/85	12.4	15.9	3.5	78.2
White Motor Co. Salary	11/30/81	0.1	3.3	3.2	2.4
Godchaux-Henderson	05/31/85	1.2	4.4	3.2	27.6
Schatz Federal Bearing Co.	02/20/81	2.4	5.6	3.2	43.1
Lebanon Steel Foundry	06/30/83	4.6	7.8	3.2	59.4
Amerace Corp.	07/31/74	0.9	4.0	3.1	22.6
Evans Products Co. Local 2340	07/31/76	2.1	5.2	3.1	40.1
Dayton Walther Corp. Dayton	10/31/84	9.0	12.1	3.1	74.4
Universal Foundry Co.	04/08/85	0.9	4.0	3.1	23.1

TABLE A–13 *(concluded)*

Plan Name	*Date of Termination*[§]	*Plan Assets*	*Reserve for Guaranteed Benefits*	*Plan Underfunding*	*Funding Ratio*
Bristol Industries	01/21/83	2.2	5.1	2.9	43.0
Bohack Corp. Nonbargaining	10/31/77	0.0	2.8	2.8	1.2
Standard Tube of Detroit	12/30/83	0.0	2.8	2.7	1.2
Williams Press	12/13/85	0.0	2.7	2.7	1.2
PF Industries Bristol Plant	01/30/81	1.8	4.5	2.7	40.9
Totals—Largest 100 Plans		$971.3	$3,167.4	$2,196.2	30.6%
Totals—All Terminations		$1,353.2	$3,879.6	$2,526.4	34.8%
Percentage Largest Plans to All Terminations		71.8%	81.6%	86.9%	

Note: Duplicate names may appear in list: This is because a single insurance event like bankruptcy of a plan sponsor may result in more than one terminated underfunded pension plan.

*Claims are measured as plan underfunding at date of termination. Claims amounts, on average, are 20 percent lower than total underfunding. This is because some portion of underfunding is paid by plan sponsors before a final settlement is reached with the PBGC.

†WPSC: Wheeling-Pittsburg Steel Company.

‡Entry is not one of the four so-called LTV terminations in 1986.

§Termination dates after 9/30/87 are estimates of termination dates for pending cases as of the end of the 1987 fiscal year.

TABLE A–14 Participants in Pay Status

Year	*Participants in Pay Status*	*Amount Paid (millions)*	*Average* *$ Current*	*Average* *$ 1986*
1975	N/A	$ 1.5	—	—
1976	N/A	9.5	—	—
1977	N/A	13.0	—	—
1978	N/A	28.1	—	—
1979	N/A	32.3	—	—
1980	28,000	36.2	$1,292	$1,699
1981	36,400	56.8	1,560	1,884
1982	50,900	94.2	1,850	2,110
1983	55,400	136.6	2,465	2,692
1984	64,700	169.3	2,616	2,754
1985	74,800	170.2	2,275	3,325
1986	90,750	260.5	2,870	2,870
1987	109,700	300.2	2,736	2,631

SOURCE: PBGC, *Annual Reports*.

TABLE A–15 Maximum Monthly Benefits, by Year

	Age of First Receipt	
Year	*55*	*65*
1974	$337	$ 750
1975	360	801
1976	391	869
1977	421	937
1978	452	1,005
1979	483	1,073
1980	521	1,159
1981	567	1,261
1982	621	1,380
1983	682	1,517
1984	721	1,602
1985	759	1,687
1986	805	1,789
1987	836	1,857
1988	859	1,909

TABLE A–16 Stock Price Indexes, 1950–1986

Year	*NYSE Composite*	*Dow Jones Industrial*	*S&P Composite*	*CPI Index*
1950	10.8	216.3	18.4	72.1
1951	13.0	257.6	22.3	77.8
1952	13.8	270.7	24.5	79.5
1953	13.6	275.9	24.7	80.1
1954	16.1	333.9	29.6	80.5
1955	21.5	442.7	40.4	80.2
1956	24.4	493.0	46.6	81.4
1957	23.6	475.7	44.3	84.3
1958	24.5	491.6	46.2	86.6
1959	30.7	632.1	57.3	87.3
1960	30.0	618.0	55.8	88.7
1961	35.3	691.5	66.2	89.6
1962	33.4	639.7	62.3	90.6
1963	37.5	714.8	69.8	91.7
1964	43.7	834.0	81.3	92.9
1965	47.3	910.8	88.1	94.5
1966	46.1	873.6	85.2	97.2
1967	50.7	879.1	91.9	100.0
1968	55.3	906.0	98.7	104.2
1969	54.6	876.7	97.8	109.8
1970	45.7	753.1	83.2	116.3
1971	54.2	884.7	98.2	121.3
1972	60.2	950.7	109.2	125.3
1973	57.4	923.8	107.4	133.1
1974	43.8	759.3	82.8	147.7
1975	45.7	802.4	86.1	161.2
1976	54.4	974.9	102.0	170.5
1977	53.6	894.6	98.2	181.5
1978	53.7	820.2	96.0	195.4
1979	58.3	844.4	103.0	217.4
1980	68.1	891.4	118.7	246.8
1981	74.0	932.9	128.0	272.4
1982	68.9	884.3	119.7	289.1
1983	92.6	1,190.3	160.4	298.4
1984	92.4	1,178.4	160.4	311.1
1985	108.0	1,328.2	186.8	322.2
1986	136.0	1,792.7	236.3	328.4
1987	161.7	2,275.9	286.8	340.4

SOURCE: *Economic Report of the President*, 1988.

TABLE A–17 Long-Term Bond Rates

Year	Moody's Aaa	30-Year Treasuries*	10-Year Treasuries
1950	2.62%		—
1951	2.86		—
1952	2.96		—
1953	3.20		2.85%
1954	2.90		2.40
1955	3.06		2.82
1956	3.36		3.18
1957	3.89		3.65
1958	3.79		3.32
1959	4.38		4.33
1960	4.41		4.12
1961	4.35		3.88
1962	4.33		3.95
1963	4.26		4.00
1964	4.40		4.19
1965	4.49		4.28
1966	5.13		4.92
1967	5.51		5.07
1968	6.18		5.65
1969	7.03		6.67
1970	8.04		7.35
1971	7.39		6.16
1972	7.21		6.21
1973	7.44		6.84
1974	8.57		7.56
1975	8.83		7.99
1976	8.43		7.61
1977	8.02	7.75%	7.42
1978	8.73	8.49	8.41
1979	9.63	9.29	9.44
1980	11.94	11.30	11.46
1981	14.17	13.44	13.91
1982	13.79	12.76	13.00
1983	12.04	11.18	11.10
1984	12.71	12.39	12.44
1985	11.37	10.79	10.62
1986	9.02	7.80	7.68
1987	9.38	8.59	8.39

*Data not available prior to 1977.

SOURCE: *Economic Report of the President,* 1988.

TABLE A–18 Treasury Bill Rates (3 months)

Year	*Nominal*	*Inflation Rate*	*Real*
1950	1.21%	.98%	.23%
1951	1.55	7.90	−6.35
1952	1.76	2.18	−.42
1953	1.93	.75	1.18
1954	.95	.49	.46
1955	1.75	−.37	2.12
1956	2.66	1.49	1.17
1957	3.26	3.56	−.30
1958	1.84	2.72	−.88
1959	3.40	.80	2.60
1960	2.92	1.60	1.32
1961	2.37	1.01	1.36
1962	2.77	1.12	1.65
1963	3.15	1.21	1.94
1964	3.54	1.31	2.23
1965	3.95	1.72	2.23
1966	4.88	2.85	2.03
1967	4.32	2.88	1.44
1968	5.33	4.20	1.13
1969	6.67	5.37	1.30
1970	6.45	5.91	.54
1971	4.34	4.29	.05
1972	4.07	3.29	.78
1973	7.04	6.22	.82
1974	7.88	10.96	−3.08
1975	5.83	9.10	−3.27
1976	4.99	5.76	−.77
1977	5.26	6.45	−1.19
1978	7.22	7.65	−.43
1979	10.04	11.25	−1.21
1980	11.50	13.52	−2.02
1981	14.03	10.30	3.73
1982	10.68	6.13	4.55
1983	8.63	3.21	5.42
1984	9.58	4.25	5.33
1985	7.48	3.56	3.92
1986	5.98	1.92	4.06
1987	5.82	3.65	2.17
Simple average			.94%
Geometric average			1.01%

SOURCE: *Economic Report of the President,* 1988.

APPENDIX B

Adjusting Liabilities to Common Interest Rates

A common problem in analyzing funding ratios across pension plans is that actuaries calculate liabilities based on different assumptions (most notably, different interest rates). For example, suppose two plans have an obligation to pay a single-life annuity of $1,000 for 15 years, but one actuary uses a discount rate of 10 percent per year, and the other uses 9 percent. Reported liabilities will be $7,760 and $8,230, respectively, even though both face the same obligation. For comparison, it is useful to evaluate all liabilities on the same basis.

In the above case, the adjustment factor is easy to determine. If both plans are to express liabilities based on a 9 percent interest rate, then the first plan's reported liabilities would be multiplied by a factor of 1.06 (=8,230/7,760). In general, however, it is difficult to determine exactly what the conversion factor should be. It depends on the level of the interest rate and the length of the annuity period. For example, in Table B–1, the above conversion is made for changes in the interest rates from 2 percent to 1 percent and 10 percent to 9 percent for annuity periods extending to 15 years, 30 years, and infinity. For the infinite annuity, a 100-basis-point conversion from a 2 percent to a 1 percent interest rate requires a conversion factor of 2, compared to 1.06 for the same 100-basis-point conversion for a 15-year annuity at the 10 percent interest rate level.

One obvious way to adjust liabilities in all plans is to ask actuaries for each plan to recalculate liabilities for a new common interest rate. This approach is feasible for a particular firm to test the sensitivity of its liabilities to interest rates. But for research purposes, usually the only data available are reported on the Form 5500 Annual Pension Plan Reports. These data include liabilities, assets, and assumed interest rates. The age distribution of participants is not reported, except insofar

TABLE B–1 Illustrative Interest Rate Conversion Factors

Period of Annuity	*Decrease in Interest Rate*	
	2 Percent to 1 Percent	*10 Percent to 9 Percent*
Infinity	2.000	1.110
30	1.149	1.091
15	1.074	1.060

as liabilities are separately reported for active participants and retirees. As suggested by the numbers in Table B–1, the liability adjustment is less sensitive for retirees because the discount period is shorter.

Actuarial Model

Algorithms are generated to convert liabilities to common interest rates in two ways. One way used by actuaries is to build a model plan with "typical" pension benefits and age and service distributions of active participants and retirees. Liabilities for participants in the model are generated for different interest rates. These relations form the basis for adjusting liabilities in a larger sample.

An example of this approach is presented in Table B–2, which summarizes the results of model simulations performed by Towers-Perrin as part of a study submitted to the PBGC in 1981. The model plan used in the study has average ages for active participants and retirees (weighted by liability levels) of 57 and 62, respectively. The results suggest that immediate liabilities (retirees) should be adjusted

TABLE B–2 Sensitivity of Liabilities to Interest Rates within Plans

Increase in Valuation Interest Rate		*Estimated Reduction in Value of Vested Benefits*	
From	*To*	*Immediate Annuities*	*Deferred Annuities*
4%	5%	7.8%	12.1%
5	6	7.4	11.7
6	7	7.0	11.2
7	8	6.6	10.8
8	9	6.3	10.4
9	10	5.9	10.1
10	11	5.6	9.8
11	12	5.3	9.5
12	13	5.1	9.2

SOURCE: Towers, Perrin, Forster & Crosby, Inc., *Forecasting of PBGC Liabilities under Terminated Pension Plans,* Final report submitted to the PBGC, September 1981.

TABLE B–3 Sensitivity of Liabilities to Interest Rates across Plans

Liabilities	*Coefficients*
Immediate (retirees)	−.077
Deferred (actives)	−.057
Number of plans	4,414

SOURCE: Richard A. Ippolito, *Pensions, Economics and Public Policy* (Homewood, Ill.: Dow Jones-Irwin, 1986), p. 65.

to a common interest rate using a factor that changes liabilities roughly 6 percent for each one percentage point change in the interest rate. The conversion factor for deferred annuities (active workers) is roughly 10 percent.

Cross-Section Estimation

If models to simulate interest rate changes are not available to researchers, another approach is to estimate the relation between liabilities and assumed interest rates using a cross-section of pension plans. An illustrative equation might be:

$$L(i)/PN = Ae^{bi} \tag{B–1}$$

where

$L(i)$ = Liabilities evaluated at interest i
P = Average pension paid in the plan
N = Number of participants in the plan

If this relation is estimated over the sample of plans that use different interest rates in their calculations, an estimate of the parameter b can be obtained. The parameter b is an estimate of the percent change in liabilities affiliated with a change in the reported interest rate.

Results of one study that estimated such relationships using data from the 5500 forms (Schedule B, question 6) are shown in Table B–3. The results reveal adjustment factors for active and retiree liabilities in the ranges of 8 and 6 percent. These were the adjustment factors used throughout the text of the book. Thus, if active liabilities are reported as $100,000 at a 10 percent interest rate, the conversion to a 7 percent rate implies liabilities of $127,000 [equal to $e^{.08 \times 3.0}$ = 1.27 × $100,000].

APPENDIX C

Factors that Affect PBGC Interest Rates

The method used by the PBGC to arrive at interest rates to discount liabilities is little understood. Its calculations are designed to replicate private-sector insurance prices, though the method used to attain this consistency sometimes generates misunderstanding from those who are not familiar with it.

This appendix is intended merely to illustrate some selected aspects of the PBGC interest rates to make them easier to compare to private-sector interest rate quotations. It is neither a description of the determination of PBGC interest rates nor a full explanation of why PBGC rates might be different than some private-sector insurance company interest rate quotations. A full-scale comparison of PBGC and private-sector rates would take into account other factors that might affect published quotations not mentioned here and would take us far beyond what is necessary.[1]

Instead, my intention is limited to illustrating (1) how the use of different mortality tables can generate correspondingly different interest rate quotations yet produce the same annuity purchase prices and (2) how different methods to set interest rates for deferred annuities can be consistent with the same market price quotations.

Immediate Annuity Rates

Prior to loading expenses, private insurance companies use discount rates presumably related to long-term bond rates (and other investments typically held by carriers). The PBGC immediate annuity rate

[1]These include the treatment of such factors as subsidized early retirement, administrative expenses, profit, and investment expenses.

tends to be lower than these rates. For example, in 1985 the PBGC immediate rate averaged approximately 9.75 percent; the average Moody's Aaa and 10-year Treasury bond rates were 11.37 and 10.62 percent, respectively. In 1977, the PBGC immediate rate was roughly 6.75 percent; the Moody's Aaa and 10-year Treasury rates were 8.02 and 7.42 percent, respectively.[2]

One reason this disparity exists is attributable to the mortality table used by the PBGC. This table generally assumes higher mortality than many tables currently referenced in private-sector annuity purchase rate quotations.

The PBGC starts with an estimate of private-sector annuity purchase prices. It then chooses an interest rate that, *when combined with the PBGC mortality table,* approximates the average private annuity purchase price. In this section, I will illustrate how the use of different mortality tables requires corresponding use of different interest rates to generate the same annuity purchase price.

Suppose, for example, that a private insurance firm assumes a 65-year-old will die with certainty at age 80. Based on long-term bond rates of, say, 7 percent and using continuous discounting, the price for an annuity for 65-year-olds is $9.29. If the PBGC used the same mortality assumption and did not reduce the interest rate to reflect administrative expenses, it also would quote a 7 percent immediate annuity rate. But instead, the PBGC uses an older mortality table; suppose this table assumes that all 65-year-olds die at age 79 instead of 80. Instead of updating its mortality table, the PBGC makes an offsetting adjustment in its choice of interest rates so as to generate the same net price as typical private sector insurance companies. The PBGC in this case would solve for some interest rate i that generates a price of $9.29; that is, if it used a continuous compounding model, it would search for the solution to the equation:

$$PVA\,(i;\,65{,}79) = (1/-i)\,[e^{-i(79-65)}-1] = \$9.29 \qquad \text{(C–1)}$$

where $PVA(i;\,65{,}79)$ denotes the present value of a one-dollar annuity from age 65 to 79 discounted at the interest rate i.

This equation is satisfied for the interest rate 6.325 percent. Thus, in this example, if the PBGC used a continuous compounding model, it would announce an immediate rate of 6.325 percent,[3] even though long-term bond rates and (pre-expense) private insurance company quotations are 7 percent. In practice, however, the PBGC rate is

---

[2] *Economic Report of the President,* 1987, p. 324.

[3] In practice, the PBGC usually rounds its rates to the nearest .25 percent. The PBGC would also add its estimate of administrative expenses to the $9.29 before solving Equation (C–1).

calculated using a discrete interest rate formula and a mortality table (instead of certain death at a particular age).

Deferred Rates

The method used by the PBGC to choose deferred rates is also different than that used by most private-sector firms. In this section, I want to illustrate how different methods can generate the same deferred annuity purchase price.

When quoting immediate annuities for retirees, private insurers generally rely on prevailing long-term interest rates. The problem of matching bonds against liabilities is not large, and reinvestment risk is not prohibitive.

For progressively younger individuals, it becomes harder to exactly match assets against liabilities (it is harder to find assets with durations as long as liabilities), and reinvestment risk becomes large. To accommodate this uncertainty, private firms scale down interest rate assumptions for periods further in the future. Thus, if the 10-year-long term bond rate is 7 percent, an insurance company might quote 7 percent for the ensuing 10 years, 6.5 percent for the next 5 years, 6 percent for the 5 years beyond this, and so on. Thus, if a pension termination occurs in 1987, a private insurance firm might use an interest rate of 7 percent for all calculations to the year 1997, then use 6.5 percent for 1997 until 2002, 6 percent from 2002 until 2007, and so on.

For example, consider a two-person pension plan that pays 10-year annuities starting at age 65. Both individuals are certain to live for 10 years. The two individuals at termination are 65 and 60 years old. For the sake of the example, suppose a 7 percent interest rate applies to the period 1987 through 1997 for both individuals; a 4 percent rate is then applied from 1997 to 2002 (when the youngest retiree receives his last benefit). These rates are shown in the first two rows in Table C–1.

The PBGC bases its deferred rate structure to match private-sector prices. Though it sets a structure to match private-sector prices, it does so in a different way. In particular, consider the simple two-person example discussed above. If the annuity per year is one dollar, the private-sector rates for the deferred individual can be presented in the following way:

$$
\begin{aligned}
PV(\#2 \text{ private}) &= e^{-(65-60).07} PVA(.07;\ 65,70) \\
&\quad + e^{-(70-60).07} PVA(.04;\ 70,75) \\
&= 2.97 + 2.25 \\
&= \$5.22 \qquad \text{(C–2)}
\end{aligned}
$$

Individual #2's annuity for the first five years from age 65 to age 70 (1992–97) is discounted back to 1987 at 7 percent [first entry on the righthand side of Equation (C–2)]; his annuity from age 70 to age 75

TABLE C–1 Illustration: Deferred Interest Rates, Private versus PBGC

Individual	*Age at Termination*	*Years* 1987–1992	1992–1997	1997–2002
Private				
#1	65	7.00%	7.00%	—
#2	60	7.00	7.00	4.00%
PBGC				
#1	65	7.00	7.00	—
#2	60	6.40	7.00	7.00

Note: Example assumes 10-year annuity, age 65 to 75; death occurs after age 75.

(1997–2002) is discounted back to age 70 at 4 percent and then discounted back from 1997 to 1987 at 7 percent. The present value of this annuity is $5.22.

In this example, the PBGC would assign a deferred rate in a different way. Ignoring the mortality risk difference (there is a fixed 10-year annuity in the example, and death is certain not to occur prior to age 75), the PBGC also would choose the 7 percent rate as the immediate annuity rate. *Its method, however, would apply the immediate annuity rate to all present and future retirees during the period of retirement, regardless of when retirement occurred.* Thus, in terms of Table C–1, a 7 percent rate would be applied to the 65-year-old in payment status at the time of termination. For the 60-year-old, the same 7 percent rate would be used for his annuity period, from age 65 to age 75, but some lower rate would be used to discount the value of this annuity from age 65 to age 60. Using the method described below, this rate turns out to be 6.4 percent.[4]

This choice of rates is shown in the third and fourth rows of Table C–1. From 1997 to 2002, the PBGC discounts at a 7 percent rate, compared to 4 percent in the private sector. During the 1987–92 period, it applies a discount rate of 7 percent to individual #1 and 6.40 percent to individual #2. This structure of rates appears inconsistent with a typical investment model because it assumes the existence of different interest rates for different participants at the same point in time. But the rate levels are chosen to approximate private price quotations.

In particular, the deferred interest rate is chosen to satisfy the following equation:

$$\begin{aligned} PV(\#2, \text{PBGC}) &= e^{-(65-60)i} PVA(.07; 65{,}75) \\ &= \$5.22 \end{aligned} \qquad \text{(C–3)}$$

[4]Again ignoring the PBGC practices of (1) loading prices before solving for the interest rate and (2) rounding the resulting rates to the nearest .25 percent.

TABLE C–2 PBGC Interest Rates, 1974–1988

Year	Month*	Immediate Rate	Deferred Rates† (1)	(2)	(3)
1974	September	8.00%	7.25%	5.75%	4.25%
1975	October	7.75	7.25	5.75	4.25
1976	January	8.00	7.25	5.25	4.00
	March	7.25	7.00	5.00	4.00
	June	7.25	6.75	4.75	3.50
	September	7.00	6.00	4.75	3.50
	December	7.00	6.25	4.75	3.75
1977	March	7.00	6.00	4.75	3.50
	June	6.75	6.25	4.50	3.75
	December	6.75	6.25	4.50	3.75
1978	March	7.00	6.25	4.75	3.75
	June	7.25	6.75	4.75	3.50
	September	7.25	6.75	4.75	3.50
1979	March	7.50	6.75	5.50	4.00
	June	7.50	6.75	5.50	4.00
	September	7.75	7.00	5.75	4.00
	December	8.50	7.75	6.50	4.00
1980	March	8.75	8.00	6.75	4.00
	June	8.75	8.00	6.75	4.00
	September	9.00	8.25	7.00	4.00
	December	9.25	8.50	7.25	4.00
1981	January	9.50	8.75	7.50	4.00
	February	9.75	9.00	7.75	4.00
	April	10.00	9.25	8.00	4.00
	June	10.25	9.50	8.25	4.00
	July	10.50	9.75	8.50	4.00
	August	10.25	9.50	8.25	4.00
	October	10.50	9.75	8.50	4.00
	November	10.75	10.00	8.75	4.00
	December	11.00	10.25	9.00	4.00
1982	January	10.50	9.75	8.50	4.00
	February	10.75	10.00	8.75	4.00
	March	11.00	10.25	9.00	4.00
	June	10.75	10.00	8.75	4.00
	August	11.00	10.25	9.00	4.00
	October	10.75	10.00	8.75	4.00
	November	10.50	9.75	8.50	4.00
	December	10.25	9.50	8.25	4.00
1983	January	10.00	9.25	8.00	4.00
	February	9.75	9.00	7.75	4.00
	April	9.50	8.75	7.50	4.00
	June	9.25	8.50	7.25	4.00
	September	9.50	8.75	7.50	4.00
1984	February	9.75	9.00	7.75	4.00
	March	9.50	8.75	7.50	4.00
	April	9.75	9.00	7.75	4.00
	May	10.00	9.25	8.00	4.00
	July	10.50	9.75	8.50	4.00
	August	10.75	10.00	8.75	4.00
	September	10.50	9.75	8.50	4.00
	November	10.25	9.50	8.25	4.00
	December	10.00	9.25	8.00	4.00

TABLE C–2 (*concluded*)

Year	Month*	Immediate Rate	Deferred Rates† (1)	(2)	(3)
1985	January	9.75	9.00	7.75	4.00
	March	9.50	8.75	7.50	4.00
	April	9.75	9.00	7.75	4.00
	May	10.00	9.25	8.00	4.00
	June	9.75	9.00	7.75	4.00
	July	9.25	8.50	7.25	4.00
	October	9.00	8.25	7.00	4.00
1986	January	8.75	8.00	6.75	4.00
	February	8.50	7.75	6.50	4.00
	April	8.00	7.25	6.00	4.00
	May	7.75	7.00	5.75	4.00
	October	7.50	6.75	5.50	4.00
	November	7.75	7.00	5.75	4.00
	December	7.50	6.75	5.50	4.00
1987	March	7.25	6.50	5.25	4.00
	June	7.50	6.75	5.50	4.00
	July	7.75	7.00	5.75	4.00
	October	8.00	7.25	6.00	4.00
	November	8.25	7.50	6.25	4.00
1988	March	8.00	7.25	6.00	4.00
	April	7.75	7.00	5.75	4.00
	June	8.00	7.25	6.00	4.00
	September	8.25	7.50	6.25	4.00
	November	7.75	7.00	5.75	4.00

Note: The method used by the PBGC to set immediate and deferred rates is provided in this appendix.

*All rates effective the first day of the month.

†Immediate rates are applied to all retirees in pay status. For participants within seven years of pay status, the first deferred rate is used; thus a worker seven years from pay status has his annuity discounted over his retirement period at the immediate rate, then discounted back seven years at the first deferred rate. Those between 7 and 15 years prior to pay status are discounted the incremental 8 years at the second deferred rate; and those further than 15 years from pay status are discounted over the incremental period at the third deferred rate. Prior to 1979, the length of the deferral periods were slightly different than these.

The solution to Equation (C–3) is approximately $i = 6.4$ percent.

The PBGC has established a fixed relationship between immediate and deferred rates. To do this, it presumably used methods similar to that shown in Equation (C–3) to determine the average relationship of deferred rates to the immediate rate. A fixed relationship between the immediate rate and deferred rates was found. The PBGC adopted a deferred rate for seven years prior to pay status 75 basis points below the immediate rate; the second eight years are discounted at 125 basis points below this number; and longer periods are discounted at a fixed 4 percent rate.

These relations were fixed so that tables of manageable size could be issued to actuaries and plan administrators who needed to perform these types of calculations. The book, entitled *Prospective and Actuarial Mortality Tables*, provides conversion rates for different ages and interest rate assumptions.

Table C–2 shows the history of immediate and deferred interest rates used by the PBGC from 1974 through 1988.

APPENDIX D

The Largest PBGC Claims

The purpose of this appendix is to briefly review the issues raised by the largest claims made against the PBGC. The circumstances surrounding these cases illustrate the essence of the so-called PBGC problem.

Introduction

Through the end of the 1986 fiscal year, approximately 1,000 companies had terminated over 1,300 single-employer pension plans, resulting in total net claims of almost $4 billion against the PBGC's single-employer termination insurance program. The 13 companies listed in Table D–1 account for roughly four fifths of this amount. The two most striking features of the table are that (1) 8 of the claims events were from the steel industry and (2) 11 occurred after 1981, which explains why the PBGC problem is relatively new. In addition, all of the companies in the table were in financial trouble at the time their pension plans terminated. All were in the process of renegotiating credit arrangements—11 were undergoing reorganization under the protection of the federal bankruptcy courts.

Generous Pension Amounts

The steel and automobile industry terminations, as a group, illustrate one of the central problems with PBGC insurance; namely, its guarantee of pension benefits is much more generous than the average benefits of PBGC premium payers. Instead of the normal retirement age of 62 or 65 with actuarial reductions for earlier retirement, the largest claims typically have "30-and-out" normal retirement ages, which means workers could retire with full (that is, unreduced) benefits after 30 years of service.

TABLE D–1 Largest PBGC Claims

Plan Sponsor	*Date of Termination*
Steel	
Alan Wood Steel	1978
Wisconsin Steel	1980
Phoenix Steel	1983
McLouth Steel	1983
Continental Steel	1986
Wheeling-Pittsburgh	1986
LTV Corporation	1986
Kaiser Steel	1987
Automobile/Trucks/Farm equipment	
White Motors	1982
White Farm	1982
Allis-Chalmers	1985
Other	
Rath Packing	1982
Braniff Airlines	1982

In addition, the steel industry plans for hourly workers included so-called shutdown benefits: the payment of unreduced pension benefits to older workers affected by a plant shutdown who otherwise did not qualify for full benefits. Usually a "rule of 65" applied: a 45-year-old worker with 20 years' service (the sum of 45 and 20 is 65) could immediately qualify for full benefits on a plant shutdown.

Instead of guaranteeing full benefits at, say, age 62 or age 65 and then providing actuarially reduced guarantees for earlier ages, the PBGC guarantees full benefits at earlier ages, including shutdown benefits.[1]

The potential magnitude of the guarantee of early retirement benefits became evident in the *Alan Wood Steel* termination in 1978, where over one fourth of the claim was attributable to such benefits. The problem grew in importance during the 1980s, culminating with the termination of three LTV plans in 1986, where almost 50 percent of the $2 billion claim was attributable to special early benefits.

Specific Attributes of Selected Large Terminations

Underfunding. Many of the large terminations highlight one or more fundamental defects of the pension insurance system. Through its short history, the PBGC has accepted hundreds of pension plans with

[1]These guarantees are limited to shutdown prior to plan termination and are subject to the maximum guaranteed benefits schedule (see Table 5–2). In addition, restrictions apply to benefits exceeding the single-life benefit annuity available at normal retirement age (see 29 CFR 2613.4).

low funding ratios. Table 7–2 in the text lists 35 PBGC claims—involving almost $1 billion in underfunding—that were less than 20 percent funded at termination. Some of the large terminations made it apparent why funding rules did not work well.

Waivers. Under ERISA, an employer is required to contribute an annual amount that will satisfy statutory funding requirements. Employers may, however, obtain funding waivers and thus defer contributions to the plan. Funding waivers were notable problems in two of the large termination cases: *Rath Packing and Continental Steel.*

When Rath terminated in 1982, five consecutive waivers to Rath's plans granted by the IRS were discovered. These waivers accounted for roughly half of the $60 million claim against the PBGC.

Interestingly, virtually the same pattern of waivers was found when Continental terminated in 1986. The IRS had also given this firm five consecutive waivers, yielding results virtually identical to Rath. Of Continental's roughly $60 million claim, approximately half was attributed to waivers.

Unpaid contributions. Employers are required to continue to fund a pension plan up to the date of termination. However, when financial problems become acute, employers often defer contributions; then, if the plan terminates, the plan has large amounts due and unpaid contributions. For example, when the *LTV Corporation* plans were terminated in 1986, the plan sponsor had not made its required contributions for the 1985 plan year.[2] A study of large terminations also showed a pattern of plan sponsors failing to pay required minimum contributions prior to termination. A 1986 GAO study of the largest terminations between 1980 and 1983 showed that almost 25 percent of claims were attributable to unpaid contributions (see Table 7–11).

Lump sums. The most notable characteristic of the *LTV Republic Steel* plan for salaried employees was its unrestricted payment of lump sums to participants eligible for normal or early retirement. During the period prior to termination, a large portion of those eligible chose lump sums. This created two problems: (1) the lump-sum procedure resulted in the use of assets to pay a significant amount of nonguaranteed benefits; and (2) few assets were left to pay ongoing benefit amounts to retirees in the plan.

Due in large part to these lump-sum payments, the plan was underfunded at termination by $230 million and had available assets of only $7,700 with which to pay more than $2 million in monthly benefits to retirees. The Republic Steel plan had been in compliance

---

[2]LTV had obtained waivers from the IRS for contributions required in the 1984 plan year; these waivers were secured by a pledge of common stock in LTV Aerospace.

with the minimum funding standards and had received no minimum funding waivers.

Minimum funding standard. Perhaps the best example of the inadequacy of ERISA funding standards was found in the termination of the *Allis-Chalmers* plans in 1986. One of the terminated plans had underfunding of $170 million and had enough assets to pay only one month of benefit payments. Yet Allis-Chalmers had made all required contributions to the plan and had no minimum funding waivers. This situation developed because the 30-year amortization rules for past service liability were too long for a plan with large underfunding that was dominated by retirees (see Chapter 7).

Transferring exposure to financially troubled firms. Another problem area that surfaced after ERISA was the large potential exposure for the PBGC if viable employers could shift poorly funded plans to weak employers. In the event of a subsequent termination, if only the weak employer was liable, the PBGC would have a large claim and the predecessor employer would have effectively shifted the liability to the PBGC.

The *Wisconsin Steel* termination illustrates this problem. Wisconsin Steel had been a part of International Harvester (now Navistar International) for 75 years until it was sold in 1977 in a leveraged transaction to a financially weak subsidiary of Envirodyne Industries, a small consulting company. However, Wisconsin Steel continued to be involved in certain aspects of the administration of the plan. The bankruptcy of Wisconsin Steel followed in 1980. The PBGC contended that a company cannot escape financial responsibility for its pension plans by transferring them to a weak third party that cannot successfully continue the business or fund the pension plans. This case remained in litigation in the fall of 1988.

Follow-on plans. When a plan is terminated with insufficient assets and the PBGC must pay guaranteed benefits, the PBGC has opposed the employer's establishing certain kinds of follow-on plans, and in particular, plans, which when added to the benefits provided by the PBGC, provide participants with benefits substantially equal to those that would have been provided by the terminated plan if it had continued. In effect, establishment of a follow-on plan allows an employer to shift to the PBGC a substantial portion of the cost of funding an ongoing pension plan for its employees.

In August 1986, *Wheeling-Pittsburgh* and the union submitted follow-on plans to the PBGC for its approval. In December 1986, the PBGC disapproved the proposed follow-on plans on the basis that such plans constituted a de facto continuation of the terminated plans. On February 9, 1987, Wheeling-Pittsburgh and the union filed suit in district court, seeking an order allowing them to establish the proposed follow-on plans and denying the PBGC authority to restore the assets and liabilities of the terminated plans on the establishment of such follow-on plans. The case was pending as of the fall of 1988.

The proposed follow-on plans of Wheeling-Pittsburgh consist of two components: one new plan covering active employees and a supplemental plan covering both active employees and retirees. The proposed supplemental plan is designed to provide retirees with 95 percent of the difference between the benefits they would have received under the terminated plan and the benefits guaranteed by the PBGC.

Size of termination. *LTV Corporation* entered Chapter 11 bankruptcy proceedings in 1986. The PBGC terminated four of its pension plans in late 1986 and early 1987. This event raised many issues for the PBGC, but perhaps none were more important than the sheer size of the claim. This single claim doubled the PBGC deficit from approximately $2 billion to almost $4 billion.

Historically, several large impending claims were facing the PBGC (notably, Chrysler Corporation and International Harvester), but none actually occurred. All of the premium requests made to Congress assumed "large" claims would not be made. The LTV termination essentially forced policymakers to face the reality that potential exposure to the PBGC was many billions of dollars higher than previously realized. This realization was perhaps the most important stimulus to enactment of the Pension Protection Act of 1987. It also intensified the issue of follow-on plans and the notion of restoration.

In June 1987, LTV and its union agreed to the collective bargaining agreement that included a follow-on plan for hourly workers. A similar follow-on plan was formulated for salaried employees. On July 30, 1987, the bankruptcy court approved the follow-on plans over the PBGC's objection.

The PBGC restored three of the LTV plans to their pretermination status on September 22, 1987. The bases for the PBGC's decision to restore were

1. The abuse of the termination insurance program caused by LTV's establishment of follow-on plans that, along with the PBGC's guaranteed benefits payments, essentially continued the terminated plans.
2. The improvement in LTV's and LTV/Steel's financial conditions.
3. The demonstrated willingness of LTV Steel to fund retirement programs.

LTV opposed the restoration, and the dispute was the subject of a district court case—*Chateaugay Corporation, Reomar, Inc., LTV Cor-*

poration, et al. Among other rulings, the district court found insufficient evidence that the follow-on plans were so abusive of the insurance system so as to justify restoration. As of fall 1988, the case had been appealed by the PBGC in the U.S. Court of Appeals for the Second Circuit.

APPENDIX E

Summary of Major Pension Protection Act Provisions Affecting Single Employer Plans

	Old Law	Pension Protection Act		
		PPA Section	*ERISA Section*	*Provision*
A. Single-employer premium				
1. Per cap ccharge	$8.50 per participant	9331(a)	4006(a)(3)(A)	$16 per participant
2. Additional premium	No provision	9331(b)	4006(a)(3)(E)	$6/$1,000 (or fraction thereof) of unfunded vested benefits as of close of preceding plan year.*
a. Maximum additional premium	No provision	9331(b)	4006(a)(3)(E)	$34/participant, less $3 for each of the 5 plan years beginning before 1988 for which contributions were the maximum deductible under IRC Sec. 404. Reduction of maximum funding charge applies for 5 plan years.
3. Liability for premiums	Plan administrator	9331(c)(2)	4007(a)	Plan administrator or joint and several liability for contributing sponsor and members of its controlled group.
4. Effective date		9331(f)		Plan years beginning on or after 1/1/88.
5. Deposit of premiums in new revolving fund	Deposited in basic benefits revolving fund	9331(d)	4005(f)	Premium in excess of $8.50 per participant, and interest and penalty thereon, to be deposited in a separate revolving fund. Fund may not be used to pay administrative costs or benefits under plans terminated before 10/1/88, unless no other amounts are available. The fund may be invested in any obligations that the PBGC considers appropriate.
B. Minimum funding standards—payment of contributions				
1. Due date for contributions	2½ months after plan year and 6-month extension	9304(a)	302(c)(10)(A)	8½ months after plan year. Effective: Plan years beginning on or after 1/1/88.

2. Quarterly estimated contribution	None	9304(b)	302(e)	Requires quarterly installments equal to "applicable percent" of lesser of 90% of required annual payment for the current plan year or 100% of required annual payment for the preceding plan year. (Rules for short plan years under regulation of the Secretary of the Treasury.) Applicable percent for plan year beginning: 1989 6.25 1990 12.50 1991 18.75 1992 & on 25.00 First installment is due 4/15/89 for calendar-year plans. Special rule for unpredictable contingent event benefits.†
3. Interest on late payments	Interest rate consistent with rate used to compute plan costs	9304(b)	302(e)	Greater of old law interest rate or 175% of the federal midterm rate in effect under IRC Sec. 1274 for the first month of the plan year. Interest runs until payment is made. Payments are credited first to the oldest outstanding contributions. Effective: Plan years beginning after 1988.
4. Excise tax on late contributions	Initial rate 5%	9304(c)	IRC 4971(a)	Initial rate 10%. Effective: Plan years beginning after 1988.
5. Notice of failure to make a required contribution payment	No provision	9304(d)	101(d)	Employer must notify participants, beneficiaries, and alternate payees within 60 days after a missed payment or denial of a funding waiver request. Notice need not be given while waiver request is pending or if waiver is granted. Effective:Date of enactment.

	Old Law	Pension Protection Act		
		PPA Section	ERISA Section	Provision
6. Liability for contributions and excise tax for unpaid contributions	Contributing sponsor	9305	302(c)(11) IRC 4971(e)	Contributing sponsor and controlled group members are jointly and severally liable. Effective: Plan years beginning after 1987.
C. Minimum funding standards—amount of required contributions				
7. Amortization periods				
a. Experience gains and losses	15 years	9307(a)	302(b)(2)(B)(iv) and 3(B)(ii)	5 years—Effective: Plan years beginning after 1987.
b. Waived funding deficiencies	15 years	9307(a)	302(b)(2)(C)	5 years—Effective: Plan years beginning after 1987.
c. Gains and losses due to changes in actuarial assumptions	30 years	9307(a)	302(b)(2)(B)(v) and (3)(B)(iii)	10 years—Effective: Plan years beginning after 1987.
8. Reasonability test for actuarial assumptions	Must be reasonable in the aggregate and in combination offer the actuary's best estimate of anticipated experience under the plan	9307(b)	302(c)(3)	Each assumption must be individually reasonable (in view of the experience of the plan and reasonable expectations) or, in the aggregate, assumptions must result in a contribution equivalent to that which would be determined if each assumption and method were reasonable. Effective: Plan years beginning after 1987.

9. Additional contribution for underfunded plans	No provision	9303	302(d)	(1) Excess of "deficit reduction contribution" over the sum of the charges to the funding standard account (excluding amortization of net experience losses and losses due to changes in actuarial assumptions), reduced by credits for amortization of decreases in unfunded liability, due to amendments and (2) "unpredictable contingent event amount" for events that occur after October 17, 1987. Additional contribution shall not exceed the amount needed to reach 100%-funded current liability percentage. See Notes for definitions of terms.
a. Small-plan exceptions				Plans with 100 or fewer participants are exempt. Plans with 101–150 participants. Additional contribution is amount for larger plans × .02 × highest number of participants above 100. All defined benefit plans of controlled group to be treated as a single plan.
b. Effective date				Effective: Plan years beginning after 1988.
c. Steel transition rule for plan years beginning before 1994.				Additional contribution is limited to the sum of: (1) a 1% per year increase in the funded current liability percentage excluding unpredictable contingent event liability and (2) 10-year amortization of unpredictable contingent event liability for events that occur after 12/17/87.
10. Limitations on amount of deductible contributions for a plan year				

	Old Law	Pension Protection Act		
		PPA Section	*ERISA Section*	*Provision*
a. Full funding limitation‡	Deduction for a plan year is limited to the excess of the accrued liability (including normal cost) over the lesser of the actuarial value or the fair market value of plan assets	9301	302(c)(7)	Deduction for a plan year is limited to the excess of the lesser of: (1) 150% of current liability or (2) accrued liability (including normal cost) over the lesser of the actuarial value or the fair market value of plan assets. (Note: Accrued liability often includes benefits projected to normal retirement age. Current liability includes only benefits accrued through the end of the plan year.)
b. Limitation on amortization of past service credits used to determine limitation on deduction	Limitation refers to amortization of past service and supplementary credits	9307(d)	IRC 404(a)(1)(A)(iii)	Limitation refers to amortization of the unfunded cost attributable to past service and supplementary credits.
c. Unfunded current liability is deductible	Full funding and other limitations on deductible amounts may preclude deduction of amounts equal to unfunded current liability	9307(c)	IRC 404(a)(1)(D)	Maximum deductible amount shall not be less than unfunded current liability under IRC Sec. 412(1) (computed without reducing assets by the credit balance in the funding standard account). Rule applies only to plans with more than 100 participants. All plans of the same controlled group are aggregated for purposes of this rule. Effective: Plan years beginning after 1987.

11. Limitation on interest rate for determining current liability and additional contributions	Must meet the reasonable-in-the-aggregate test together with other assumptions. Must be consistent with the rate used to determine costs	9307(e)	302(b)(5)	(1) Must be within "permissible range" of 10% above or below weighted average of 30-year Treasuries for the 4 years preceding the plan year. (2) Must be determined without regard to plan experience or reasonable expectations but consistent with annuity purchase rates to provide plan liabilities. (3) If Secretary of Treasury finds that lowest end of permissible range is too high, Secretary may lower the rate but not below 80% of the average of the range before the rate is lowered.
D. Funding waivers				
1. Due date for waiver applications	No provision	9306(a)	303(d)	2½ months after close of plan year. Effective: Plan years beginning after 1987. Transition rule for plan year beginning in 1988: 5½ months after close of plan year.
2. Hardship criterion for funding waiver	Substantial business hardship of contributing sponsor	9306(a)	303(a),(b) and (d)	Entire controlled group (viewed as a single employer) must be suffering *temporary* hardship. Effective: Waiver applications submitted after 12/17/87
3. Frequency of waivers	5 in 15 consecutive years	9306(b)	303(a)	3 in 15 consecutive years. Waivers for plan years beginning before 1/1/88 are disregarded. Effective: Waiver applications submitted after 12/17/87.
4. Interest on waived contributions and extensions of amortization periods	Rate for late taxes	9306(c)	303(a) and 304(a)	Greater of: (1) 150% of the federal midterm rate under IRC Sec. 1274 for the first month of the plan year or (2) the interest rate used to determine plan costs. Effective: Applications submitted after 12/17/87.

	Old Law	Pension Protection Act		
		PPA Section	ERISA Section	Provision
5. Notice of waiver application	No provision	9306(d)	303(e)(1)	Notice must be given to the plan, participants, beneficiaries, alternate payees, and union. Notice must state extent to which guaranteed benefits and benefit liabilities are funded. Effective: Waiver applications submitted more than 90 days after date of enactment.
E. Lien for unpaid, unwaived contributions				
1. Plans affected	None	9304(e)	302(f)	Lien may arise only if aggregate unpaid contributions (with interest) exceed $1 million and unfunded current liability percentage is less than 100%.
2. Amount of lien	None	9304(e)	302(f)	Lesser of: (1) aggregate outstanding unpaid amounts (with interest), less $1 million or (2) aggregate unpaid amounts outstanding for plan years beginning after 1987 (with interest).
3. Period of lien	None	9304(e)	302(f)	Lien runs from the 60th day after payment was due to the end of the plan year in which payment is made.
4. Nature of lien	None	9304(e)	302(f)	Statutory lien in favor of the plan on all real and personal property of the contributing sponsor and controlled group. Amount underlying the lien shall be treated as a tax due and owing the United States. Rules similar to ERISA Sec. 4068 (c)–(e) (employer liability lien) shall apply to lien and underlying amount.

5. Notice to PBGC of missed contribution	Reportable event by plan administrator under 4043	9304(e)	302(f)	Person failing to make a required payment for which a lien arises must notify the PBGC within 10 days of the due date.
6. Enforcement	None	9304(e)	302(f)	Lien may be perfected and enforced only by the PBGC or by a contributing sponsor or controlled group member at the PBGC's direction.
7. Effective date	None	9304(e)		Plan years beginning after 1987.
F. Security for new underfunding				
1. Benefit increases subject to security requirement	No provision	9341	307	Security required if abenefit increase will bring ratio of assets to current liability below 60%. Plan loses qualification if security is not provided.
2. Amount of security		9341	307	The excess of the lesser of: (1) amount needed to increase funded ratio to 60% or (2) the increase in current liability due to the benefit increase amendment, over $10 million.
3. Form of security		9341	307	Surety bond, escrowed cash or short-term Treasuries, or other security satisfactory to Treasury and involved parties.
4. Release of security		9341	307	Security is released at the end of the plan year after security is provided and funded current liability percentage is at least 60%. Secretary of Treasury may allow partial releases based on improvements in funded current liability percentage.
5. Effective date		9341		Security rules apply to amendments made after enactment of Pension Protection Act excluding amendments made under collective bargaining agreements ratified before enactment.

	Old Law	Pension Protection Act		
		PPA Section	*ERISA Section*	*Provision*
G. Standard terminations				
1. Sufficiency criterion	Assets sufficient to distribute benefit commitments	9313(a)	4041(b)	Assets sufficient to distribute benefit liabilities.
2. Enrolled actuary certifications for insured plans described in IRC Sec. 412(i) (plans fully funded by paid-up insurance contracts)	Required	9314(a)	4041(b)(2)(A)	Requirement eliminated.
H. Limitations on reversions of excess assets from terminated plans				
1. Waiting period before effective date of an amendment permitting reversion to contributing sponsor or controlled group member	No provision	9311(a)	4044(d)(2)	5-year waiting period unless plan is less than 5 years old and has provided for reversion since inception. 5-year waiting period also applies to assets transferred to another plan. Effective: Reversion provisions adopted after 12/17/87. (Exceptions: for existing plans silent on ownership of reversions, a one-year period was granted during which these plans could amend plan to make provisions for reversion ownership without triggering the new five-year rule.)

2. Formula for excess assets derived from mandatory employee contributions	No provision. The PBGC has issued regulations that include a presumptive formula and require PBGC approval of other formulas.	9311(b)	4044(d)(3)	Excess attributable to mandatory contributions is determined by ratio of mandatory employee contributions (plus such amounts paid out in lump sums and annuity purchases of entire nonforfeitable benefits in the 3 years before termination) to total benefit values. Effective: Notices of intent to terminate filed and termination proceedings initiated by the PBGC after 12/17/87.
I. Distress termination				
1. Controlled group members that must meet a distress test	Contributing sponsors and substantial controlled group members	9313(b)	4041(c)(2)(B)	Contributing sponsors and all controlled group members.
2. Bankruptcy reorganization distress test	Must enter reorganization before termination date and bankruptcy court approves termination	9313(b)	4041(c)(2)(B)	Must enter reorganization before proposed termination date. Bankruptcy court must approve the termination and find it necessary for the company to pay its debts and stay in business outside of reorganization.§
3. Submit to the PBGC a copy of request of court approval of termination	No provision	9313(b)(5)	4041(c)(2)(B)	Copy of request of court approval of termination must be filed with the PBGC.
4. Effective date				Notices of intent to terminate filed after 12/17/87.
5. Enrolled actuary certifications for insured plans described in IRC Sec. 412(i) (plans fully funded by paid-up insurance contracts)	Required	9314(a)	4041(c)(2)(A)	Requirement eliminated.

	Old Law	Pension Protection Act		
		PPA Section	ERISA Section	Provision
J. Section 4049 trust				
1. Liability above guarantees	Lesser of 75% of outstanding benefit commitments or 15% of total benefit commitments	9312(b)(2)	4062(b)(1)(A)	100% of unfunded benefit liabilities as of termination date, plus interest.
2. Collection of liability above guarantees	Sec. 4049 trust	9312(b)(2)	4062(b)(1)(A) 4068(a)	4049 trust is eliminated. The PBGC is responsible for collecting the entire unfunded benefit liabilities. The PBGC's tax-status claim/lien remains at 30% of controlled group net worth.
3. Determination of amounts payable to participants in excess of guaranteed and funded nonguaranteed benefits	Amounts collected by Sec. 4049 trust are distributed annually to participants based on outstanding benefit commitments	9312(b)(3)	4022(c)	The PBGC shall allocate to participants in accordance with Sec. 4044(a) benefit priorities, the product of the outstanding benefit liabilities and the "recovery ratio."¶
4. Effective date		9312(d)(1)		Notices of intent to terminate filed or termination proceedings instituted by the PBGC after 12/17/87. Transitional rule. For notices of intent to terminate filed before 12/17/90, the recovery ratio is determined based on plan data and not on historical data, provided the recovery ratio can be calculated on plan data by 12/17/90.
5. Sec. 4049 trust expenses for prior terminations	Cannot be paid until Sec. 4049 trust collects enough assets to cover them	9312(d)(2)	4049(a)	Contributing sponsor and controlled group responsible for reasonable administrative expenses of Sec. 4049 trust before collections by the trust and employer liability will be reduced accordingly.

*Unfunded vested benefits means unfunded current liability under Sec. 302(d)(8)(A), taking into account vested benefits only and valuing vested benefits using an interest rate equal to 80 percent of the annual yield on 30-year Treasury securities for the month preceding the month in which the plan year begins.

†Unpredictable contingent event benefits are disregarded in computing the required annual payment. However, the required quarterly installment is increased by the greater of (1) the amount of such benefits paid during the three months preceding the month in which the installment is due (including the cost of annuities purchased and lump sums paid) or (2) 25 percent of the charge for the plan year for amortizing over seven years the benefit liability for unpredictable contingent events, with amortization beginning in the plan year in which the event occurs.

‡Secretary of Treasury required to study effect of change in full funding limitation on benefit security and report results to the Ways and Means and Finance Committees by 8/15/88. (NOTE: As of fall 1988, this study had not been completed.)

§The liquidation distress test also tightened to require commencement of proceeding before proposed termination date.

¶Benefit liabilities means the benefits of employees and their beneficiaries under the plans [within the meaning of IRC Sec. 401(a)(2)].

Outstanding amount of benefit liabilities means the value of benefit liabilities [under assumptions prescribed by the PBGC for purposes of Sec. 4044] minus the value of such liabilities funded by plan assets or guaranteed by the PBGC.

The recovery ratio is the ratio of the values of the PBGC's recovery under 4062–4064, as applicable, to unfunded benefit liabilities. If outstanding benefit liabilities exceed $20 million, the recovery ratio is based on plan data. In smaller cases, an average of prior terminations after 12/17/87 is used. The PBGC's calculations are binding unless shown by clear and convincing evidence to be unreasonable.

Definitions of terms

Deficit reduction contribution means the sum of the unfunded old liability amount and the unfunded new liability amount.

Unfunded old liability amount is the amount needed to amortize in equal annual installments over 18 years unfunded current liability in the plan at the start of the first plan year beginning after 12/31/87.

Unfunded new liability amount is the product of the applicable percentage and the unfunded current liability determined without regard to (1) unamortized unfunded old liability and (2) liability related to unpredictable contingent event benefits (whether or not the event has occurred).

The *applicable percentage* is .30 − [.25 × (Funded current liability percentage − .35)] or .3, whichever is lower.

Current liability means all liabilities to employees and beneficiaries. The rate of interest used to determine current liability is restricted (see item C.11 of this summary). Unpredictable contingent event benefits are not taken into account until the event occurs. *Conference Report* states that current liability is determined on a termination basis.

Unfunded current liability means the excess of (1) current liability over (2) plan assets, reduced by any credit balance in the funding standard account.

Definitions of terms (*concluded*)

Unpredictable contingent event amount means the greater of:

(1) the applicable percentage of (1-Funded current liability percentage) × Unpredictable contingent event benefits paid during the plan year

Plan years beginning in:	*Applicable percentage*
1989 and 1990	5%
1991	10
1992	15
1993	20
1994–2001	Increases 10 percentage points a year, reaching 100% in 2001 and remaining at 100% thereafter

or

(2) the amount needed to amortize in equal annual installments over seven years the unpredictable contingent event benefit liabilities, beginning with the plan year in which the event occurs.

Unpredictable contingent event benefit means a benefit contingent on an event other than age, service, compensation, death, disability, or an event that is reasonably and reliably predictable as determined by the Secretary of the Treasury.

Funded current liability percentage means the ratio of plan assets to current liability. Assets are valued under any reasonable actuarial method that takes into account fair market value and is permitted by regulations of the Secretary of the Treasury. Current liability is determined using the rate of interest for determining required contributions [IRC 412(b)(5) rate of interest].

APPENDIX F

References

The Pension Contract

Pension–Wage Trade-Off

Ehrenberg, Ronald G. "Retirement System Characteristics and Compensating Wage Differentials in the Public Sector." *Industrial Labor Relations Review* 33 (1980), pp. 470–483.

Ehrenberg, Ronald G., and Robert Smith. *Modern Labor Economics*. Glenview, Ill.: Scott, Foresman, 1985.

Schiller, Bradley R., and Randall D. Weiss. "Pensions and Wages: A Test for Equalizing Differences." *Review of Economics and Statistics* 62 (1980b), pp. 529–38.

Smith, Robert S. "Compensating Differentials for Pensions and Underfunding in the Public Sector." *Review of Economics and Statistics* 63 (1981), pp. 463–68.

Rate of Pension Savings over Tenure

Clark, Robert, and Ann A. McDermed. "Earnings Response to Pension Coverage and Eligibility." Paper presented at the American Economic Association Meetings, New York, 1985.

———. "Life Cycle Patterns of Earnings, Pension Wealth, and Total Compensation." *Quarterly Journal of Economics* 101 (1986), pp. 341–62.

Ippolito, Richard A. "The Labor Contract and True Economic Pension Liabilities." *American Economic Review* 75 (December 1985), pp. 1031–43.

Mitchell, Olivia, and S. Pozzenbon. "Wages, Pensions, and the Wage-Pension Trade-Off." Paper presented at the American Economic Association Meetings, New Orleans, 1986.

Pensions and Job Mobility

Allen, Steven; Robert Clark; and Daniel Sumner. "Job Mobility, Older Workers, and the Role of Pensions." Final report submitted to the U.S. Department of Labor, 1986a.

Bartel, Ann P., and George J. Borjas. "Middle-Age Job Mobility: Its Determinants and Consequences." In *Men in Their Pre-Retirement Years*. Philadelphia: Temple University School of Business Administration, 1977.

Ippolito, Richard A. "Why Federal Workers Don't Quit." *Journal of Human Resources* 22 (Spring 1987), pp. 281–99.

Mitchell, Olivia S. "Fringe Benefits and Labor Mobility." *Journal of Human Resources* 17 (Spring 1982), pp. 286–98.

Schiller, Bradley R., and Randall D. Weiss. "The Impact of Private Pensions on Firm Attachments." *Review of Economics and Statistics* 62 (1980a), pp. 369–80.

Other Studies

Allen, Steven; Robert Clark; and Daniel Sumner. "Post-Retirement Adjustments of Pensions." *Journal of Human Resources* 21 (1986), pp. 118–37.

Clark, R.; S. Gohmann; and A. McDermed. "Declining Use of Defined Benefit Pension Plans: Is Federal Regulation the Reason?" Mimeograph. North Carolina State University, Raleigh, N.C.: April 1988.

Hay-Huggins Company. *Pension Plan Terminations with Asset Reversions*. Final report submitted to the U.S. Department of Labor, 1986.

Ippolito, Richard A. "The Implicit Pension Contract: Developments and New Directions." *Journal of Human Resources* 22 (Summer 1987), pp. 441–67.

________. *Pensions, Economics and Public Policy*. Pension Research Council Monograph. Homewood, Ill.: Dow Jones-Irwin, 1986.

Pension Insurance

Ippolito, Richard A. "The Economic Function of Underfunded Pension Plans." *Journal of Law and Economics* 28 (October 1985), pp. 511–51.

________. "A Study of the Regulatory Effect of ERISA." *Journal of Law and Economics* 31 (April 1988), pp. 85–125.

McGill, Dan M. *Guarantee Fund for Private Pension Obligations*. Homewood, Ill.: Richard D. Irwin, 1970.

Munnell, Alicia H. "Guaranteeing Private Pension Benefits: A Potentially Expensive Business." *New England Economic Review*, March/April 1982, pp. 24–47.

Government Studies of the PBGC Problem

Congressional Budget Office. *Federal Insurance of Private Pension Benefits*. Washington, D.C.: U.S. Government Printing Office, October 1987.

Pension Benefit Guaranty Corporation. *Pension Promises at Risk*. Washington, D.C.: 1987.

U.S. General Accounting Office. "Pension Plans: Government Insurance Program Threatened by Its Growing Deficit." Report to the Subcommittee on Oversight, Committee on Ways and Means, House of Representatives, March 1987.

Studies of Underfunding Exposure

Regan, Patrick, and Jack Treynor. *The Financial Reality of Pension Funding under ERISA*. Homewood, Ill.: Dow Jones-Irwin, 1976.

"Unfunded Pension Liabilities." *Business Week*. July 18, 1977, pp. 86–88.

U.S. Departments of Treasury and Labor. *Study of Pension Plan Terminations, 1972*. Washington, D.C.: U.S. Government Printing Office, August 1973.

———. *Study of Pension Plan Terminations, 1974*. Washington, D.C.: U.S. Government Printing Office, May 1976.

U.S. Senate, Subcommittee on Labor of the Committee on Labor and Public Welfare. *Legislative History of ERISA*, 3 vols. 94th Congress (2nd Session). Washington, D.C.: U.S. Government Printing Office, 1976.

———. *Preliminary Report of the Private Welfare and Pension Plan Study*. 92nd Congress (1st Session). Washington, D.C.: U.S. Government Printing Office, 1971.

PBGC Studies of Premium Needs

Pension Benefit Guaranty Corporation. "Premium Requirements for the Single-Employer Basic Benefits Insurance Program." Mimeograph. Washington, D.C.: 1977.

———. "Premium Requirements for the Single-Employer Basic Benefits Insurance Program." Mimeograph. Washington, D.C.: May 1982.

———. "Variable-Rate Premium for the PBGC's Single-Employer Insurance Program." Mimeograph. Washington, D.C.: October 1986.

Other Studies

Lebowitz, Martin. "The Dedicated Bond Portfolio in Pension Funds: Motivations and Basics." *Financial Analysts Journal* 42 (January–February 1986a), pp. 69–75.

———. "The Dedicated Bond Portfolio in Pension Funds: Immunization, Matching, and Contingent Procedures." *Financial Analysts Journal* 42 (March-April 1986b), pp. 47–57.

Marcus, Alan J. "Corporate Pension Policy and the Value of PBGC Insurance." National Bureau of Economic Research, Working Paper no. 1217, October 1983.

Pesando, James. "Projecting Exposure, Terminations, and Claims among

Single-Employer Plans." Final report submitted to the Pension Benefit Guaranty Corporation, 1985.

Towers, Perrin, Forster & Crosby, Inc. *Forecasting of PBGC Liabilities under Termination Pension Plans*. Final report submitted to the PBGC, September 1981.

VanDerhei, Jack. "An Empirical Analysis of Risk-Related Insurance Premiums for the Pension Benefit Guaranty Corporation." Final report submitted to the PBGC, 1988.

VanDerhei, Jack, and F. P. Jonette. "Economic Determinants for the Choice of Actuarial Cost Methods." *Journal of Risk and Insurance*, 60 (March 1988), pp. 59–74.

White, Michelle. "Pension Liabilities and the Bankruptcy Process: A Report to the PBGC." Final report submitted to the Pension Benefit Guaranty Corporation, August 1987.

Data Sources

Bankers Trust. *Corporate Pension Plan Study*, annual.

Beller, Dan, and John Turner. *Pension Trends*. Washington, D.C.: U.S. Department of Labor, forthcoming.

Ibbotson Associates. *Stocks, Bonds, Bills, and Inflation: 1987 Yearbook*. Chicago: 1987.

Ippolito, Richard, and Walter Kolodrubetz (eds.), *The Handbook of Pension Statistics, 1985*. Chicago: Commerce Clearing House, 1986.

Ippolito, Richard, and John Turner. "Turnover, Fees, and Pension Plan Performance." *Financial Analysts Journal* 43 (November/December 1987), pp. 16–26.

McCarthy, David. *Findings from the Survey of Private Pension Benefit Amounts*. Washington, D.C.: U.S. Department of Labor, 1985.

Pension Benefit Guaranty Corporation. *Annual Report*, annual.

________. *Prospective Actuarial and Mortality Tables*, 1980.

U.S. Council of Economic Advisors. *Economic Report of the President*. Washington, D.C.: U.S. Government Printing Office, 1988.

U.S. Department of Labor. *Employee Benefits of Medium and Large Firms*. Washington, D.C.: Bureau of Labor Statistics, 1983.

Wyatt Company. *1987 Survey of Actuarial Assumptions and Funding*. Washington, D.C.: 1988.

Dissenting Comments

Statement of Howard Young

This book contains a wealth of data about PBGC experience. However, it does not provide a complete or balanced presentation of the development or operation of the program. Instead, the analysis is shaped by the author's desire to develop a private-market approach to the issue. While that may be an interesting academic exercise, readers should consider the following questions.

First, is it a utilitarian approach? Major efforts were made prior, and subsequent, to the enactment of ERISA (which established the PBGC) to encourage the development of such private-market insurance. None of that activity is discussed in the book. No significant entities were willing to underwrite the risk, and there still isn't any indication that insurers would be available.

Second, would the resulting private-market insurance be more acceptable to plan sponsors than the present system? For example, the proposal in Chapter 10 includes a requirement that the insurer be the plan administrator. That seems more onerous than many of the regulatory provisions that plan sponsors have opposed. (The "private" nature of the insurer shouldn't make much difference—federal or state regulators regularly intervene in insurers' operations.) Also, the vast majority of plan sponsors (and participants) bear PBGC annual premiums below $35 per participant under the new law (see Table 6–9). How many of them would be willing to pay the $240 lump-sum transition charge, in addition to ongoing premiums, as suggested at the very end of Chapter 10?

Third, would the private-market insurance meet the protection goals that stimulated enactment of ERISA and the PBGC? Throughout the book, there is an emphasis on real cuts in protection against loss of benefits. If such arrangements had applied during the severe dislocations of the U.S. economy in the 1970s and 80s, even greater hardships would have occurred, and it is likely that support for the existing pension system would be much weaker. Dissatisfaction with the system as it then existed produced ERISA/PBGC; an unsatisfactory private-market arrangement would invite additional legislation.

In the absence of positive answers to those three questions, there is little justification for expecting the public program to mimic the supposed characteristics of a nonimplementable private-market approach. Public and private programs each have interrelated strengths and weaknesses, which ought to be considered in their own context rather than on the basis of an ideal standard.

Certainly the PBGC encountered difficulties, and abuses have occurred; but those arose from the objections and obstacles raised by the program's opponents as well as from the overly optimistic good intentions of its supporters. For example, at a very early date, the supporters made proposals (such as changes in the bankruptcy laws) that would have produced a sounder program. Additional problems need to be overcome, but there should also be recognition of its public-program advantages, such as the ability to allocate costs across firms in our interdependent economy.

Students interested in improving protection against benefit loss should focus on how to develop a more effective public program rather than use private-market concepts as a justification for reducing benefits of participants in plans where no abuse has occurred.

Statement of Michael S. Gordon

The Economics of Pension Insurance, by Richard A. Ippolito, contains so much that is valuable and well reasoned (and, incidentally, with which the undersigned agrees) that it is painful to point out that the book is significantly flawed, if not disfigured, by the author's unwillingness to confront—except by innuendo and disparagement—the politics of pension insurance. Indeed, although the author explicitly or implicitly indicts Congress or prior regimes at the PBGC for their collective willingness to open loopholes or their failure to close them—all at the expense of what the author perceives, often correctly, as sound insurance principles—he either is not aware of, or overlooks, innumerable efforts both in the drafting stages of ERISA and thereafter to structure the law on some of the very principles he advocates.

To give just a few examples: he does not acknowledge that the early precursors of Title IV confined the insurable event to "distress" terminations, nor does he seek to inquire as to why that approach was subsequently abandoned. He seems unaware of, or oblivious to, the fact that (1) the Senate Labor and Public Welfare Committee reported Title IV provisions making an employer liable up to 50 percent of his net worth (some members of the committee would have preferred 100 percent), (2) the Senate Finance Committee insisted under organized business pressure that net worth liability be restricted to 10 percent (the bulk of that committee would have preferred no employer liability whatsoever), and (3) 30 percent was a last-ditch compromise preventing a Senate floor fight that would have unglued the entire legislation.

He also neglects to note that the original premium formula in the bills of both Senate and House labor committees was tied to the PBGC's exposure (i.e., to the degree of unfunded vested liabilities) and that even after the *per capita* premium tax method was adopted, the law still authorized the PBGC to prescribe exposure-related premiums, subject to congressional ratification. The PBGC never seriously sought to exercise that authority until 1987. Moreover, there is no mention that (1) all the original ERISA bills adopted Professor McGill's recommendation and prohibited insurance coverage with respect to plan amendments occurring within five years of plan termination and (2) the original Williams-Javits bill precluded insurance coverage for unfunded vested liabilities accrued before the bill's enactment (which goes a long way toward explaining why, as a matter of legislative design, a 30-year amortization funding period was considered adequate).

Finally, and most significantly in terms of the author's heavy reliance on a private insurance model to guide his analysis, there is no mention that, as enacted, ERISA authorized the creation of private insurance for the 30 percent net worth liability exposure—so-called contingent employer liability insurance (CELI)—which was exhaustively studied by the PBGC, found unworkable, and, on the basis of recommendations made by the PBGC, repealed in 1980 as part of the multiemployer plan amendments to ERISA (MEPPAA). The failure to touch on CELI's demise is inexplicable.

This is not the place to indicate in detail the nature of the political value judgments that influenced the adoption of departures from what otherwise might be regarded as sound insurance principles. Suffice it to say that free market criteria, which Ippolito extols as the highest good, were not then, and may not be even now, controlling. In the first chapter, Ippolito announces—somewhat snidely, in my opinion—that "PBGC can be viewed as the embodiment of a national research project," that he will assume that "Congress intended to erect a bona fide pension insurance firm," and that for purposes of writing his book he has rejected the possibility that "a pricing and insurance contract could have been enacted in 1974, but was not because of deliberate attempts to effect transfers to workers and shareholders in troubled firms."

Of course, what the author rejects happens to be the only authentic explanation for what occurred in 1974. Lest we forget, this was the era of the Chrysler and Lockheed bailouts. The supposition that Congress was prepared to accept loss of jobs and further industrial decline in return for sound insurance principles is preposterous and is why, even today, there will be stiff resistance to redesigning pension insurance along the lines he proposes.

Ippolito seems to regard the political value judgments that led to the subordination of sound insurance principles as distasteful, irrational, or even immoral. Not so. Legislative policy (and even economic policy) vis-à-vis private pensions cannot be judged primarily by free market criteria or the competitive impact on those affected by it, but rather by political standards. What might appear on the surface to be only a technical question involving PBGC design may be in reality another example of the ceaseless struggle to maintain the economic strength of the greatest democracy in the world and the major defender of freedom everywhere. This being the case, the national interest requires close attention and action with respect to declining industries, which is, after all, the real problem underlying pension insurance. The obsession with free market criteria—while it may serve as a useful corrective to inappropriate, politically based proposals—should not distract us from the essential political task—to reconcile the need to arrest this nation's precipitous industrial deterioration with the further redesign of Title IV along more solid insurance principles.

All of this suggests to me that the incremental approach to Title IV amendments will continue. In this respect, Ippolito has much to say that is of great importance, and no one, with the possible exception of Professor McGill, has said it better. Rather than catalog here all the specific areas of my agreements and disagreements, let me close by noting my judgment that overall, the most fruitful areas to explore for the next administration would be the concept of a risk-related premium and its collateral aspects, and revision of the latest overkill funding rules created by the Pension Protection Act of 1987. I should add that in this last respect, the PBGC cannot escape responsibility for a miserable legislative strategy that virtually invited a tax committee ambush. Let us hope that next time—if there is a next time—more attention will be paid to the nuances of the legislative process and less attention to scoring ideological points.

Index

A

Actuarial interest rate assumptions
  changes prior to termination, 118–20
  relation to funding ratios, 120
  rules affecting, 134, 136
Alan Wood Steel, 42, 44, 54–55, 115, 235
Allis Chalmers, 39, 42, 44, 56, 59, 114–15, 237
Amortization rules; *see also* Minimum funding standards
  congressionally enacted changes in, 135–39
  PBGC proposed changes in, 133–34
Assigned risk pool, 14, 179, 199–201

B

Bankruptcy rules, 12, 40, 153–54, 165–66
Benefit guarantees
  levels, 37, 75, 220
  proposals for alternatives, 77–78, 150–52
  reductions for early retirement, 5, 38, 75–77

C

Capital losses, 19–23
Catastrophic risk, 34, 167, 177–78
Claims; *see* Pension Benefit Guaranty Corporation, claims
Coinsurance, 10, 21–24, 26, 37, 183–84
Contributions, unpaid; *see* Minimum funding standards *and* Unpaid contributions
Control group, 73–75, 237
Cross subsidies
  PBGC pricing proposal, 94–100
  Pension Protection Act, 100–102

D

Default risk, 57–60, 88–91, 94–100, 185–86
Deficit; *see* Pension Benefit Guaranty Corporation, deficit
Defined benefit plan
  contract, 16–21
  coverage; *see also* Participants, in defined benefit plans
    by industry, 211
    by plan size, 212
  facts, 7

Defined benefit plan—*Cont.*
funding of; *see* Funding ratios
growth in, 7–8, 209
Defined contribution plans, 7–9, 171
tax advantages in OBRA, 167–73

E

Efficiency concepts, 157–59
Efficiency of pension insurance rules
bankruptcy rules, 165–66
benefit levels, 163; *see also* Benefit guarantees, proposals for alternatives
funding, 163–65
mandatory participation, 160–62, 166–67
prices, 159–60
Employee Retirement Income Security Act (ERISA), 3–4, 9–10, 39, 50, 105–7
Exposure
control of; *see* Pension Benefit Guaranty Corporation, reform efforts
as enacted in PPA, 100–102
estimates of, 46, 57–60, 91–92
increases prior to termination; *see* Funding ratios, reductions in
market system, 88–91, 94–100
PBGC proposal, 91–94

F

Follow-on plans, 22, 69–73, 86–87, 237
Formations, 7–8, 210
Full funding limit
changes enacted, 13, 144–45
comparison to pre-1988 rules, 145–48
impact of changes on tax advantages, 167–73
Funding ratios; *see also* Underfunding
distribution of
ongoing basis, 47–48, 106–8, 196, 213
termination basis, 46, 91, 106–8, 212
in terminated plans, 4, 39, 51, 54, 123–27, 215–19
in termination versus ongoing plans, 49, 108, 147
reductions in, 11, 39, 89–90, 95, 114–23, 140–41
estimates of, 123–26
relation to interest rate assumption, 120

I

Insurance; *see also* Private-sector pension insurance
event, 40
pricing, 88–91, 94–100
principles, 36, 41, 53
reform proposals; *see* Pension Benefit Guaranty Corporation, reform efforts
Interest rates, 222–23; *see also* Pension Benefit Guaranty Corporation, interest rates
impact on claims, 24–27, 43, 45–46, 50
impact on liabilities, 224–26

L

Liens, 12, 84, 152–153; *see also* Unpaid contributions
LTV Corporation, 14–15, 42, 56, 59, 72–73, 118, 238
Lump sum payouts, 120–22, 236

M

McGill, Dan, 3–4, 175–76, 187–88
Market for pension insurance, 29–34
Minimum funding standards
changes in, 85, 135–39
flat benefit plan, 56, 108–10, 112–14

Minimum funding standards—*Cont.*
inadequacy of old rules, 39, 56, 237
salary-related plan, 111–14
shortcoming of new rules, 140–44
Multiemployer pension plan, 14
Multiemployer Pension Plan Amendments Act (MPPAA), 82–83, 150–51

O

Omnibus Budget Reconciliation Act (OBRA), 13, 144; *see also* Full funding limit, *and* Pension Protection Act (PPA) provisions
impact on funding ratios, 145–48
impact on PBGC exposure, 148–50
impact on pension tax advantages, 167–73

P

Participants
in defined benefit plans, 7–8, 209
in PBGC pay status, 4, 219
PBGC; *see* Pension Benefit Guaranty Corporation (PBGC)
Pension
capital losses; *see* Capital losses
contract; *see* Defined benefit plan, contract
formations; *see* Formations
reversions; *see* Reversions
terminations; *see* Terminations
Pension Benefit Guaranty Corporation (PBGC)
claims, 4, 41–45, 51, 53–57, 60–62, 214
largest, 100, 215, Appendix D
deficit, 4, 41, 52, 215
exposure; *see* Exposure
facts, 4
insurance event, 40, 84
interest rates, 45, 231–32
derivation of, 227–30
PBGC—*Cont.*
premiums
enacted in PPA, 100–102
historical, 41
proposed, 91–94
premium studies, 4, 11, 50–53, 60–65, 91–94
reform efforts, 11
benefit guarantees, 75–77
MPPAA, 82–83
PPA, 83–85, 135–39
proposals, 77–78, 91–100, 132–35, 150–54
regulation and litigation, 69–75
SEPPAA, 80–82
summary of, 70, 136, 151
Pension Protection Act (PPA) provisions, 12, 83–84, 100–102, 135–39
distress terminations, 254–55
full funding limit; *see* Full funding limit
funding waivers, 248–49
liens for unpaid contributions, 250–51
minimum funding, 242–48
premiums, 241–42
reversions, 253–54
section 4049 trust, 255–56
security for new funding, 251–52
standard terminations, 252–53
Portfolio immunization
nominal pension contract, 27–29
real pension contract, 31–32
Portfolio risk, 192–97
PPA; *see* Pension Protection Act (PPA) provisions
Price indexing
of insured benefits, 29–31, 62–63
of post-retirement benefits, 23
proposal for, 182–83
Private-sector pension insurance, 5, 10, 36, 40, 49, 88–91
administration of, 191–92
congressional constraints, 176
exposure calculation, 190–91
exposure control of, 187–90
insurable event, 197

Private-sector pension insurance—
Cont.
role for industry group, 177–79
summary of features, 180

R

Rath Packing, 42, 54–55, 59, 115, 236
Reversions, 7, 213
Risk
in portfolio; *see* Portfolio risk
of default; *see* Default risk

S

Shutdown benefits, 38, 55, 79–80, 117–18, 151–52
Single Employer Pension Plan Amendments Act (SEPPAA), 41, 80–82
Steel industry; *see* Terminations, steel
Supplemental early benefits, 78–80; *see also* Shutdown benefits

T

Terminations
all plans, 7–8, 210
steel, 42–44

U

Underfunding
impact of ERISA, 105–7, 127–31
ongoing, 47–48
reasons for, 160–61; *see also* Funding ratios, reductions in *and* Minimum funding standards, inadequacy of old rules
at termination; *see* Funding ratios, in terminated plans
Unpaid contributions, 117, 141, 236

V

VanDerhei, Jack, 4, 94–100, 116–17, 120–21, 123–24, 186
Variable rate premium
enacted by Congress, 100–102
market estimates, 94–100
proposed by PBGC, 91–94

W

Waivers, 39, 54–55, 84, 114–17, 135, 140, 236
Wheeling Pittsburg, 42, 44, 56, 71, 237